TIME FOR KIDS®

WORLD ATLAS

Keep your *TFK World Atlas* up-to-the-minute
with changes and news from around the world
at *www.timeforkids.com/atlas*

Continue your travel adventures online with Go Places!
Explore countries, test your knowledge, and hear
languages at *www.timeforkids.com/goplaces*

Your special web-access code is **TFKNews**

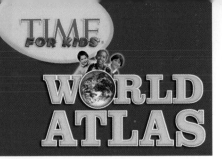

TIME FOR KIDS World Atlas

EDITORIAL DIRECTOR: Keith Garton
EDITOR: Nelida Gonzalez Cutler
DEPUTY EDITOR: Leslie Dickstein
MAPS: Joe LeMonnier. **Additional maps:** Joe Lertola,
Jean Wisenbaugh. **Research:** Kathleen Adams
PHOTOGRAPHY EDITOR: Joan Menschenfreund
CONTRIBUTORS: Claudia Atticot, David Bjerklie, Jeremy Caplan,
Borden Elniff, Jennifer Marino, Butch Phelps, Lisa Jo Rudy,
Kathryn R. Satterfield, Tiffany Sommers, Elizabeth Winchester
COPY EDITORS: Barbara Collier, Steve Levine, Peter McGullam,
Elsie St. Léger
INDEXING: Marilyn Rowland
ART DIRECTION AND DESIGN: Raúl Rodriguez/Rebecca Tachna for
R studio T, NYC
COVER DESIGN: Elliot Kreloff

TIME INC. HOME ENTERTAINMENT

PRESIDENT: Rob Gursha
VICE PRESIDENT, BRANDED BUSINESSES: David Arfine
VICE PRESIDENT, NEW PRODUCT DEVELOPMENT: Richard Fraiman
EXECUTIVE DIRECTOR, MARKETING SERVICES: Carol Pittard
DIRECTOR, RETAIL & SPECIAL SALES: Tom Mifsud
DIRECTOR OF FINANCE: Tricia Griffin
ASSISTANT MARKETING DIRECTOR: Ann Marie Doherty
PREPRESS MANAGER: Emily Rabin
BOOK PRODUCTION MANAGER: Jonathan Polsky
RETAIL MANAGER: Bozena Bannett
ASSOCIATE PRODUCT MANAGER: Kristin Walker

SPECIAL THANKS: Alexandra Bliss, Bernadette Corbie, Robert Dente,
Gina Di Meglio, Anne-Michelle Gallero, Peter Harper, Suzanne Janso,
Robert Marasco, Natalie McCrea, Mary Jane Rigoroso, Steven
Sandonato, Grace Sullivan

SPECIAL THANKS TO IMAGING: Patrick Dugan, Eddie Matros

Contents

Contents

South America..................... 46

Europe.......................... 58

Asia 94

Africa 124

Australia and the Pacific Islands 144

Antarctica...................... 152

World Guide

The Arctic
16

Scandinav
62

The Lo
Countr
70

United Kingdom
and Ireland
60

France and
Monaco
66

Italy, Malta,
San Marino and
Vatican City
78

The Iberian
Peninsula
64

Western Canada
and Alaska
22

Eastern Canada
20

United States
of America:
Midwest
32

United States
of America:
New England
28

United States of
America: West
38

United States
of America:
South
34

United States
of America:
Middle Atlantic
30

United States
of America:
Southwest
36

Western
Africa
132

Mexico and
Central America
40

Caribbean
44

Northwestern
South America
48

Northeastern
South America
52

Southern
South America
56

Austria, Liechtenstein
and Switzerland
74

Central Europe
76

Ukraine, Moldova
and the Caucasus
Republics
88

The Baltic
States and
Belarus
86

Western
Russia
90

any

The Balkans
80

utheastern
Europe
82

Turkey and Cyprus
98

Israel, Jordan,
Lebanon and Syria
100

Afghanistan,
Iran and
Pakistan
106

The
Arabian
Peninsula
102

Central Asia
104

Indian
Subcontinent
108

Eastern Russia
96

China, Mongolia
and Taiwan
112

Japan,
North Korea and
South Korea
116

Southeast
Asia
118

Maritime
Southeast
Asia
122

uwestern
frica
130

Northeastern
Africa
126

Central
Africa
134

East Central
Africa
136

Southern
Africa
140

Australia and
Papua New
Guinea
146

New Zealand and
the Pacific Islands
150

Antarctica
152

How to Use the TFK World Atlas

Take a trip around the world with the *TIME FOR KIDS World Atlas.* This book divides the world into continents, countries and regions. Each of the book's sections begins with a map of the continent and an explanation of the continent's features. Throughout the atlas, 14 Fact File pages will introduce you to real kids who will share information about their countries. The "World-at-a-Glance" chapter at the end of the book gives vital statistics for every country in the world. But before you begin to explore the world, take a few moments to find out about planet Earth and its place in the universe by reading pages 8 through 15.

Abbreviations

ft	feet
h	hectare
kg	kilogram
I	island
L	lake
lb	pound
Mt.	Mount
Mtns.	Mountains
m	meter
mi	mile
NA.	not available
R.	River
St.	Saint
sq km	square kilometer
sq mi	square mile
U.K.	United Kingdom

Key to Map Symbols

- ✪ State, province or territory capital
- ✪ Country capital
- ● City
- ▲ Mountain or volcano

Introduction
These paragraphs give a brief overview of the continent's physical and geographic features.

Color Tabs
Each continent has a different color tab so that you can easily locate countries within continents.

Lines of Longitude and Latitude
Lines of longitude run in a north-south direction. Lines of latitude run in an east-west direction.

Continent

Continent Facts
Here you will find the size of the continent, its countries and other information.

Scale
Use the scale to measure distances. The scale is given in kilometers and miles.

Wow Zone!
This is where you will find amazing facts about the continent.

Locator Globe
The globe shows the continent's location in the world.

Introduction
These paragraphs give a brief overview of states, provinces, territories or countries.

Compass Rose
The compass rose will help you locate north, south, east, west and points in between.

Map Grid
A color-coded grid surrounds the country and regional maps. Use the grid to quickly locate places.

Data Bank
Each section has a Data Bank with important information about area, population, the capital and the languages. Look for Data Bank entries about Canadian provinces on pages 20-23 and each state in the United States on pages 26-39.

Locator Globe

Scale

Did You Know?
This is where you will discover surprising facts about the states, provinces, territories or countries.

Country/Region

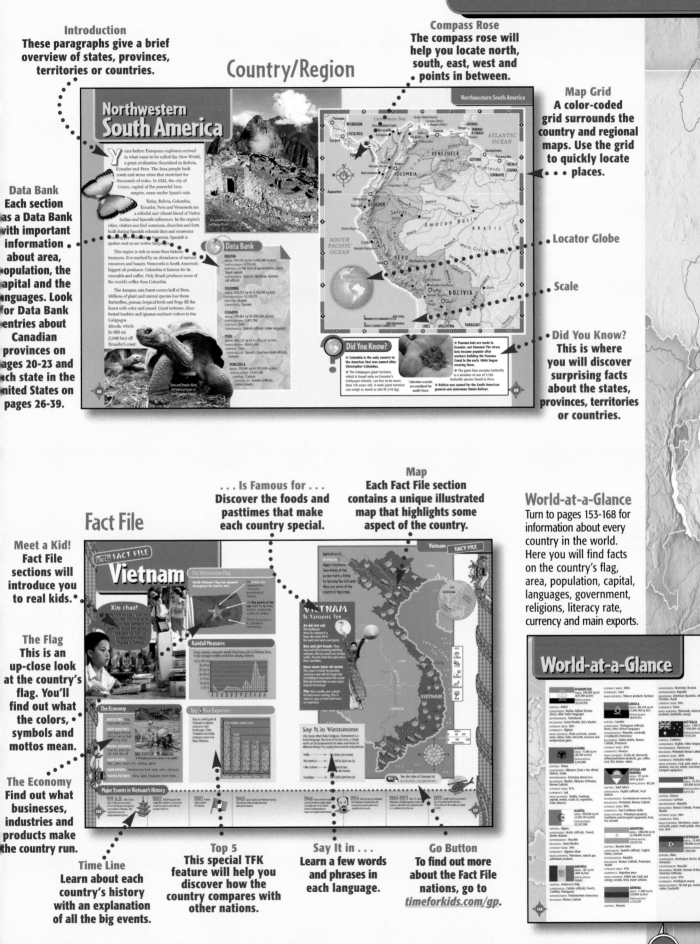

... Is Famous for ...
Discover the foods and pasttimes that make each country special.

Map
Each Fact File section contains a unique illustrated map that highlights some aspect of the country.

World-at-a-Glance
Turn to pages 153-168 for information about every country in the world. Here you will find facts on the country's flag, area, population, capital, languages, government, religions, literacy rate, currency and main exports.

Fact File

Meet a Kid!
Fact File sections will introduce you to real kids.

The Flag
This is an up-close look at the country's flag. You'll find out what the colors, symbols and mottos mean.

The Economy
Find out what businesses, industries and products make the country run.

Time Line
Learn about each country's history with an explanation of all the big events.

Top 5
This special TFK feature will help you discover how the country compares with other nations.

Say It in ...
Learn a few words and phrases in each language.

Go Button
To find out more about the Fact File nations, go to *timeforkids.com/gp*.

The Living Earth

When did life on Earth begin, and how? What were the conditions that made life possible? Did life arise only once? For centuries, scientists have struggled with these difficult questions.

We know from studying tiny microfossils of simple marine bacteria that life on Earth began at least 3.5 billion years ago. For the first billion years of Earth's history, bacteria were the only life on the planet. Some types of marine bacteria formed large colonies, and their fossil remains, called stromatolites, can be found along the coasts of South Africa and Australia.

Gradually, more complex animals began to evolve in the sea. An explosion in the diversity of animals took place between 500 million and 550 million years ago. This was followed by the appearance of the first creatures with backbones, fish. The next 100 million years saw the first plants and the first animals and insects to live on land. Dinosaurs appeared nearly 250 million years ago. They ruled Earth until 65 million years ago, when they disappeared. Scientists believe that an asteroid hit Earth and caused mass extinctions.

Today, life in all of its forms and glory is present in every nook and cranny of the globe, from the coldest, darkest depths of the ocean to ice-covered lakes in Antarctica to desolate Himalayan mountaintops. Earthlings now include microscopic flower mites that hitch rides on the beaks of hummingbirds, awesome 100-foot-long blue whales—and humans.

Biologists categorize the amazing diversity of the world's plant and animal life by habitat. The Arctic tundra, for example, with its polar bears and seals, is one habitat. The tropical rain forest along the Amazon River is another. Habitats range from the grasslands of bison and prairie dogs to the coral reefs of clownfish and moray eels. As the number of human beings on the planet grows larger and larger, it is our responsibility to make sure that these habitats and the precious creatures that depend on them are kept healthy and safe.

Major Events in Earth's History

4.5 billion years ago
Earth forms.

3.5 billion years ago
The oldest forms of life, such as bacteria, appear.

2 billion years ago
Simple microbes called protists appear.

1 billion years ago
Plants and fungi emerge.

Atmosphere

Lithosphere

Biosphere

Hydrosphere

Did You Know?

● Scientists divide Earth into four spheres. The atmosphere includes the gases that surround Earth. The biosphere includes all the living organisms. The hydrosphere contains all the planets water. The lithosphere is Earth's hard crust, which includes the tallest craggy mountains and the dirt in our gardens.

● There have been periods in Earth's history when many plants and animals have died all at once. These mass extinctions were probably caused by climate change or something like an asteroid hitting Earth.

● Bacteria, the first living things on Earth, are still the most plentiful organisms on the planet. They are found on land, in water and in the air.

● Each type of plant and animal is called a species. Biologists use the word biodiversity to describe the many different species on Earth. Even though scientists have identified only 1.5 million species, there may be as many as 10 million to 30 million in the world.

600 million years ago
More-complex soft-bodied animals emerge.

500 million years ago
Animals with backbones (jawless fish) emerge.

7 million years ago
Human ancestors emerge.

The Changing Planet

The earth is 4.5 billion years old. Like all other planets, it was formed from dust and debris by the powerful pull of the Sun's gravity. Scientists believe a smaller planet crashed into Earth when it was still a ball of molten rock. This collision created our moon. Gradually, the surface of Earth cooled and hardened. But most of the planet is still molten. What we think of as solid ground is only the outer layer, or the crust, less than 50 mi (80 km) thick. In some places it is only a couple of miles (kilometers) thick.

The earth's crust is on the move. Think of it as a giant jigsaw puzzle floating on a hot lava ball that is nearly 8,000 mi (13,000 km) across! The slowly shifting pieces of crust are called tectonic plates. Scientists believe that 220 million years ago, our seven continents were actually squashed together into one supercontinent called Pangea. Right now, the plates that meet in the middle of the Atlantic Ocean are pulling apart. That movement makes the Atlantic grow an inch wider each year.

Even though shifting plates move as slowly as snails, the shifts create dramatic results. Mountains are caused by plates crashing into one another. Earthquakes happen when two plates grinding against each other suddenly slip. Volcanoes are spots where the molten rock beneath the crust leaks out, sometimes explosively. And though we can't see them, many of the most spectacular formations on earth—from the biggest mountains to the deepest canyons—are actually underneath the water of the oceans, which covers two-thirds of the planet.

How a Volcano Works

1 Hot liquid rock (magma) from deep within the earth carves out a chamber as much as 6 mi (10 km) below the surface. As the magma rises, gases trapped in it expand and bubble off.

2 The gases exert tremendous outward pressure that pushes the magma upward. As the magma comes into contact with groundwater, the water turns to steam and exerts more pressure.

3 The magma and gases push through cracks in the mountain. (That's why warning signs of an eruption include higher levels of carbon dioxide, sulfur dioxide and other gases.) When the magma and gases reach the surface, the pressure is suddenly released. The volcano erupts, shooting out rocks, ash, gases and lava.

Magma chamber

Sources: U.S. Geological Society, The Smithsonian

Students in Taiwan inspect a track after a quake.

Danger Spots

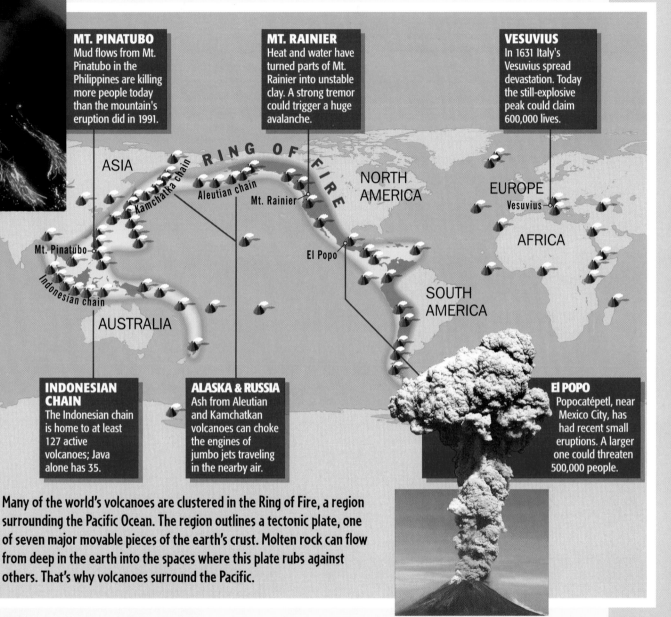

MT. PINATUBO
Mud flows from Mt. Pinatubo in the Philippines are killing more people today than the mountain's eruption did in 1991.

MT. RAINIER
Heat and water have turned parts of Mt. Rainier into unstable clay. A strong tremor could trigger a huge avalanche.

VESUVIUS
In 1631 Italy's Vesuvius spread devastation. Today the still-explosive peak could claim 600,000 lives.

ASIA

RING OF FIRE

Kamchatka chain

Aleutian chain

Mt. Rainier

NORTH AMERICA

EUROPE

Vesuvius

Mt. Pinatubo

El Popo

AFRICA

Indonesian chain

AUSTRALIA

SOUTH AMERICA

INDONESIAN CHAIN
The Indonesian chain is home to at least 127 active volcanoes; Java alone has 35.

ALASKA & RUSSIA
Ash from Aleutian and Kamchatkan volcanoes can choke the engines of jumbo jets traveling in the nearby air.

El POPO
Popocatépetl, near Mexico City, has had recent small eruptions. A larger one could threaten 500,000 people.

Many of the world's volcanoes are clustered in the Ring of Fire, a region surrounding the Pacific Ocean. The region outlines a tectonic plate, one of seven major movable pieces of the earth's crust. Molten rock can flow from deep in the earth into the spaces where this plate rubs against others. That's why volcanoes surround the Pacific.

Did You Know?

● In 1999, a team of scientists used satellite equipment to calculate a more accurate height for Mount Everest. The new height is 29,035 ft (8,850 m) above sea level. That is 7 ft (2 m) higher than before.

● Volcanoes can form where two plates meet. They can also form as the sea-floor plate passes over a "hot spot," an area where the crust is thin and the molten rock below has broken through. As the moving crust passes over the hot spot, volcanoes form, sometimes one after another. This is how the Hawaiian Islands were formed.

● There are thousands of volcanic eruptions each year. Most of them are minor. Many occur underwater. In 1963, an underwater eruption created a new island near Iceland.

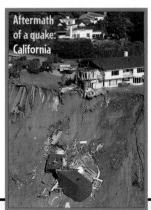

Aftermath of a quake: California

● The Richter scale measures the strength of earthquakes. The scale goes from a magnitude 1 to 9, with 9 being the strongest quake. An earthquake measuring 8 on the Richter scale is 10 times more powerful than a quake that measures 7. In 1908, a magnitude-8 earthquake nearly destroyed San Francisco, California.

Weather and Climate

The San Miguel River in Ecuador

When it comes to the day's forecast, climate is what you expect and weather is what you get. You can expect that it will be hot in Houston in July and cold in Chicago in January. It's impossible to know whether it will be sunny or raining or what the temperature will be.

The Sun is the ultimate climate-and-weather machine for our planet. The Sun's energy doesn't fall evenly on Earth—and that makes all the difference in the world! The tilt of our planet as it orbits the Sun causes the four seasons and contributes to the patterns of air circulation that create wet and dry seasons in parts of the world. Because Earth is curved, the Sun's rays hit the planet at different angles. Places located near the equator get more direct sunlight and more intense heat. The Sun also drives the weather on a daily basis. The collision of warm and cold air can produce a spring shower or a swarm of tornadoes. The circulation patterns in oceans also play a role in creating weather conditions. Some ocean currents keep northern Europe warm. Other currents fuel hurricanes and monsoons.

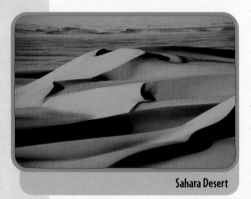
Sahara Desert

Climate is stable from year to year. But over long periods of time, climate can change dramatically. Fifteen thousand years ago, large parts of Europe, Canada, and the United States were stuck in a long, deep freeze called the Ice Age. Scientists are now busy taking the planet's temperature and measuring polar ice caps and mountaintop glaciers to determine how much our climate is changing. Scientists believe that the burning of fossil fuels is causing global warming.

Earth's atmosphere is divided into five layers: the troposphere, 0 mi to 7 mi (0 km to 11 km) high, where our weather occurs; the stratosphere, 7 mi to 30 mi (11 km to 48 km) high; the mesosphere, 30 mi to 50 mi (48 km to 80 km) high; the thermosphere, 50 mi to 300 mi (80 km to 483 km) high; and the exosphere, at 300 mi to 500 mi (483 km to 804 km) high and above, the edge of outer space.

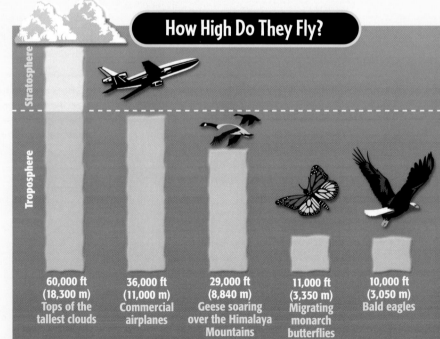

How High Do They Fly?

Stratosphere

Troposphere

| 60,000 ft (18,300 m) Tops of the tallest clouds | 36,000 ft (11,000 m) Commercial airplanes | 29,000 ft (8,840 m) Geese soaring over the Himalaya Mountains | 11,000 ft (3,350 m) Migrating monarch butterflies | 10,000 ft (3,050 m) Bald eagles |

A Hurricane's Life

Hurricanes get their start over Africa. The swirling storms are fueled by wet weather, winds and warm ocean water.

3 Tropical storms and hurricanes
If the storm holds together, a column-shaped "eye" forms at its center. Winds spin around it faster and faster. When winds reach 40 miles per hour, the system is called a tropical storm. When winds reach 74 miles per hour, it's a hurricane.

2 Across the Atlantic
Some storms remain small. But a few gather warm ocean moisture and speed up as they travel west. When bands of these thunderstorms form a swirling pattern, the system is called a tropical depression.

4 After the storm
Hurricanes weaken after they reach land. Some never hit land but turn northeast and die out over the Atlantic Ocean.

NORTH AMERICA

Hurricane

Atlantic Ocean

AFRICA

Sahara

Storm system

Sahel

Pacific Ocean

Upper-level and lower-level winds

SOUTH AMERICA

1 Born in West Africa
When hot, dry air from the Sahara Desert meets cooler, moist air from the Sahel region to the south, little storms form.

Other winds help build the storm
Upper- and lower-level winds blowing nearby in the same direction help hurricanes gather strength. Winds blowing in different directions or at different speeds can blow the storm apart.

Did You Know?

● The end of the Ice Age, about 10,000 years ago, was also the time of giant animals such as the mastodon, the woolly mammoth and the saber-toothed tiger. We know from fossils that Ice Age peoples used stone spears to hunt animals. Did these animals disappear because of overhunting or because the climate was getting warmer? Scientists don't know.

Glaciers in Antarctica

● In the past million years, ice ages have been common. It is the warm periods between them, such as the one we are in now, that are unusual. Some scientists believe that the next ice age is right around the corner. Don't worry: That could be about 10,000 years away!

● Is Earth getting warmer? The average worldwide surface temperature has been above normal for the past 25 years. The 10 warmest years on record for at least a century also occurred during that time. This warming trend is a concern to a lot of scientists—and probably some polar bears!

The Universe

Have you ever looked up at the starry night sky and wondered how big the universe is? On a clear night, away from the lights of towns and cities, you can see thousands of twinkling stars against the inky blackness. But it is only with the help of powerful telescopes that we can know just how awesomely big the universe really is.

Our neighborhood in space is the solar system. It contains nine planets and their moons, along with asteroids and comets. All orbit the Sun. The planet closest to the Sun is Mercury, which is 35 million miles (56 million km) away. Earth is 93 million miles (150 million km) away from the Sun. The planet farthest from the Sun, Pluto, is 3.5 billion miles (5.6 billion km) away. Beyond Pluto lies the Kuiper (*kie*-pur) Belt, a disk-shaped region filled with icy objects that stretches for an additional 6 billion miles.

Our nearest stellar neighbor is Proxima Centauri. It is 25 trillion miles (40 trillion km) away! That is only 4.2 light-years. Because the distances in the universe are so vast, astronomers don't measure them in miles but in light-years. A light-year is the distance that light travels in a year. Light travels at an incredibly fast rate—186,000 miles (299,000 km) per second. It takes only eight minutes for light to travel the 93 million miles (150 million km) from the Sun to Earth.

Our solar system is part of a gigantic, spiral-shaped cluster of stars and planets known as the Milky Way galaxy. Although the Milky Way contains 200 billion stars and is 90,000 light-years across, it is just one galaxy. Astronomers believe there may be 100 billion other galaxies in the universe! The universe is like a small bag of sparkling sand scattered in a dark and endless ocean.

Our Place in Space

Earth's solar system is just a tiny dot in the gigantic Milky Way galaxy. This chart shows the location of our solar system.

Neptune

The rocky Martian landscape

Solar system

Milky Way galaxy

Kuiper Belt

Sun
Mercury | Venus
Earth | Mars

Asteroid belt

Saturn

Pluto

Jupiter

Uranus

A star is born.

Did You Know?

● Even before there were telescopes, people saw patterns of stars in the sky. They called the patterns constellations and gave them names such as Orion, the hunter, and Leo, the lion.

● Stars are "born" in huge clouds of gas and dust when gravity concentrates them into dense balls of matter.

● Since 1995, astronomers have discovered dozens of planets orbiting nearby stars. Does life exist somewhere else in the universe?

● When some large stars die, they become novas, or exploding stars. The gas and dust that they leave behind can, in turn, be used to form new stars.

● If you could take a jet that traveled at 600 mph (970 kph), it would take you 17 weeks to fly to the Sun and 690 years to get to Pluto.

● In January 2004, two NASA probes, *Spirit* and *Opportunity*, landed on Mars after seven-month journeys. The probes explored the surface, took pictures and sent data back to Earth.

The Arctic

The Arctic region is the northernmost place on the planet. Strictly speaking, it is the area that falls inside the Arctic Circle. But many scientists define the Arctic as the area centered around the North Pole, including everything north of the tree line (the point beyond which no trees can grow). That region includes parts of Alaska, Canada, Greenland, Iceland, Russia and Norway.

The Arctic climate is cold and harsh. Winter at the North Pole lasts six months, and the sun never rises! The average temperature is about –22°F (–33°C). Summer at the top of the world is nearly opposite, with six months of constant daylight and relatively mild temperatures of around 32°F (0°C).

Night Lights: The aurora borealis dances across the Canadian sky.

Despite the forbidding environment, some hardy animals—including humans!—thrive in the frozen north. Giant polar bears, walruses, seals and some 23 other animal species survive year-round in the polar climate. The people of the Arctic, including the Inuit of North America, the Lapps (Sami) of Scandinavia and the Nenets and Chukchis of Russia, have also adapted to their surroundings. It is not possible to grow food, so nourishment must come from land and sea animals. In the past, native Arctic communities were isolated from the rest of the world. But in recent years, tourism and the discovery of oil and mineral deposits have started to bring more outsiders to the region.

Regional Facts

ARCTIC CIRCLE AREA: 8,000,000 sq mi (21,000,000 sq km)
ARCTIC OCEAN AREA: 5,427,000 sq mi (14,056,000 sq km)
ARCTIC OCEAN DEPTH: 13,123 ft (4,000 m)
LOWEST POINT: Fram Basin, 15,305 ft (4,665 m)
LARGEST ISLAND: Greenland, 836,222 sq mi (2,166,086 sq km)

Polar bears can weigh as much as 1,000 lbs (453 kg)!

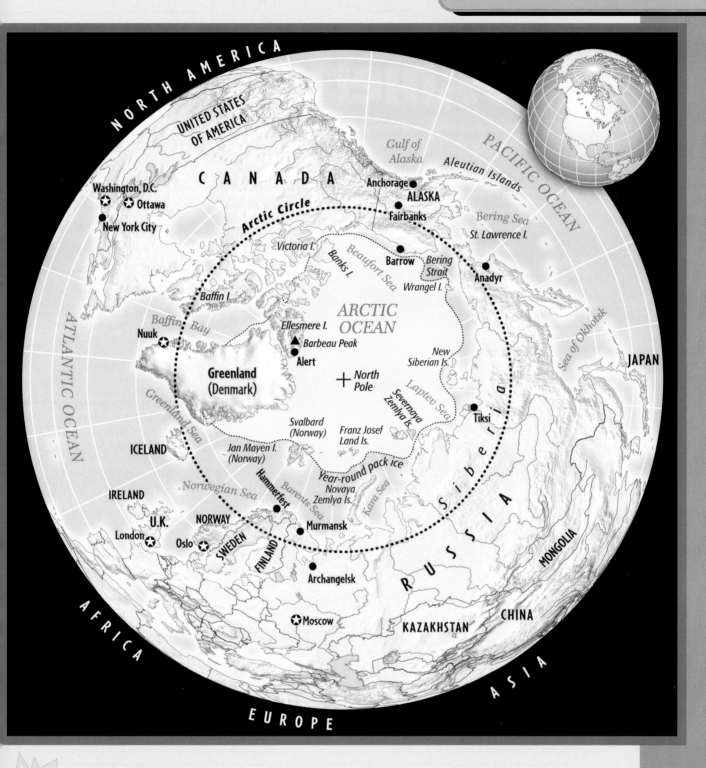

The Arctic map showing North America, Canada, United States of America, Washington D.C., Ottawa, New York City, Gulf of Alaska, Anchorage, ALASKA, Aleutian Islands, PACIFIC OCEAN, Fairbanks, Arctic Circle, Bering Sea, St. Lawrence I., Victoria I., Beaufort Sea, Banks I., Barrow, Bering Strait, Wrangel I., Anadyr, Baffin I., Baffin Bay, ARCTIC OCEAN, Nuuk, Ellesmere I., Barbeau Peak, Alert, New Siberian Is., Sea of Okhotsk, JAPAN, Greenland (Denmark), North Pole, Laptev Sea, Severnaya Zemlya Is., Siberia, Tiksi, Greenland Sea, Svalbard (Norway), Franz Josef Land Is., ICELAND, Jan Mayen I. (Norway), Year-round pack ice, Novaya Zemlya Is., Kara Sea, RUSSIA, IRELAND, Hammerfest, Barents Sea, Norwegian Sea, U.K., NORWAY, Murmansk, London, Oslo, SWEDEN, FINLAND, MONGOLIA, Archangelsk, CHINA, KAZAKHSTAN, Moscow, AFRICA, EUROPE, ASIA, ATLANTIC OCEAN

Wow Zone!

Dog sledding is an Arctic mode of transportation.

● The Arctic Ocean is the smallest ocean in the world.

● Ilulissat, also called Jakobshavn, is the third-largest town in Greenland. The town is home to 4,000 people and some 6,000 sled dogs!

● The word Arctic comes from the Greek word *arktos*, which means "bear." It refers to the northern constellation of stars called Bear.

● The aurora borealis, or northern lights, can be seen in the Arctic night sky. It is caused by solar winds interacting with Earth's atmosphere.

North America

The Grand Canyon in Arizona

Stretching 9 million square miles (24 million sq km), North America is the world's third-biggest continent. The region extends from the icy Arctic Ocean in the north to the warm, turquoise waters of the Caribbean Sea. In between lies nearly every landscape imaginable: massive glaciers, snow-covered mountains, vast canyons, fertile plains and tropical rain forests.

North America is made up of 23 nations, including Canada, the world's second-largest country, and the U.S., the world's third-largest country. The continent is rich in natural resources—abundant water, minerals and fertile soil—and has one of the world's most developed economies. North Americans have a higher income per person than those living on any other continent.

Beyond its physical beauty, North America is also known for its dynamic cities. From New York City to Los Angeles, Mexico City to Vancouver, world-class museums, universities and concert halls beckon those hungry for cultural and intellectual fare.

Continent Facts

AREA: 9,361,791 sq mi (24,247,039 sq km)

COUNTRIES AND TERRITORIES: Antigua and Barbuda, Anguilla (U.K.), Aruba (Netherlands), Bahamas, Barbados, Belize, Bermuda (U.K.), Canada, Cayman Islands (U.K.), Costa Rica, Cuba, Dominica, Dominican Republic, El Salvador, Greenland (Denmark), Grenada, Guadeloupe (France), Guatemala, Haiti, Honduras, Jamaica, Martinique (France), Mexico, Montserrat (U.K.), Netherlands Antilles (Netherlands), Nicaragua, Panama, Puerto Rico (U.S.), Saint Barthélemy (Guadeloupe), Saint Kitts and Nevis, Saint Lucia, Saint Maarten/Saint Martin (Netherlands Antilles/ Guadeloupe), Saint Vincent and the Grenadines, Trinidad and Tobago, Turks and Caicos (U.K.), United States, Virgin Islands (U.S. and U.K.)

HIGHEST POINT: Mount McKinley (Denali), Alaska, 20,320 ft (6,194 m)

LOWEST POINT: Death Valley, California, 282 ft (86 m) below sea level

LARGEST LAKE: Lake Superior, 31,820 sq mi (82, 414 sq km)

LONGEST RIVER: Missouri-Mississippi river system, 3,710 mi (5,971 km)

LARGEST COUNTRY: Canada, 3,855,085 sq mi (9,984670 sq km)

SMALLEST COUNTRY: Saint Kitts and Nevis, 101 sq mi (262 sq km)

Wow Zone!

● The oldest rocks in the world are from Canada. Scientists believe they are close to 4 billion years old!

● Greenland is the world's largest island. It is nearly covered with ice.

● Lake Superior, on the U.S.-Canadian border, is the world's largest freshwater lake.

● The Everglades covers about 4 million acres (1.6 million hectares). It is home to more than 400 species of birds, 25 species of mammals, 60 species of amphibians and reptiles and 125 species of fish.

● North America includes two of the world's most populous cities, New York City and Mexico City. Both have populations in excess of 8 million.

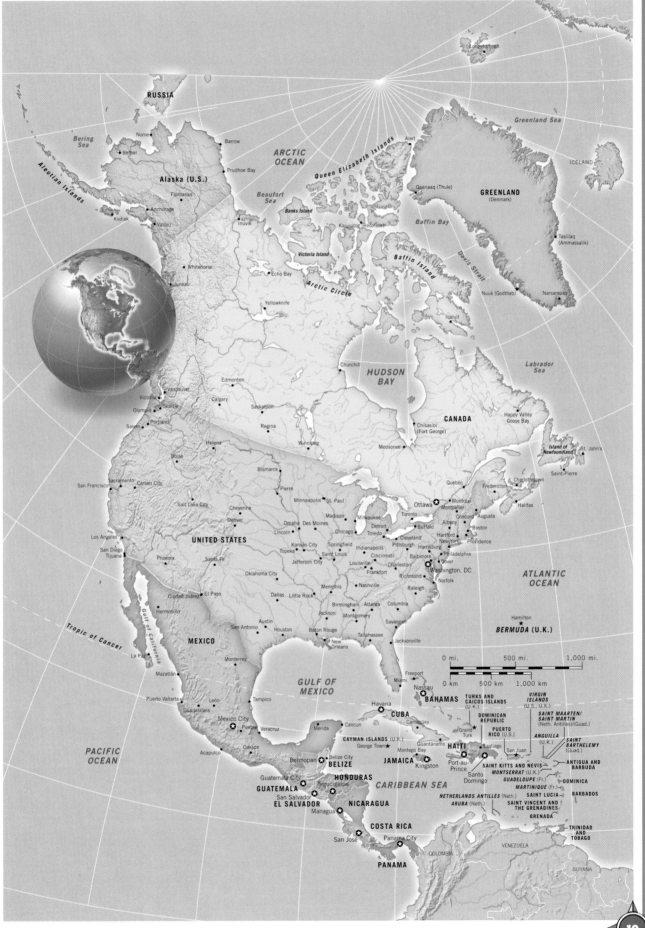

RUSSIA

Bering
Sea

Aleutian Islands

Nome
Bethel
Barrow
Prudhoe Bay

ARCTIC
OCEAN

Queen Elizabeth Islands

Longyearbyen

Greenland
Sea

Alert

ICELAND

Alaska (U.S.)

Fairbanks
Anchorage
Kodiak
Valdez

Beaufort
Sea

Banks Island

Inuvik

Kangiqtugaapik (Resolute)

Baffin Bay

Qaanaaq (Thule)

GREENLAND
(Denmark)

Davis Strait

Tasiilaq
(Ammassalik)

Whitehorse
Juneau

Echo Bay

Victoria Island

Arctic Circle

Baffin Island

Nuuk (Godthåb)

Narsarsuaq

Yellowknife

Iqaluit

Edmonton

Churchill

HUDSON
BAY

Labrador
Sea

Happy Valley
Goose Bay

Vancouver
Victoria
Seattle
Olympia
Salem
Portland

Calgary

Saskatoon

Regina

Winnipeg

Moosonee

Chisasibi
(Fort George)

CANADA

Island of
Newfoundland

St. John's

Saint-Pierre

Helena
Boise

Bismarck

Québec

Fredericton

Charlottetown

Halifax

San Francisco
Sacramento
Carson City

Salt Lake City

Cheyenne

Pierre

Minneapolis   St. Paul

Montréal
Ottawa   Montpelier
Concord   Augusta
Toronto   Albany   Boston
Buffalo   Hartford   Providence
New York
Harrisburg   Philadelphia

Los Angeles

San Diego
Tijuana

Phoenix

Denver

Madison

Milwaukee

Detroit
Chicago   Toledo   Cleveland
Pittsburgh

UNITED STATES

Lincoln

Santa Fe

Omaha   Des Moines

Kansas City
Topeka
Jefferson City

Springfield
Indianapolis
Saint Louis
Louisville   Cincinnati
Frankfort

Baltimore
Dover
Washington, DC
Richmond
Norfolk

ATLANTIC
OCEAN

Oklahoma City

Memphis

Nashville

Charleston

Raleigh

Ciudad Juárez   El Paso

Hermosillo

Dallas   Little Rock

Birmingham   Atlanta   Columbia

Jackson   Montgomery

Savannah

Hamilton

BERMUDA (U.K.)

Tropic of Cancer

MEXICO

La Paz

Mazatlán

Puerto Vallarta

Guadalajara

León
Mexico City
Puebla

Monterrey

San Antonio   Austin

Houston
Baton Rouge
New
Orleans

Tampico

Veracruz

Merida

GULF OF
MEXICO

Miami

Freeport

Nassau

Havana

Cancun

Camagüey

Tallahassee

Jacksonville

0 mi.   500 mi.   1,000 mi.

0 km   500 km   1,000 km

BAHAMAS

TURKS AND
CAICOS ISLANDS
(U.K.)

VIRGIN
ISLANDS
(U.S. & U.K.)

SAINT MAARTEN/
SAINT MARTIN
(Neth. Antilles)/(Guad.)

PACIFIC
OCEAN

Acapulco

Oaxaca

Belmopan   Belize City

BELIZE

CUBA

Guantánamo

Montego Bay

JAMAICA

Kingston

DOMINICAN
REPUBLIC

Santiago

HAITI
Port-au-
Prince

Santo
Domingo

PUERTO
RICO
(U.S.)

San Juan

CAYMAN ISLANDS (U.K.)
George Town

Grand
Turk

ANGUILLA
(U.K.)

SAINT
BARTHELEMY
(Guad.)

ANTIGUA AND
BARBUDA

SAINT KITTS AND NEVIS
MONTSERRAT (U.K.)
GUADELOUPE (Fr.)
MARTINIQUE (Fr.)

DOMINICA

Guatemala City

GUATEMALA

San Salvador

EL SALVADOR

HONDURAS

Tegucigalpa

Managua

NICARAGUA

CARIBBEAN SEA

NETHERLANDS ANTILLES (Neth.)
ARUBA (Neth.)

SAINT LUCIA

SAINT VINCENT AND
THE GRENADINES

GRENADA

BARBADOS

TRINIDAD
AND
TOBAGO

COSTA RICA

San José

Panama City

PANAMA

COLOMBIA

VENEZUELA

GUYANA

Eastern Canada

Measuring nearly 4 million sq mi (10 million sq km), Canada is the world's second-largest country. Only Russia is larger. Canada is divided into 10 provinces and three territories. It stretches from the Atlantic Ocean in the east to the Pacific Ocean in the west. More than half of Canada's population lives in the eastern region. The east is also the location of the country's capital, Ottawa, and its two largest cities, Montreal and Toronto. Many of Canada's early settlers were from France and Britain. Both countries believed that Canada should belong to them, which led to years of war and conflict. In 1763, at the end of the Seven Years' War, France was forced to give its Canadian territory to Britain. In 1867, Canada's colonies joined to form the Dominion of Canada. The country's government included a governor general, who represented Britain's monarch.

Niagara's Horseshoe Falls

Canadians today are proud of their freedom, but they have not forgotten their heritage. French is spoken by about one-third of the population; Britain's queen is still pictured on some Canadian money; and the customs and traditions of native people are valued and respected.

Data Bank

CANADA
AREA: 3,855,085 sq mi (9,984,670 sq km)
POPULATION: 32,507,874
CAPITAL: Ottawa
LANGUAGES: English, French (both official)

Eastern Canada's Provinces

ONTARIO
AREA: 412,582 sq mi (1,068,587 sq km)
POPULATION: 10,084,885
CAPITAL: Ottawa

NEW BRUNSWICK
AREA: 28,345 sq mi (73,433 sq km)
POPULATION: 723,900
CAPITAL: Fredericton

NEWFOUNDLAND AND LABRADOR
AREA: 156,185 sq mi (404,519 sq km)
POPULATION: 568,474
CAPITAL: Saint John's

NOVA SCOTIA
AREA: 21,425 sq mi (55,491 sq km)
POPULATION: 899,942
CAPITAL: Halifax

PRINCE EDWARD ISLAND
AREA: 2,184 sq mi (5,657 sq km)
POPULATION: 129,765
CAPITAL: Charlottetown

QUEBEC
AREA: 594,860 sq mi (1,553,637 sq km)
POPULATION: 6,895,963
CAPITAL: Quebec

The fishing industry provides more than 120,000 jobs for Canadians.

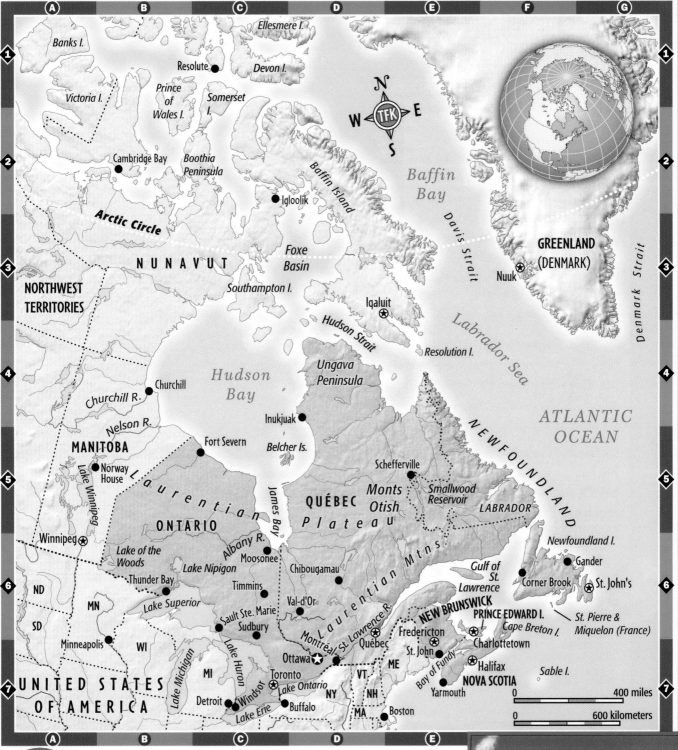

Map of Eastern Canada

Grid references: A B C D E F G (columns), 1 2 3 4 5 6 7 (rows)

Banks I.
Ellesmere I.
Devon I.
Resolute
Victoria I.
Prince of Wales I.
Somerset I.
Cambridge Bay
Boothia Peninsula
Igloolik
Baffin Island
Baffin Bay
Arctic Circle
GREENLAND (DENMARK)
Nuuk
Davis Strait
NUNAVUT
NORTHWEST TERRITORIES
Foxe Basin
Southampton I.
Iqaluit
Hudson Strait
Labrador Sea
Resolution I.
Denmark Strait
Hudson Bay
Ungava Peninsula
Churchill
Churchill R.
Nelson R.
MANITOBA
Norway House
Lake Winnipeg
Fort Severn
Inukjuak
Belcher Is.
Schefferville
Smallwood Reservoir
NEWFOUNDLAND
ATLANTIC OCEAN
LABRADOR
Monts Otish
QUÉBEC
Plateau
James Bay
Laurentian
ONTARIO
Winnipeg
Lake of the Woods
Albany R.
Moosonee
Lake Nipigon
Chibougamau
Newfoundland I.
Gander
Thunder Bay
Timmins
Val-d'Or
Laurentian Mtns.
Gulf of St. Lawrence
Corner Brook
St. John's
ND
MN
SD
Lake Superior
Sault Ste. Marie
Sudbury
St. Lawrence R.
NEW BRUNSWICK
PRINCE EDWARD I.
Cape Breton I.
St. Pierre & Miquelon (France)
Minneapolis
WI
MI
Lake Michigan
Lake Huron
Montréal
Québec
Fredericton
Charlottetown
Ottawa
Toronto
Lake Ontario
ME
VT
St. John
Halifax
Sable I.
UNITED STATES OF AMERICA
Detroit
Windsor
Lake Erie
Buffalo
NY
NH
MA
Boston
Bay of Fundy
Yarmouth
NOVA SCOTIA

0 — 400 miles
0 — 600 kilometers

Did You Know?

● Canada has the world's longest coastline. Its length of 151,614 mi (244,000 km) would circle the earth more than six times!

● In winter, the Rideau Canal, in Ottawa, is the world's longest skating rink. It is 4.8 mi (7.72 km) long.

● Canada is considered the birthplace of ice hockey. More than half the players in the U.S.'s National Hockey League are Canadian.

● Niagara Falls has two sides, one in Canada and one in the United States. The Canadian Falls, or Horseshoe Falls, is 170 ft (52 m) high. As much as 40 million gal of water (151 million l) rushes over the rim of the Canadian Falls each minute.

● The word *Canada* is from an Iroquois Indian word that means "community."

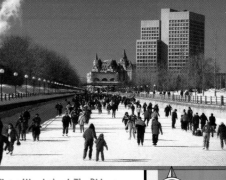

Winter Wonderland: The Rideau Canal is a giant ice-skating rink.

Western Canada and Alaska

Vancouver is Canada's third-largest city.

Snowcapped mountains, icy glaciers, grassy prairies and fertile farmland are the landscapes that cover the vast area that makes up western Canada. This region has four provinces and three territories. Nunavut—a sprawling region of tundra, Arctic islands and frozen fjords—was carved out of the Northwest Territories in 1999.

Most of western Canada's residents live near the country's southern border, where temperatures are milder. Alberta, Saskatchewan and Manitoba are known for their oil and gas reserves, plentiful fields of wheat and large cattle ranches. British Columbia, which is Canada's westernmost province, features the beautiful city of Vancouver.

West of Canada lies Alaska. It is the largest state in the United States but has the fewest people per square mile. In 1867, the U.S. bought Alaska from Russia for $7.2 million. Many people thought it was a foolish purchase. But they changed their minds when gold was discovered in 1896. Today, oil is Alaska's largest industry.

RUSSIA Anadyr

St. Lawrence I.

Bering Sea

Aleutian Islands

Arctic Circle

Data Bank

Western Canada's Provinces

ALBERTA
AREA: 255,285 sq mi (661,188 sq km)
POPULATION: 2,545,553
CAPITAL: Edmonton

BRITISH COLUMBIA
AREA: 366,255 sq mi (948,600 sq km)
POPULATION: 3,282,061
CAPITOL: Victoria

MANITOBA
AREA: 250,934 sq mi (650.930 sq km)
POPULATION: 1,091,942
CAPITAL: Winnipeg

SASKATCHEWAN
AREA: 251,700 sq mi (651,903 sq km)
POPULATION: 988,928
CAPITAL: Regina

NORTHWEST TERRITORIES
AREA: 532,643 sq mi (1,379,028 sq km)
POPULATION: 39,672
CAPITAL: Yellowknife

NUNAVUT
AREA: 772,260 sq mi (2,000,671 sq km)
POPULATION: 24,730
CAPITAL: Iqaluit

YUKON TERRITORY
AREA: 207,076 sq mi (536,327 sq km)
POPULATION: 27,797
CAPITAL: Whitehorse

U.S. State

ALASKA
AREA: 656,424 sq mi (1,700,135 sq km)
POPULATION: 628,932
CAPITAL: Juneau
MOTTO: North to the Future

Cold-Weather Gear: Girls in Nunavut

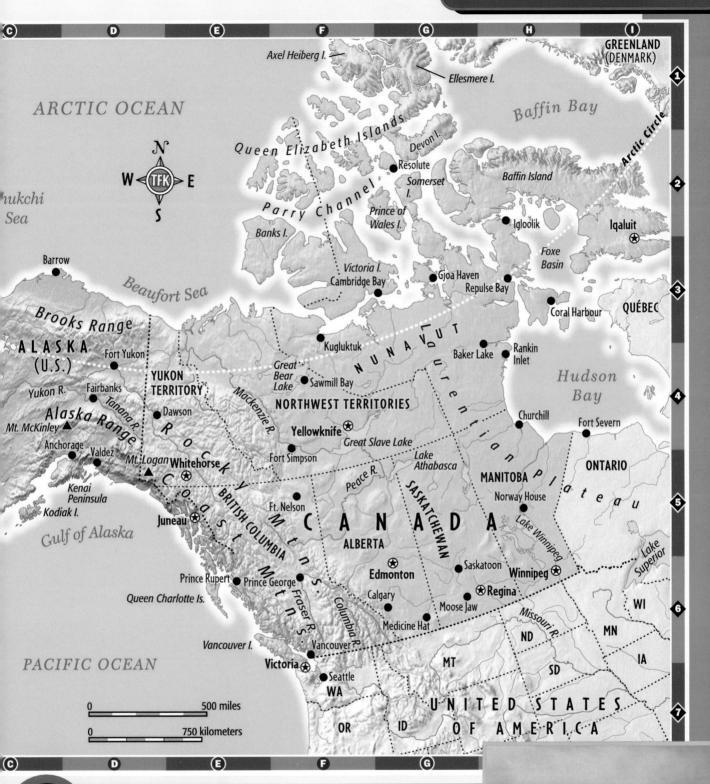

C **D** **E** **F** **G** **H** **I**

GREENLAND
(DENMARK)

ARCTIC OCEAN

Arctic Circle

Axel Heiberg I.

Ellesmere I.

Baffin Bay

Queen Elizabeth Islands

Devon I.

Resolute

Baffin Island

Somerset I.

Parry Channel

Prince of Wales I.

Igloolik

Iqaluit

hukchi Sea

Banks I.

Foxe Basin

Barrow

Beaufort Sea

Victoria I.
Cambridge Bay

Gjoa Haven
Repulse Bay

Coral Harbour

QUÉBEC

Brooks Range

Kugluktuk

N U N A V U T

Baker Lake

Rankin Inlet

ALASKA
(U.S.)

Fort Yukon

Great Bear Lake

Sawmill Bay

Hudson Bay

Yukon R.   Fairbanks

YUKON TERRITORY

Mackenzie R.

NORTHWEST TERRITORIES

Churchill

Fort Severn

Tanana R.

Dawson

Yellowknife

Laurentian Plateau

Alaska Range

Mt. McKinley ▲

Great Slave Lake

Anchorage

Fort Simpson

Lake Athabasca

ONTARIO

Valdez

Mt. Logan ▲ Whitehorse

Peace R.

MANITOBA

Kenai Peninsula

Juneau

BRITISH COLUMBIA

Ft. Nelson

C A N A D A

SASKATCHEWAN

Norway House

Kodiak I.

Gulf of Alaska

ALBERTA

Lake Winnipeg

Lake Superior

Prince Rupert   Prince George

Edmonton

Saskatoon

Winnipeg

Queen Charlotte Is.

Fraser R.

Calgary

Regina

WI

Columbia R.

Medicine Hat

Moose Jaw

Missouri R.

MN

Vancouver I.

Vancouver

ND

MT

SD

IA

PACIFIC OCEAN

Victoria

Seattle
WA

UNITED STATES
OF AMERICA

OR   ID

0   500 miles

0   750 kilometers

C **D** **E** **F** **G**

23

Canada

Hi, Bonjour!

I'm Dalhi, and I'm 12 years old. I live with my mom and my dog Ginny on Galiano Island, off Canada's west coast. My background is French Canadian, and I go to a French-immersion school. To get there, I take a one-hour ride on a ferry. My favorite sports are soccer and hockey, and I play the saxophone. My jazz band is called the Brass Buttons! Join me on a tour of my home, Canada.

The Canadian Flag

The maple-leaf flag first flew in 1965. The design of Canada's earlier flag included a small British flag.

Red and **white** are the country's official colors.

The maple leaf is a national symbol. Canada's native people used the sap from maple trees as food. Today Canada produces 85% of the world's supply of maple syrup!

Canadian Heritage

Though most Canadians have British or French roots, Canada is a country that is a blend of many cultures.

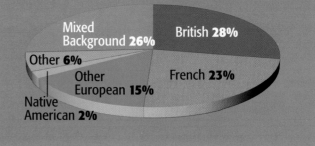

- Mixed Background **26%**
- British **28%**
- Other **6%**
- Other European **15%**
- French **23%**
- Native American **2%**

The Economy

AGRICULTURE: Wheat, barley, corn, oats, potatoes, vegetables, soybeans, sugar beets

MANUFACTURING: Food products, paper and printing products, lumber and wood products

MAJOR EXPORTS: Machinery, transportation equipment, oil and gas, lumber, newsprint, paper products

MAJOR IMPORTS: Chemical products, automobiles, food

TRADING PARTNERS: U.S., Japan, Britain, Mexico, China

An oil rig in Alberta

Top 5 Forest-Product Exporters

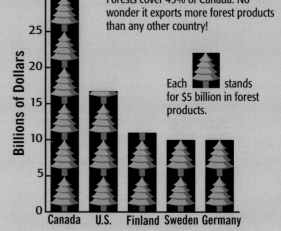

Forests cover 45% of Canada. No wonder it exports more forest products than any other country!

Each ▲ stands for $5 billion in forest products.

Billions of Dollars — Canada, U.S., Finland, Sweden, Germany

Major Events in Canada's History

30,000 B.C.–15,000 B.C. The first people arrive in the area. They had crossed a land bridge from northeast Asia to North America.

1000 A.D. The Vikings explore what is now Nova Scotia, Newfoundland and New Brunswick.

1497 Explorer John Cabot sails to Canada's east coast and claims it for England.

1534 Explorer Jacques Cartier claims what is now Quebec Province for France. He uses the Huron-Iroquois word for village or community, *kanata*, to describe it.

CANADA
NORTH AMERICA

KEY

Gas		Logging	
Wheat		Sheep	
Oil		Cattle	
Mining		Hogs	
Maple Syrup		Fishing	
Manufacturing			

SCALE
Miles
0   250   500
0   250   500
Kilometers

GREENLAND (DENMARK)

UNITED STATES

Yukon Territory

Northwest Territories

Nunavut

Arctic Circle

PACIFIC OCEAN

British Columbia

Alberta

CANADA

Churchill

Saskatchewan

Manitoba

HUDSON BAY

LABRADOR SEA

Newfoundland

Vancouver

Ontario

Quebec

St. Lawrence Seaway

New Brunswick

Quebec City

Nova Scotia

OTTAWA

Montreal

Lake Superior

UNITED STATES

Lake Michigan

Lake Huron

Lake Ontario
Toronto
Lake Erie

ATLANTIC OCEAN

From its untamed frozen north to its rich cropland in the south, Canada is a country of extremes. Most Canadians live near the Canadian-U.S. border.

CANADA Is Famous for ...

Ice hockey Though the ancient Egyptians, Greeks and Romans played forms of the sport on dry land, Canadians developed the modern game on ice in the mid-1850s.

Curling A winter sport in which players slide heavy stones on a field of ice toward a target.

Poutine (poo-teen) A French-Canadian dish of french fries smothered in cheese curds and beef gravy. It's so popular, you can find it in fast-food restaurants!

Tourtière (tor-tee-air) A meat pie cooked with herbs and gravy is another French-Canadian favorite.

The Royal Canadian Mounted Police, or Mounties, are known for their scarlet uniforms, dashing hats and skillful police work.

Say It in Canadian Slang

Can you talk like a **Canuck**? Bet you a loonie that you can! These words and phrases are Canadian slang. They're fun, eh?

Eh? ⟶ Do you know what I mean?

Canuck ⟶ Nickname for a Canadian

Loonie ⟶ Dollar coin

Toonie ⟶ Two-dollar coin

Hang up the skates ⟶ Retire

Tuque (took) ⟶ Woolen winter cap

 To learn more about Canada, go to *timeforkids.com/gpcanada*.

1763 The Treaty of Paris ends seven years of fighting between France and England. France gives its Canadian settlements to England.

1896 Gold is discovered in the Klondike region of western Canada.

1982 The Charter of Rights and Freedoms becomes the law of the land. It outlines rights for all Canadians.

1999 Nunavut, which was part of the Northwest Territories, becomes a self-governing Inuit territory. It is the first territory to have a majority native population.

United States of America

The U. S. Capitol in Washington, D. C.

The United States of America stretches across the North American continent and beyond. It includes a vast range of climates and geographic regions, from temperate forests to arid deserts. In 1776, the 13 original British colonies revolted against their rulers and formed a new nation. Since the Revolution, the United States has grown to 50 states and become a destination for immigrants from around the world. Over the centuries, these very diverse cultures have found a means to coexist in a democracy. For this reason, the population of the United States is often referred to as a "melting pot" of people.

The United States includes 49 states on the North American continent, one state in the Pacific Ocean and a number of possessions. Puerto Rico and the Virgin Islands are in the Caribbean Sea; American Samoa and Guam are in the Pacific Ocean. The nation is governed by an elected President and a Congress, made up of a Senate and a House of Representatives. Washington, D.C., is the nation's capital. In addition to the President and Congress, each state has its own elected government. Although an American national culture exists, each region has its own particular accent, customs and cuisines. Among the regions are New England, the Middle Atlantic, the South, the Midwest, the Southwest and the West.

Since its founding, the United States has steadily increased in physical size and political power. Today, as a superpower, the nation wields a great deal of economic and cultural influence around the world.

Data Bank

UNITED STATES OF AMERICA
AREA: 3,717,776 sq mi (9,629,091 sq km)
POPULATION: 293,027,571
CAPITAL: Washington, D.C.
LANGUAGES: English, Spanish

Monumental Presidents:
Mount Rushmore in South Dakota

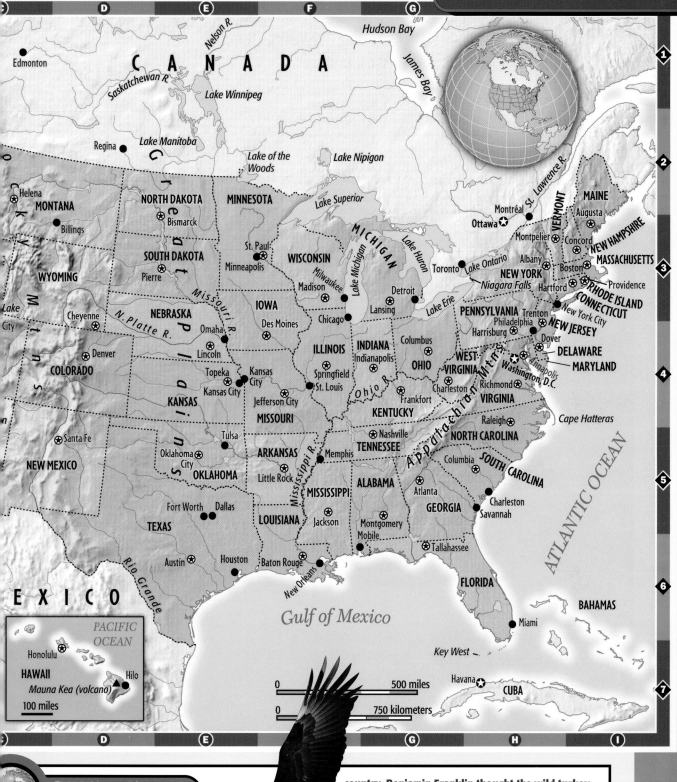

Edmonton

Nelson R.

C A N A D A

Hudson Bay

James Bay

1

Saskatchewan R.

Lake Winnipeg

St. Lawrence R.

2

Regina

Lake Manitoba

Lake of the Woods

Lake Nipigon

MAINE

Augusta

Helena
MONTANA

NORTH DAKOTA

MINNESOTA

Lake Superior

Montréal

VERMONT

NEW HAMPSHIRE

Billings

Bismarck

MICHIGAN

Ottawa

Montpelier

Concord

MASSACHUSETTS

3

SOUTH DAKOTA

WISCONSIN

Lake Huron

Toronto

Lake Ontario

Albany

Boston

Providence

WYOMING

St. Paul
Minneapolis

Milwaukee
Madison

Lake Michigan

Detroit

Niagara Falls

NEW YORK

Hartford

RHODE ISLAND
CONNECTICUT

Pierre

Lansing

Lake Erie

PENNSYLVANIA

Trenton

New York City

Lake
City

Cheyenne

NEBRASKA

IOWA
Des Moines

Chicago

Philadelphia
Harrisburg

NEW JERSEY
Dover

Omaha

INDIANA

Columbus

WEST
VIRGINIA

DELAWARE

Denver

Lincoln

ILLINOIS
Indianapolis

OHIO

Washington, D.C.

Annapolis

MARYLAND

4

COLORADO

Topeka

Kansas
City

Springfield
St. Louis

Richmond

Santa Fe

KANSAS

Kansas City

Jefferson City

Frankfort

Charleston

VIRGINIA

Raleigh

Cape Hatteras

MISSOURI

KENTUCKY

Nashville

NORTH CAROLINA

Tulsa

TENNESSEE

Columbia

SOUTH
CAROLINA

5

NEW MEXICO

Oklahoma
City

OKLAHOMA

ARKANSAS

Memphis

Little Rock

ALABAMA

Atlanta

Charleston

Fort Worth

Dallas

MISSISSIPPI

Jackson

GEORGIA

Savannah

TEXAS

LOUISIANA

Montgomery

Mobile

Austin

Houston

Baton Rouge

Tallahassee

FLORIDA

BAHAMAS

6

New Orleans

Gulf of Mexico

Miami

E X I C O

Rio Grande

ATLANTIC OCEAN

PACIFIC
OCEAN

Honolulu

HAWAII

Mauna Kea (volcano)

Hilo

Key West

Havana

CUBA

7

100 miles

0   500 miles

0   750 kilometers

D E F G H I

Did You Know?

● The United States is the third-largest country in the world by size and population.

● The bald eagle is the national bird of the United States and a symbol for the nation. With its 7-ft (2-m) wingspan and powerful beak and talons, the eagle is an impressive bird of prey. Still, not all the Founding Fathers wanted the eagle to represent the country. Benjamin Franklin thought the wild turkey would be a more appropriate symbol!

● Mount Rushmore National Memorial is an enormous sculpture blasted and drilled into the side of a mountain in the Black Hills of South Dakota. The monument, which was completed in 1941, depicts Presidents Theodore Roosevelt, Abraham Lincoln, George Washington and Thomas Jefferson.

● The motto of the United States is *E pluribus unum*, which means "From many, one."

United States of America
New England

Nestled between Canada, New York and the Atlantic Ocean are the six states that make up New England. Each state has its own special identity, and together they have many unique features, including snow-capped mountains that beckon skiers during the winter; miles of scenic coastline; marshy bogs where cranberries grow; spectacular fall foliage; and bustling cities and towns.

The Atlantic Ocean forms the eastern border of all but Vermont, which is landlocked. Connecticut, Massachusetts, Maine, New Hampshire and Rhode Island touch the ocean.

Much of America's colonial history is anchored in New England. Plymouth Colony, in Massachusetts, was the first permanent European settlement in New England. The first battles of the American Revolution took place in Concord, Massachusetts, near Boston. Historically, trade, fishing and shipbuilding were important revenue sources for the region. But tourism, banking and industry have emerged as the major moneymakers for these Northeastern states.

Beacon of Light: **Portland Head Light in Maine**

The purple finch is New Hampshire's state bird.

Data Bank

CONNECTICUT
AREA: 4,845 sq mi (12,550 sq km)
POPULATION: 3,483,372
CAPITAL: Hartford
MOTTO: *Qui transtulit sustinet* (He who transplanted still sustains)

MAINE
AREA: 30,865 sq mi (79,941 sq km)
POPULATION: 1,305,728
CAPITAL: Augusta
MOTTO: *Dirigo* (I lead)

MASSACHUSETTS
AREA: 7,838 sq mi (20,300 sq km)
POPULATION: 6,433,422
CAPITAL: Boston
MOTTO: *Ense petit placidam sub libertate quietem* (By the sword we seek peace, but peace only under liberty)

NEW HAMPSHIRE
AREA: 8,969 sq mi (23,231 sq km)
POPULATION: 1,287,687
CAPITAL: Concord
MOTTO: Live free or die

RHODE ISLAND
AREA: 1,045 sq mi (2,707 sq km)
POPULATION: 1,076,164
CAPITAL: Providence
MOTTO: Hope

VERMONT
AREA: 9,249 sq mi (23,955 sq km)
POPULATION: 619,107
CAPITAL: Montpelier
MOTTO: Vermont, freedom and unity

A snowboarder takes a ride in Killington, Vermont.

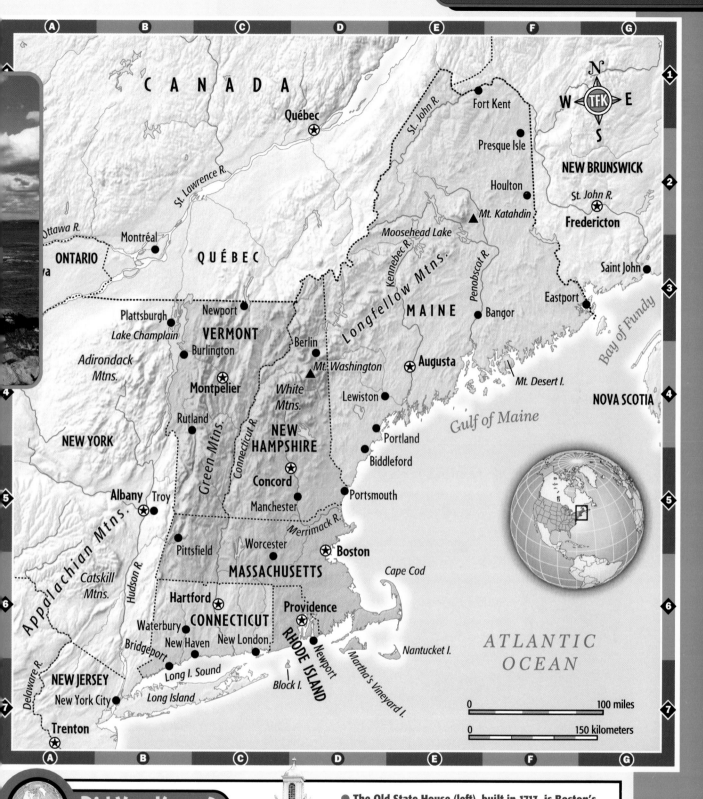

CANADA

Québec

Fort Kent

Presque Isle

NEW BRUNSWICK

Houlton

St. John R.

Mt. Katahdin

Fredericton

Moosehead Lake

Ottawa R.

Montréal

Saint John

ONTARIO

QUÉBEC

Eastport

Penobscot R.

Kennebec R.

Longfellow Mtns.

MAINE

Bangor

Bay of Fundy

Plattsburgh

Newport

Lake Champlain

VERMONT

Berlin

Mt. Washington

Augusta

NOVA SCOTIA

Burlington

Gulf of Maine

Adirondack Mtns.

Montpelier

White Mtns.

Lewiston

Mt. Desert I.

Rutland

NEW HAMPSHIRE

Portland

NEW YORK

Biddleford

Green Mtns.

Connecticut R.

Concord

Portsmouth

Albany

Troy

Manchester

Appalachian Mtns.

Hudson R.

Merrimack R.

Pittsfield

Worcester

Boston

Cape Cod

Catskill Mtns.

MASSACHUSETTS

ATLANTIC OCEAN

Hartford

Providence

Waterbury

CONNECTICUT

New London

Bridgeport

New Haven

RHODE ISLAND

Newport

Nantucket I.

Delaware R.

Long I. Sound

Martha's Vineyard I.

NEW JERSEY

Long Island

Block I.

New York City

Trenton

| 0 | | 100 miles |

| 0 | | 150 kilometers |

Did You Know?

- In 1826, the first American railroad was built, in Quincy, Massachusetts.

- West Quoddy Head Light, a lighthouse in Lubec, Maine, marks the easternmost point in the United States.

- The Old State House (left), built in 1713, is Boston's oldest public building. The Declaration of Independence was read from its balcony in 1776.

- New Hampshire became the first state to declare itself independent from England, in 1775.

- The oldest schoolhouse in the United States is in Portsmouth, Rhode Island. It was built in 1716.

- Rhode Islander Gilbert Stuart painted the portrait of George Washington that is found on the dollar bill.

United States of America
Middle Atlantic

New York City's famous skyline

The Middle Atlantic region is the most ethnically diverse, densely populated area of the United States. From New York to Delaware, people of every race and religion live in a colorful, cultural mix.

New York City is the nation's largest city, with more than 8 million residents. It is home to the United Nations and many international companies and organizations. It is also the country's financial capital. Philadelphia, the fifth-largest city in the U.S., is the birthplace of the nation. It was there that the Declaration of Independence was drafted in 1776 and the U.S. Constitution was written in 1787. Washington, D.C., the nation's capital, lies on the Potomac River, nestled between Maryland and Virginia. Washington is a federal city rather than a state; it belongs to the entire nation.

Outside the big cities, the Middle Atlantic region has fertile farmland. Pennsylvania has the largest rural population in the U.S. and is a major producer of milk, eggs and poultry. Farmland covers some 20% of New Jersey.

Industry and tourism are equally important to the region. New Jersey and Delaware are major pharmaceutical and chemical manufacturers. Maryland, famous for its delicious fresh crabs and shellfish, also produces many electronic goods and metals. New York City, with its theaters and museums, draws many visitors.

Data Bank

DELAWARE
AREA: 1,955 sq mi (5,153 sq km)
POPULATION: 817,491
CAPITAL: Dover
MOTTO: Liberty and independence

MARYLAND
AREA: 9,775 sq mi (25,316 sq km)
POPULATION: 5,508,909
CAPITAL: Annapolis
MOTTO: *Fatti maschii, parole femine*
(Manly deeds, womanly words)

NEW JERSEY
AREA: 7,419 sq mi (19,215 sq km)
POPULATION: 8,638,396
CAPITAL: Trenton
MOTTO: Liberty and prosperity

NEW YORK
AREA: 47,224 sq mi (122,310 sq km)
POPULATION: 19,190,115
CAPITAL: Albany
MOTTO: *Excelsior* (Ever upward)

PENNSYLVANIA
AREA: 44,820 sq mi (116,083 sq km)
POPULATION: 12,365,455
CAPITAL: Harrisburg
MOTTO: Virtue, liberty and independence

WASHINGTON, D.C.
AREA: 68 sq mi (177 sq km)
POPULATION: 563,384
MOTTO: *Justitia omnibus* (Justice to all)

Shore Thing: One of New Jersey's many beaches

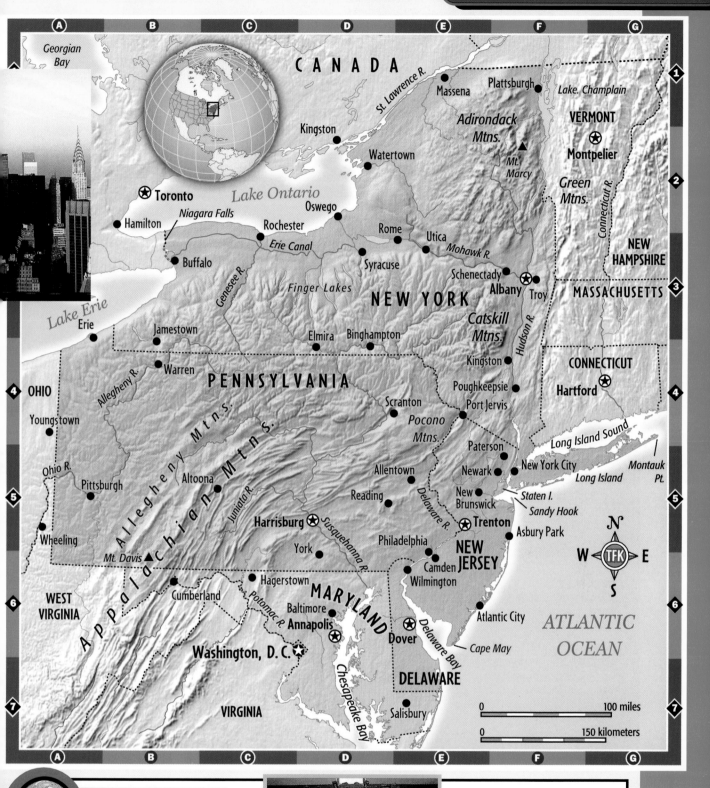

Georgian Bay

CANADA

Massena
Plattsburgh
Lake. Champlain
VERMONT

Adirondack Mtns.
Mt. Marcy
Montpelier

Kingston

Watertown

Green Mtns.

St. Lawrence R.

Toronto
Lake Ontario
Oswego

NEW HAMPSHIRE

Niagara Falls
Hamilton
Rochester
Rome
Utica
Mohawk R.
Schenectady
Albany
Troy

MASSACHUSETTS

Buffalo
Erie Canal
Syracuse

Finger Lakes

NEW YORK

Catskill Mtns.

Connecticut R.

Genesee R.

Lake Erie
Erie

Jamestown
Elmira
Binghampton
Kingston

CONNECTICUT
Hartford

Warren

Allegheny R.

PENNSYLVANIA

Poughkeepsie
Port Jervis

Hudson R.

OHIO

Youngstown

Scranton
Pocono Mtns.

Paterson

Long Island Sound

Ohio R.

Pittsburgh

Altoona

Juniata R.

Allentown

Newark
New York City

Long Island
Montauk Pt.

Allegheny Mtns.
Appalachian Mtns.

Reading

New Brunswick
Staten I.
Sandy Hook

Delaware R.

Wheeling

Harrisburg
Susquehanna R.

Trenton
Asbury Park

Mt. Davis

York

Philadelphia
Camden
NEW JERSEY

N
W TFK E
S

Hagerstown
Wilmington

WEST VIRGINIA

Cumberland
Potomac R.

MARYLAND

Baltimore
Annapolis

Dover
Delaware Bay

Atlantic City

ATLANTIC OCEAN

Washington, D.C.

Chesapeake Bay

DELAWARE

Cape May

VIRGINIA

Salisbury

0 ——— 100 miles
0 ——— 150 kilometers

Did You Know?

● Annapolis, Maryland, is home to the U.S. Naval Academy. It was founded in 1845.

● Delaware, the second-smallest state, was the first to ratify the U.S. Constitution, in 1787.

● New Jersey has the highest population density of any state in the nation.

● The Liberty Bell, housed in Philadelphia, Pennsylvania, cracked in 1835 when it was rung to announce the death of Supreme Court Chief Justice John Marshall.

● In 1961, the 23rd Amendment to the U.S. Constitution gave the citizens of Washington, D.C., the right to vote. Washington's residents cast their first ballots for President and Vice President in 1964.

United States of America
Midwest

A Great Lake: Boating on Lake Michigan in Chicago

Tucked in the middle of the United States between the country's East Coast and the West Coast are the 12 states that make up the Midwest. Much of the terrain in the Midwest is flat. Rich, fertile soil and an abundance of crops have earned the region its nickname, the nation's breadbasket. Farmers grow wheat, oats, corn and potatoes, among other crops.

The population of the Midwest grew dramatically in the 19th century. People from the Eastern states moved there as well as immigrants from Germany, Sweden and Norway. Today, the population, especially in large urban centers, is ethnically and culturally diverse.

Chicago is the biggest city in the Midwest and the nation's third largest. The city serves as a major hub for train and airline passengers. One of the country's tallest buildings, the Sears Tower, looms over Chicago's imposing skyline. Other large cities contribute to the vitality of the region. The U.S. automobile industry is based in Detroit, Michigan. Each year, Indianapolis, Indiana, hosts the Indianapolis 500, a speed-car race.

Data Bank

ILLINOIS
AREA: 55,593 sq mi (143,987 sq km)
POPULATION: 12,600,620
CAPITAL: Springfield
MOTTO: State sovereignty, national union

INDIANA
AREA: 35,870 sq mi (92,904 sq km)
POPULATION: 6,159,068
CAPITAL: Indianapolis
MOTTO: The crossroads of America

IOWA
AREA: 55,875 sq mi (144,716 sq km)
POPULATION: 2,936,760
CAPITAL: Des Moines
MOTTO: Our liberties we prize and our rights we will maintain

KANSAS
AREA: 81,823 sq mi (211,922 sq km)
POPULATION: 2,715,884
CAPITAL: Topeka
MOTTO: Ad astra per aspera (To the stars through difficulties)

MICHIGAN
AREA: 56,809 sq mi (147,135 sq km)
POPULATION: 10,050,446
CAPITAL: Lansing
MOTTO: Si quaeris peninsulam amoenam circumspice (If you seek a pleasant peninsula, look around you)

MINNESOTA
AREA: 79,617 sq mi (206,207 sq km)
POPULATION: 5,019,720
CAPITAL: Saint Paul
MOTTO: L'Etoile du nord (The north star)

NEBRASKA
AREA: 76,878 sq mi (199,113 sq km)
POPULATION: 1,729,180
CAPITAL: Lincoln
MOTTO: Equality before the law

NORTH DAKOTA
AREA: 70,704 sq mi (183,123 sq km)
POPULATION: 634,110
CAPITAL: Bismarck
MOTTO: Liberty and union, now and forever: one and inseparable

OHIO
AREA: 40,953 sq mi (106,067 sq km)
POPULATION: 11,421,267
CAPITAL: Columbus
MOTTO: With God all things are possible

SOUTH DAKOTA
AREA: 75,898 sq mi (196,575 sq km)
POPULATION: 761,063
CAPITAL: Pierre
MOTTO: Under God the people rule

WISCONSIN
AREA: 97,105 sq mi (251,501 sq km)
POPULATION: 498,703
CAPITAL: Madison
MOTTO: Equal rights

Amber Waves of Grain: A farm near Salina, Kansas

MONTANA

WYOMING

N
W TFK E
S

Cheyenne

Harney Pea
▲ ● Rapid

Black Hills

North Platte R.

South Platte R.

Denver

COLORADO

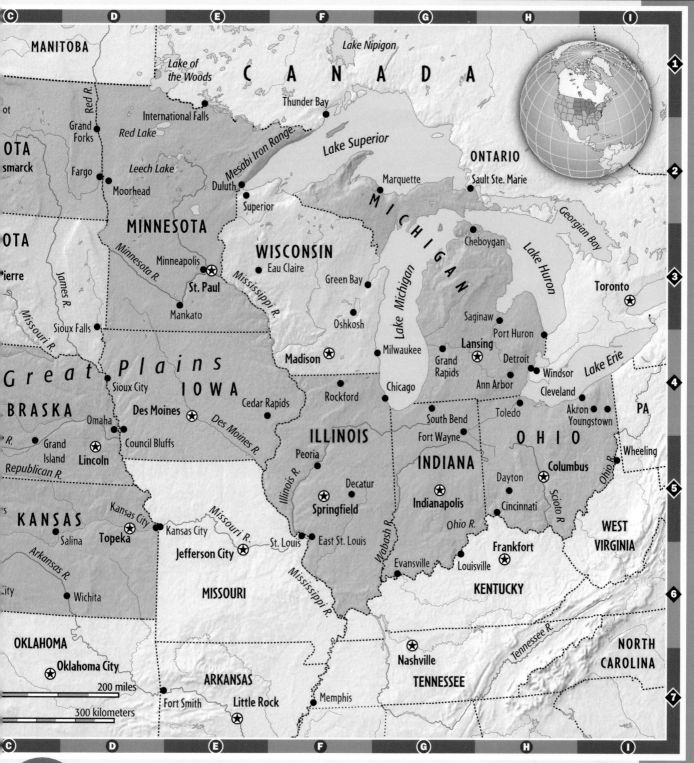

C **D** **E** **F** **G** **H** **I**

MANITOBA

Lake Nipigon

Lake of
the Woods

CANADA

Thunder Bay

International Falls

Red R.

Grand
Forks

ot

Red Lake

Mesabi Iron Range

Lake Superior

ONTARIO

smarck

Fargo

Leech Lake

Duluth

Marquette

Sault Ste. Marie

Moorhead

Superior

Georgian Bay

OTA

MINNESOTA

WISCONSIN

M I C H I G A N

Cheboygan

ierre

Minnesota R.

Minneapolis

Eau Claire

Lake Huron

Toronto

James R.

St. Paul

Mississippi R.

Green Bay

Saginaw

Port Huron

Missouri R.

Mankato

Oshkosh

Lake Michigan

Lansing

Detroit

Lake Erie

Sioux Falls

Milwaukee

Grand
Rapids

Windsor

G r e a t   P l a i n s

Sioux City

I O W A

Madison

Ann Arbor

Cleveland

Akron

PA

BRASKA

Des Moines

Cedar Rapids

Rockford

Chicago

South Bend

Toledo

Youngstown

Omaha

Council Bluffs

Fort Wayne

O H I O

Wheeling

R.

Grand
Island

Lincoln

Des Moines R.

Peoria

ILLINOIS

INDIANA

Dayton

Columbus

Ohio R.

Republican R.

Illinois R.

Decatur

Indianapolis

Cincinnati

Scioto R.

KANSAS

Kansas City

Missouri R.

Springfield

Ohio R.

WEST
VIRGINIA

Salina

Topeka

Kansas City

St. Louis

East St. Louis

Frankfort

Wabash R.

Jefferson City

Evansville

Louisville

Arkansas R.

ity

Wichita

MISSOURI

Mississippi R.

KENTUCKY

NORTH
CAROLINA

OKLAHOMA

Nashville

Oklahoma City

200 miles

ARKANSAS

Memphis

TENNESSEE

Tennessee R.

300 kilometers

Fort Smith

Little Rock

C **D** **E** **F** **G** **H** **I**

1 **2** **3** **4** **5** **6** **7**

Did You Know?

● South Dakota is the home of the Sioux
Indians. The Sioux greeting *How, kola!* means
"Hello, friend!"

● **Chewing gum was invented in Ohio in 1869.**

● Minnesota has more recreational boats per
person than any other state. There is about one
boat for every six people.

● **Michigan's shoreline is
longer than that of any
other state except Alaska.**

● Kool-Aid is the official
soft drink of Nebraska. It
was invented in Hastings
in 1927.

● Wisconsin produces
more milk than any
other state.

United States of America
South

Old Kentucky Home: Horses at play on a farm

At one time, the states that make up the Southern part of the United States were best known for their rolling fields of cotton, tobacco, soy beans and other vegetables. In the 1800s, cotton was king. Plantation owners relied on slave labor to grow and harvest the crop. From 1861 to 1865, the Southern states fought the Northern states in the bloody and destructive Civil War.

Today, agriculture is still an important industry. But Southern cities such as Atlanta, Georgia, and Miami, Florida, are commercial, industrial and cultural centers. In Miami; New Orleans, Louisiana; and Nashville, Tennessee, the sounds of uniquely Southern music set the rhythm and pace for this section for the nation.

Southerners are proud of their region's scenic beauty. The Great Smoky Mountains National Park in North Carolina and Tennessee attracts more than 9 million visitors each year. The park has more than 800 mi (1,290 km) of trails. Everglades National Park in Florida is the only subtropical preserve in North America. It is the only place in the world where alligators and crocodiles live side by side.

A riverboat on the Mississippi River

Data Bank

ALABAMA
AREA: 50,750 sq mi (131,443 sq km)
POPULATION: 4,500,752
CAPITAL: Montgomery
MOTTO: *Audemus jura nostra defendere* (We dare defend our rights)

ARKANSAS
AREA: 52,075 sq mi (134,874 sq km)
POPULATION: 2,725,714
CAPITAL: Little Rock
MOTTO: *Regnat populus* (The people rule)

FLORIDA
AREA: 54,153 sq mi (140,256 sq km)
POPULATION: 17,019,068
CAPITAL: Tallahassee
MOTTO: In God we trust

GEORGIA
AREA: 57,919 sq mi (150,010 sq km)
POPULATION: 8,684,715
CAPITAL: Atlanta
MOTTO: Wisdom, justice and moderation

KENTUCKY
AREA: 39,732 sq mi (102,907 sq km)
POPULATION: 4,117,827
CAPITAL: Frankfort
MOTTO: United we stand, divided we fall

LOUISIANA
AREA: 43,566 sq mi (112,836 sq km)
POPULATION: 4,496,334
CAPITAL: Baton Rouge
MOTTO: Union, justice and confidence

MISSISSIPPI
AREA: 46,914 sq mi (121,506 sq km)
POPULATION: 2,881,281
CAPITAL: Jackson
MOTTO: *Virtute et armis* (By valor and arms)

MISSOURI
AREA: 68,898 sq mi (178,446 sq km)
POPULATION: 5,704,484
CAPITAL: Jefferson City
MOTTO: *Salu populi suprema lex esto* (The welfare of the people shall be the supreme law)

NORTH CAROLINA
AREA: 48,718 sq mi (126,180 sq km)
POPULATION: 8,407,248
CAPITAL: Raleigh
MOTTO: *Esse quam videri* (To be rather than to seem)

SOUTH CAROLINA
AREA: 30,111 sq mi (77,988 sq km)
POPULATION: 4,147,152
CAPITAL: Columbia
MOTTO: *Animis opibusque parati* (Prepared in mind and resources) and *Dum spiro spero* (While I breathe, I hope)

TENNESSEE
AREA: 41,220 sq mi (106,759 sq km)
POPULATION: 5,841,748
CAPITAL: Nashville
MOTTO: Agriculture and commerce

VIRGINIA
AREA: 39,598 sq mi (102,558 sq km)
POPULATION: 7,386,330
CAPITAL: Richmond
MOTTO: *Sic semper tyrannis* (Thus always to tyrants)

WEST VIRGINIA
AREA: 24,087 sq mi (62,384 sq km)
POPULATION: 1,810,354
CAPITAL: Charleston
MOTTO: *Montani semper liberi* (Mountaineers are always free)

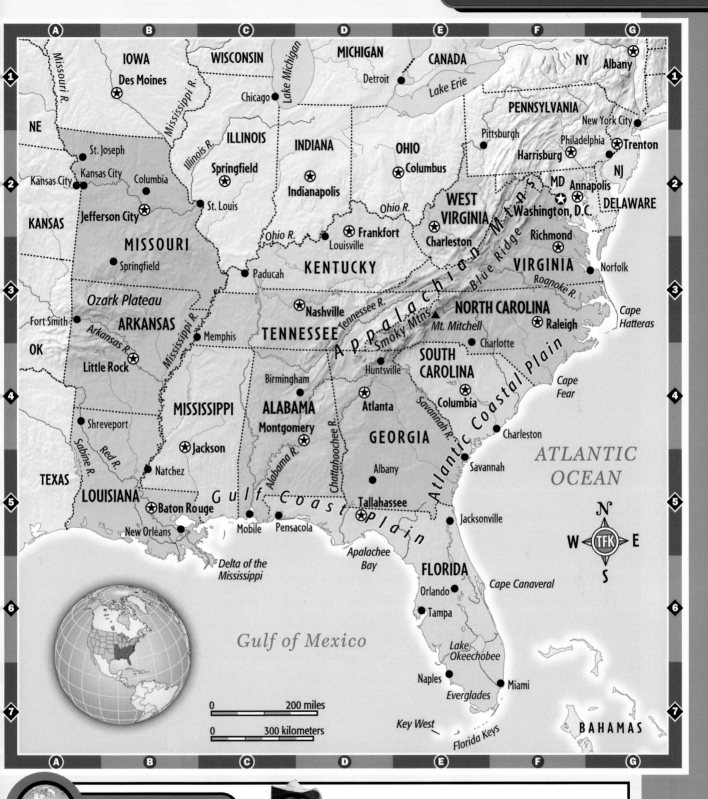

A B C D E F G

1 IOWA WISCONSIN MICHIGAN CANADA NY Albany
Des Moines Detroit Lake Erie
Missouri R. Chicago Lake Michigan PENNSYLVANIA New York City
NE St. Joseph Mississippi R. ILLINOIS INDIANA OHIO Pittsburgh Philadelphia Trenton
2 Kansas City Kansas City Columbia Springfield Indianapolis Columbus Harrisburg NJ
KANSAS Jefferson City St. Louis Ohio R. WEST MD Annapolis DELAWARE
Illinois R. VIRGINIA Washington, D.C.
MISSOURI Ohio R. Frankfort Charleston Richmond
Springfield Louisville KENTUCKY Blue Ridge VIRGINIA Norfolk
3 Ozark Plateau Paducah Roanoke R. Cape Hatteras
Fort Smith ARKANSAS Nashville Tennessee R. Appalachian Mts. NORTH CAROLINA Raleigh
OK Arkansas R. Memphis TENNESSEE Smoky Mtns. Mt. Mitchell
Little Rock Mississippi R. Huntsville SOUTH Charlotte Atlantic Coastal Plain
4 Birmingham CAROLINA Cape Fear
Shreveport MISSISSIPPI ALABAMA Atlanta Columbia
TEXAS Montgomery GEORGIA Savannah R. Charleston ATLANTIC OCEAN
Jackson Chattahoochee R. Albany Savannah
5 Natchez Alabama R. Tallahassee Jacksonville N
LOUISIANA Gulf Coast Plain W TFK E
Baton Rouge Mobile Pensacola S
New Orleans Apalachee Bay FLORIDA Cape Canaveral
Delta of the Mississippi Orlando
6 Gulf of Mexico Tampa
Lake Okeechobee
Naples Miami
7 0 200 miles Key West Everglades BAHAMAS
0 300 kilometers Florida Keys

A B C D E F G

Did You Know?

● Jamestown, Virginia, was the first permanent English settlement in North America.

● Panthers live in the Florida Everglades. There are fewer than 50 panthers left in the wild.

● In 1860, South Carolina was the first state to secede from the Union. Mississippi, Florida, Alabama, Georgia, Louisiana, Texas, Virginia, Arkansas, Tennessee and North Carolina joined it to form the Confederacy that fought against the North in the Civil War.

● Coca-Cola was first bottled in Vicksburg, Mississippi, in 1894.

● The Grand Ole Opry is the world's longest-running, live radio show.

● *Mississippi* is a Native American word meaning "great water."

35

United States of America
Southwest

The Southwest is a region of dry desert and high plains. It is rich in Native American and Hispanic culture. Geographically, the region is dominated by Texas, the second-largest state in the U.S. and an industrial giant. When it comes to oil production and cattle ranching, the Lone Star State leads the nation. Texas is also tops in farmland and in the production of cotton and cottonseed oil. The state is home to the Johnson Space Center in Houston.

To the north of Texas lies Oklahoma, another state that struck it rich with oil. Farming and cattle ranching are also vital to the state's economy. Wheat is Oklahoma's main crop. Oklahoma's Native American population—273,230—is second only to California's—333,346.

In New Mexico and Arizona, pueblos (flat-roofed stone or adobe dwellings) still dot the desert landscape, along with giant saguaro cacti. Many American Indians live in the area, including people belonging to the Hopi, Zuni and Navajo tribes. Arizona is perhaps best known for the Grand Canyon, the world's largest gorge. Carved by the Colorado River over 6 million to 10 million years ago, the etched rocky walls turn brilliant shades of red, orange and yellow at sunset each day.

Arizona's Montezuma Castle was built by Sinagua Indians more than 600 years ago.

Data Bank

ARIZONA
AREA: 113,642 sq mi (296,400 sq km)
POPULATION: 5,580,811
CAPITAL: Phoenix
MOTTO: *Ditat deus* (God enriches)

NEW MEXICO
AREA: 121,365 sq mi (314,334 sq km)
POPULATION: 1,874,614
CAPITAL: Santa Fe
MOTTO: *Crescit eundo* (It grows as it goes)

OKLAHOMA
AREA: 68,679 sq mi (177,880 sq km)
POPULATION: 3,511,532
CAPITAL: Oklahoma City
MOTTO: *Labor omnia vincit* (Labor conquers all things)

TEXAS
AREA: 261,914 sq mi (678,358 sq km)
POPULATION: 22,118,509
CAPITAL: Austin
MOTTO: Friendship

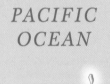

Mission Control at Houston's Johnson Space Center

ORE

NEVADA

Carson Ci

Nevada

CALIFORNIA

Los Angeles

San Diego
Tijuana

PACIFIC OCEAN

IDAHO

WYOMING

Great Salt Lake

Cheyenne

North Platte R.

NEBRASKA

IOWA

Salt Lake City

UTAH

Denver

Lincoln

Topeka

Kansas City

Kansas City

Missouri R.

Missouri R.

MISSOURI

Great Basin

COLORADO

KANSAS

Arkansas R.

Colorado R.

Grand Canyon

Colorado Plateau

Santa Fe

Canadian R.

Amarillo

Oklahoma City

Tulsa

ARKANSAS

Gallup

Humphreys Peak

Flagstaff

Albuquerque

OKLAHOMA

Lawton

Quachita Mtns.

Red R.

ARIZONA

NEW MEXICO

Lubbock

Dallas

Sabine R.

LA

Phoenix

Gila R.

Sierra Blanca

Llano Estacado

Brazos R.

Fort Worth

Tyler

Yuma

Black Range

Sacramento Mtns.

TEXAS

Waco

Tucson

Douglas

El Paso

Colorado R.

Pecos R.

Edwards Plateau

Austin

Houston

Galveston

Davis Mtns.

Rio Grande

San Antonio

Gulf Coastal Plain

Chihuahua

Nueces R.

Corpus Christi

Gulf of Mexico

Hermosillo

Sierra Madre Occidental

Gulf of California

MEXICO

Sierra Madre Oriental

Laredo

Baja California

Monterrey

Matamoros

0   300 miles

0   450 kilometers

- The Chapel of San Miguel, built in Santa Fe, New Mexico, in the 17th century, is known as the oldest church in the United States.

- The cowboy hat is based on the Mexican sombrero. The first cowboys raised cattle in Texas when the state still belonged to Mexico.

- In the 1830s, what is now Oklahoma was set aside as Indian Territory for Native Americans. Today the state is still home to more than 60 tribes.

- The Grand Canyon measures 277 mi (446 km) long, up to 18 mi (29 km) wide and more than 5,000 ft (1,500 m) deep. Some 4 million people visit the gorge each year!

United States of America
West

El Capitan in Yosemite National Park

The Mississippi River forms a natural boundary between the American East and the American West. Before the 1840s, very few pioneers had ventured beyond the Mississippi. The Gold Rush of 1849 brought an avalanche of miners to California. The following year, California became the first state west of the Mississippi. By 1900, settlers had built cities all across the West and were the laying claim to Indian territories.

Stories of the Old West are part of the heritage of the United States. So, too, are the natural wonders of the region. The area's towering mountains, wide deserts, canyons and waterfalls inspired the creation of the U.S. National Park System, which includes Yellowstone in Wyoming and Yosemite in California.

The most western of all states, Hawaii, did not become a state until 1959. Located in the South Pacific, Hawaii is a string of volcanic islands with its own history and culture.

The Seattle Space Needle

PACIFIC OCEAN

0 ——————— 300
0 ——————— 450 kilom

Kauai
Oahu
Molokai
Honolulu
Lanai

HAWAII

PACIFIC OCEAN

50 miles

Data Bank

CALIFORNIA
AREA: 155,973 sq mi (403,970 sq km)
POPULATION: 35,484,453
CAPITAL: Sacramento
MOTTO: Eureka! (I have found it!)

COLORADO
AREA: 103,730 sq mi (268,660 sq km)
POPULATION: 4,550,688
CAPITAL: Denver
MOTTO: *Nil sine numine* (Nothing without providence)

HAWAII
AREA: 6,423 sq mi (16,637 sq km)
POPULATION: 1,257,608
CAPITAL: Honolulu
MOTTO: *Ua mau ke ea o ka aina i ka pono* (The life of the land is perpetuated in righteousness)

IDAHO
AREA: 82,751 sq mi (214,325 sq km)
POPULATION: 1,366,332
CAPITAL: Boise
MOTTO: *Esto perpetua* (It endures forever)

MONTANA
AREA: 145,556 sq mi (376,991 sq km)
POPULATION: 917,621
CAPITAL: Helena
MOTTO: *Oro y plata* (Gold and silver)

NEVADA
AREA: 109,806 sq mi (284,397 sq km)
POPULATION: 2,241,154
CAPITAL: Carson City
MOTTO: All for our country

OREGON
AREA: 96,003 sq mi (248,647 sq km)
POPULATION: 3,559,596
CAPITAL: Salem
MOTTO: *Alis volat propriis* (She flies with her own wings)

UTAH
AREA: 82,168 sq mi (212,816 sq km)
POPULATION: 2,351,467
CAPITAL: Salt Lake City
MOTTO: Industry

WASHINGTON
AREA: 66,582 sq mi (172,448 sq km)
POPULATION: 6,131,445
CAPITAL: Olympia
MOTTO: *Al-ki* (By and by)

WYOMING
AREA: 97,105 sq mi (251,501 sq km)
POPULATION: 501,242
CAPITAL: Cheyenne
MOTTO: Equal rights

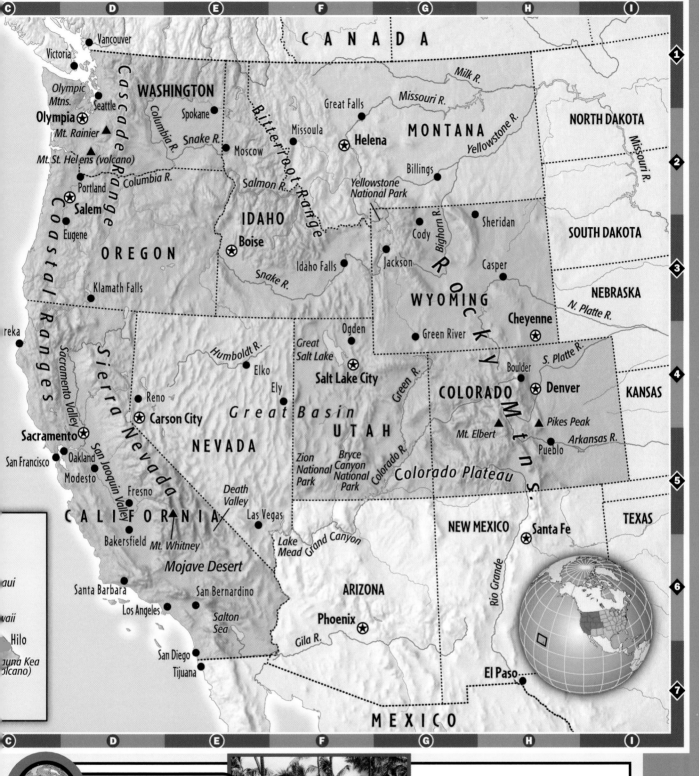

CANADA

Vancouver

Victoria

Olympic Mtns.

WASHINGTON

Seattle

Cascade Range

Olympia ✪

Mt. Rainier ▲

Columbia R.

Spokane

Great Falls

Missouri R.

Milk R.

NORTH DAKOTA

Mt. St. Helens (volcano) ▲

Portland ✪

Columbia R.

Salem

Eugene

Moscow

Snake R.

Bitterroot Range

Missoula

Helena ✪

Salmon R.

Yellowstone R.

MONTANA

Billings

Missouri R.

SOUTH DAKOTA

OREGON

IDAHO

Boise ✪

Idaho Falls

Snake R.

Yellowstone National Park

Cody

Bighorn R.

Sheridan

Jackson

Casper

NEBRASKA

Klamath Falls

Coastal Ranges

eka

Sacramento Valley

Sierra Nevada

Humboldt R.

Elko

Ely

Reno

Carson City ✪

NEVADA

Great Salt Lake

Ogden

Salt Lake City ✪

Great Basin

UTAH

Green River

WYOMING

Cheyenne ✪

ROCKY

N. Platte R.

S. Platte R.

Boulder

COLORADO

Denver ✪

Mt. Elbert ▲

▲ Pikes Peak

Arkansas R.

Pueblo

KANSAS

Mtns.

Green R.

Colorado R.

Sacramento ✪

San Francisco

Oakland

Modesto

San Joaquin Valley

Fresno

CALIFORNIA

Bakersfield

Mt. Whitney

Death Valley

Las Vegas

Zion National Park

Bryce Canyon National Park

Colorado Plateau

Mojave Desert

Santa Barbara

Los Angeles

San Bernardino

Salton Sea

Lake Mead

Grand Canyon

ARIZONA

Phoenix ✪

NEW MEXICO

Santa Fe ✪

Rio Grande

TEXAS

San Diego

Tijuana

Gila R.

El Paso

M E X I C O

aui

aii

Hilo

una Kea olcano)

Did You Know?

● The San Andreas Fault is a huge crack in the earth's crust that stretches for 600 mi (966 km) through the state of California. The fault causes dozens of earthquakes each year.

● The Seattle Space Needle, built in 1962 for the Century 21 Exposition, is a marvel of engineering. It includes a revolving restaurant and a gas torch that is 600 ft (183 m) high.

● Hawaii is famous for its huge, tubular waves, which are great for surfers.

● The hula originated in Hawaii as a dance to honor the gods.

● The 10 national forests in Idaho cover 20.4 million acres (8.2 million hectares).

Mexico and Central America

J ust south of the United States lies Mexico and Central America, the narrow landmass that connects North America and South America. From Mexico's dry plateaus to Costa Rica's tropical rain forests, this is an area of varied terrain and climate.

A hummingbird and an orchid in Costa Rica

Mexico City combines the old with the new.

Mexico was once home to several great civilizations, including the Mayan and the Aztec. Today, Mexico's language, food, culture and architecture reflect its rich history: magnificent temples and pyramids mix with sleek skyscrapers and luxurious beachfront resorts. Mexico City, the nation's capital, is the oldest continuously inhabited city in the Western Hemisphere.

To the south of Mexico sit the seven small countries that make up Central America: Belize, Costa Rica, El Salvador, Guatemala, Honduras, Nicaragua and Panama. Combined, they are less than half the size of Mexico. Rare and exotic wildlife can be found throughout the region. In tiny Costa Rica alone there are 850 species of birds, 136 species of snakes and 1,500 species of orchids.

Data Bank

MEXICO
AREA: 761,600 sq mi (1,972,550 sq km)
POPULATION: 104,959,594
CAPITAL: Mexico City
LANGUAGES: Spanish, Mayan, Nahuatl, other native languages

BELIZE
AREA: 8,865 sq mi (22,966 sq km)
POPULATION: 272,945
CAPITAL: Belmopan
LANGUAGES: English (official), Creole, Spanish, Mayan, Garifuna

COSTA RICA
AREA: 19,730 sq mi (51,100 sq km)
POPULATION: 3,956,507
CAPITAL: San José
LANGUAGES: Spanish (official), English

EL SALVADOR
AREA: 8,124 sq mi (21,040)
POPULATION: 6,587,541
CAPITAL: San Salvador
LANGUAGES: Spanish, Nahua

GUATEMALA
AREA: 42,042 sq mi (108,890 sq km)
POPULATION: 14,286,596
CAPITAL: Guatemala City
LANGUAGES: Spanish, native languages

HONDURAS
AREA: 43,278 sq mi (112,090 sq km)
POPULATION: 6,669,789
CAPITAL: Tegucigalpa
LANGUAGES: Spanish, Amerindian dialects

NICARAGUA
AREA: 49,998 sq mi (129,494 sq km)
POPULATION: 5,232,268
CAPITAL: Managua
LANGUAGES: Spanish (official), English and native languages on Atlantic coast

PANAMA
AREA: 30,193 sq km (78,200 sq km)
POPULATION: 3,000,463
CAPITAL: Panama City
LANGUAGES: Spanish (official), English

Tikal is one of Guatemala's most spectacular Mayan sites.

Map labels: CA, AZ, T H, San Diego, Tijuana, Mexicali, Nogales, Ciudad J, Hermosillo, Baja California, Gulf of California, Yaqui R., Sierra, M, Cabo San Lucas, Islas Mar, Islas Revillagigedo (Mexico)

C · D · E · F · G · H · I

1

OK

AR

TN

NC

SC

NITED STATES OF AMERICA

TX

LA

MS

AL

GA

FL

Mississippi R.

**ATLANTIC
OCEAN**

2

Houston

New Orleans

Río Grande

*Gulf of
Mexico*

Miami

3

uahua

Laredo

Nuevo Laredo

Matamoros

Monterrey

Havana

CUBA

rango

Sierra Madre Oriental

Mexican Plateau

Tampico

N
W · TFK · E
S

Yucatán Channel

4

dalajara

León

Mérida

Cancun

Santiago R.

Mexico
City

Veracruz

Campeche

*Yucatán
Peninsula*

Chichén Itzá (ruin)

JAMAICA

Kingston

Paricutín

Citlaltépetl

Puebla

*Bay of
Campeche*

Belize City

*Gulf of
Honduras*

Caribbean Sea

5

Acapulco

Sierra Madre del Sur

Oaxaca

Cobán

Belmopan

BELIZE

HONDURAS

*Gulf of
Tehuantepec*

GUATEMALA

San Pedro Sula

Tajumulco Volcano

Guatemala City

Tegucigalpa

NICARAGUA

Puerto Cabezas

6

San Salvador

EL SALVADOR

León

Granada

Bluefields

**PACIFIC
OCEAN**

Managua

Lake Nicaragua

Puerto Limón

Colón

*Panama
Canal*

San José

COSTA RICA

Panama City

Puntarenas

0 — 400 miles

0 — 600 kilometers

David

PANAMA

7

D · E · F · G · H · I

Did You Know?

● There are nearly 100 volcanoes in Mexico and Central America.

● The Panama Canal, which connects the Atlantic and Pacific oceans, took more than 10 years and some 56,000 workers to build. The U.S. owned it from 1914 until December 31, 1999, when it was given to the Panamanian people.

Costa Rica's Arenal volcano at night

● At its narrowest point, in Panama, Central America is just 50 mi (80 km) wide.

● Some of the largest and possibly oldest Mayan ruins can be found in Tikal, Guatemala. The ancient site has thousands of structures, including spectacular temples and pyramids that were used in the first *Star Wars* movie.

● Belize's barrier reef, the largest in the Western Hemisphere, stretches across 185 mi (298 km).

Mexico

¡HOLA!

My name is Maricela. I am 9 years old, and I live in San Miguel de Allende, which is about four hours from Mexico City by bus. My father is a farmer. Let me introduce you to some interesting facts about my country. ¡Bienvenidos!

The Mexican Flag

This flag has many symbols. Here is what they mean:

Green is for independence.

White is for religion.

Red represents union.

The **coat of arms** contains an eagle with a snake in its beak perched on a cactus. According to Aztec legend, the god of the sun told the Aztecs that they would find their promised land where they saw an eagle on a nopal cactus eating a snake. The Aztecs found this vision in a place they called Tenochtitlán (tay-knoch-teet-*lahn*), which means "place of the nopal cactus." Today it is called Mexico City.

The Multicultural Mix

In Mexico, Spanish colonial influence blends with Native Indian tradition. This chart shows the country's ethnic groups.

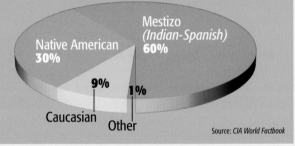

Native American 30%

Mestizo (Indian-Spanish) 60%

Caucasian 9%

Other 1%

Source: *CIA World Factbook*

The Economy

AGRICULTURE: Corn, wheat, rice, beans, soybeans, cotton, coffee, fruit, tomatoes, wood

MANUFACTURING: Processed food, chemical products, cars and trucks, electrical machinery, printing and paper products, textiles, iron and steel products

MINING: Silver, lead, mercury, zinc, sulfur, copper

MAJOR EXPORTS: Cotton, coffee, oil and oil products, manufactured goods, silver

MAJOR IMPORTS: Agricultural and metalworking machines, steel products, electrical equipment, auto parts, aircraft and aircraft parts

Top 5 Silver-Producing Countries

Rich in many types of minerals, Mexico is the world's silver capital.

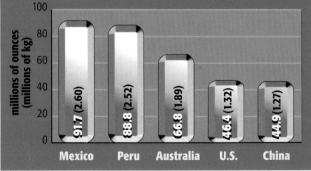

millions of ounces (millions of kg)

Mexico	Peru	Australia	U.S.	China
91.7 (2.60)	88.8 (2.52)	66.8 (1.89)	46.4 (1.32)	44.9 (1.27)

Major Events in Mexico's History

300 A.D.–900 A.D. The classical period of the ancient Maya, Zapotec and Teotihuacán civilizations. Temples were built at Chichén Itzá and Uxmal.

1519-1521 Spanish military leader Hernando Cortés and his conquistadores arrive and conquer Mexico.

1810-1821 Mexico fights for independence from Spain, winning it in 1821.

1836 Texas breaks away from Mexico, and the battles of the Alamo and San Jacinto are fought.

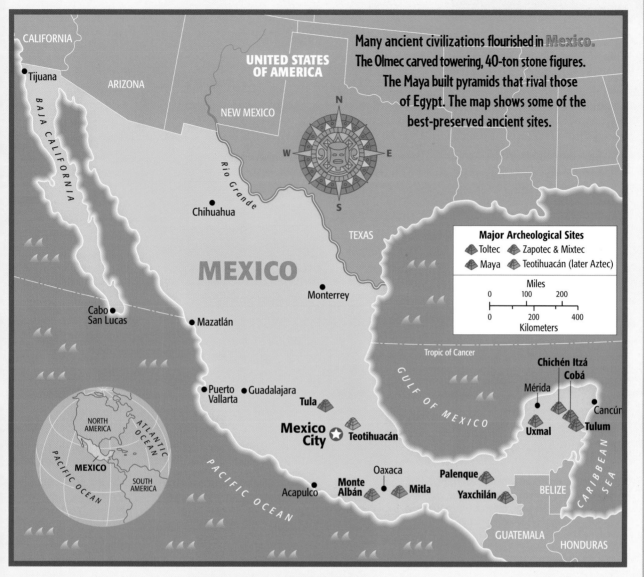

Many ancient civilizations flourished in Mexico. The Olmec carved towering, 40-ton stone figures. The Maya built pyramids that rival those of Egypt. The map shows some of the best-preserved ancient sites.

Major Archeological Sites
- Toltec
- Maya
- Zapotec & Mixtec
- Teotihuacán (later Aztec)

Miles
0   100   200

Kilometers
0   200   400

CALIFORNIA
Tijuana
ARIZONA
UNITED STATES OF AMERICA
NEW MEXICO
BAJA CALIFORNIA
Rio Grande
Chihuahua
TEXAS
MEXICO
Monterrey
Cabo San Lucas
Mazatlán
Tropic of Cancer
GULF OF MEXICO
Chichén Itzá
Cobá
Mérida
Cancún
Puerto Vallarta
Guadalajara
Tula
Uxmal
Tulum
Mexico City
Teotihuacán
CARIBBEAN SEA
NORTH AMERICA
ATLANTIC OCEAN
MEXICO
PACIFIC OCEAN
SOUTH AMERICA
Acapulco
Monte Albán
Oaxaca
Mitla
Palenque
Yaxchilán
BELIZE
GUATEMALA
HONDURAS
PACIFIC OCEAN

MEXICO
Is Famous for ...

Ranchero and mariachi These two types of music are heard throughout the land. A mariachi band is pictured below.

Mole (*mo-lay*) The national food is a spicy sauce made with chilies and usually chocolate. It is served with meat.

Fiesta Mexicans love to celebrate. A fiesta is a party.

Bullfighting Many people enjoy the national sport.

Murals These large, colorful paintings are the most widely recognized Mexican art form.

Say It in Spanish

Spanish is the official language of Mexico. Here are a few words and phrases:

Hi	Hola (*oh*-lah)
My name is	Me llamo (may *yah*-moh)
I live in	Vivo en (*vee*-vo ehn)
Thank you	Gracias (*grah*-see-as)
See you later.	Hasta luego. (*ah*-stah loo-*eh*-go)
Welcome!	¡Bienvenidos! (bee-en-veh-*nee*-dos)

 To learn more about Mexico, go to *timeforkids.com/gpmexico*.

1848 The U.S. wins the Mexican-American War and takes Mexican territory, which forms Texas, California, New Mexico and Arizona.

1910 The Mexican Revolution begins when citizens rise up against oppressive rulers. The revolution leads to a new constitution in 1917.

1968 The first Olympic Games ever held in a Latin American country open in Mexico City.

1985 An earthquake measuring 8.1 on the Richter scale strikes Mexico City. Nearly 10,000 are killed and 50,000 are injured.

Caribbean

Just Beachy: The Dominican Republic

T he Caribbean Islands, also called the West Indies, are known for their sparkling blue waters, white sand beaches and gentle tropical breezes. The multiethnic people of the Caribbean are proud of their contributions to the fields of literature, dance and music.

There are thousands of islands in the Caribbean, including 13 nations and many colonial dependencies, territories and possessions. Just 90 mi (145 km) off the coast of Florida lies the Caribbean's largest island, Cuba. Since 1960, relations between the governments of Cuba and the United States have been strained.

Data Bank

The West Indies

AREA: The islands of the West Indies are an archipelago approximately 2,000 mi (3,200 km) long. There are four island chains in the West Indies: the Bahamas, the Greater Antilles, and the eastern and southern islands of the Lesser Antilles.
POPULATION: 34.5 million
LANGUAGES: Spanish, French, English, Dutch, Creole, local dialects

Countries

ANTIGUA AND BARBUDA
AREA: 171 sq mi (443 sq km)
POPULATION: 68,320
CAPITAL: Saint John's
LANGUAGES: English (official), local dialects

BARBADOS
AREA: 166 sq mi (431 sq km)
POPULATION: 278,289
CAPITAL: Bridgetown
LANGUAGE: English

BAHAMAS
AREA: 5,380 sq mi (13,940 sq km)
POPULATION: 299,697
CAPITAL: Nassau
LANGUAGE: English

CUBA
AREA: 42,803 sq mi (110,860 sq km)
POPULATION: 11,308,764
CAPITAL: Havana
LANGUAGE: Spanish

DOMINICA
AREA: 290 sq mi (754 sq km)
POPULATION: 69,278
CAPITAL: Roseau
LANGUAGES: English (official), French patois

DOMINICAN REPUBLIC
AREA: 18,815 sq mi (48,730 sq km)
POPULATION: 8,833,634
CAPITAL: Santo Domingo
LANGUAGE: Spanish

GRENADA
AREA: 133 sq mi (344 sq km)
POPULATION: 89,357
CAPITAL: Saint George's
LANGUAGES: English (official), French patois

HAITI
AREA: 10,714 sq mi (27,750 sq km)
POPULATION: 7,656,166
CAPITAL: Port-au-Prince
LANGUAGES: French, Creole (both official)

JAMAICA
AREA: 4,244 sq mi (10,991 sq km)
POPULATION: 2,713,130
CAPITAL: Kingston
LANGUAGES: English, patois English

SAINT KITTS AND NEVIS
AREA: 101 sq mi (261 sq km)
POPULATION: 38,836
CAPITAL: Basseterre
LANGUAGE: English

SAINT LUCIA
AREA: 238 sq mi (616 sq km)
POPULATION: 164,213
CAPITAL: Castries
LANGUAGES: English (official), French patois

SAINT VINCENT AND THE GRENADINES
AREA: 150 sq mi (389 sq km)
POPULATION: 117,193
CAPITAL: Kingstown
LANGUAGES: English, French patois

TRINIDAD AND TOBAGO
AREA: 1,980 sq mi (5,128 sq km)
POPULATION: 1,096,585
CAPITAL: Port-of-Spain
LANGUAGES: English (official), Hindi, French, Spanish, Chinese

U.S. Territories

PUERTO RICO (Commonwealth)
AREA: 3,515 sq mi (9,104 sq km)
POPULATION: 3,885,877
CAPITAL: San Juan
LANGUAGES: Spanish, English

VIRGIN ISLANDS (Unincorporated territory)
AREA: 135 sq mi (349 sq km)
POPULATION: 124,778
CAPITAL: Charlotte Amalie
LANGUAGES: English (official), Creole, Spanish

FLORIDA (U.S.)

Miami

Strait Flori

Havana

Pinar del Río

Cienfuegos

I. of Pines

Cayman Is. (U.K.)

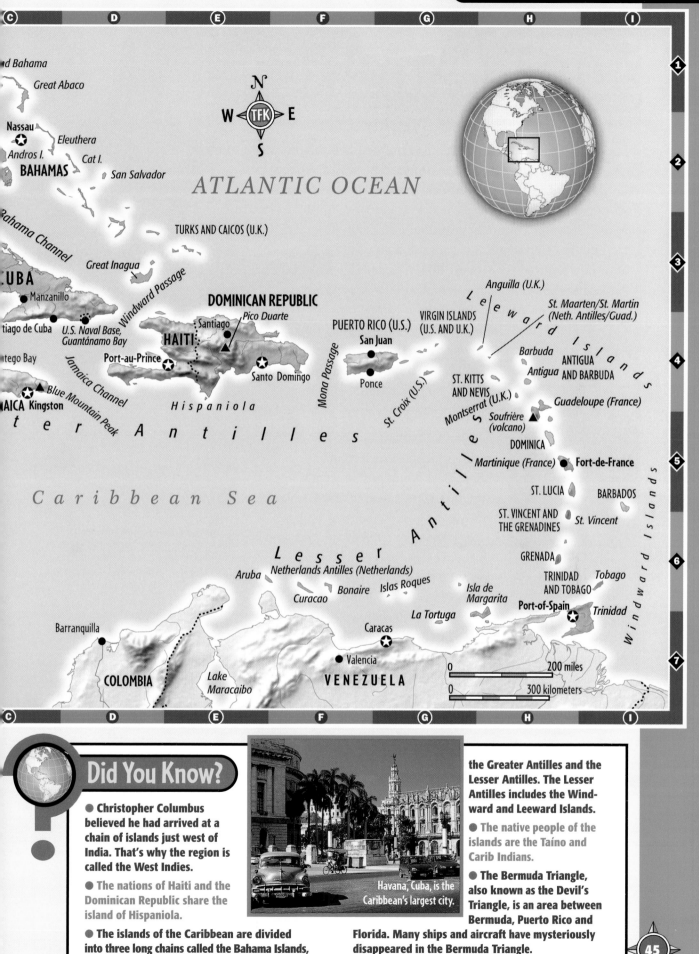

C D E F G H I

1 2 3 4 5 6 7

d Bahama
Great Abaco

Nassau
Eleuthera
Andros I.
Cat I.
San Salvador
BAHAMAS

N
W TFK E
S

ATLANTIC OCEAN

Bahama Channel

TURKS AND CAICOS (U.K.)

Great Inagua

CUBA
Manzanillo

tiago de Cuba
U.S. Naval Base,
Guantánamo Bay

tego Bay
Jamaica Channel

AICA Kingston
Blue Mountain Peak

ter Antilles

Caribbean Sea

Windward Passage

DOMINICAN REPUBLIC
Pico Duarte
Santiago
HAITI
Port-au-Prince
Santo Domingo

Hispaniola

Mona Passage

PUERTO RICO (U.S.)
San Juan

Ponce

St. Croix (U.S.)

Anguilla (U.K.)

Leeward Islands

St. Maarten/St. Martin
(Neth. Antilles/Guad.)

VIRGIN ISLANDS
(U.S. AND U.K.)

Barbuda
ANTIGUA
Antigua AND BARBUDA

ST. KITTS
AND NEVIS
Montserrat (U.K.)
Soufrière
(volcano)

Guadeloupe (France)

DOMINICA

Martinique (France) Fort-de-France

ST. LUCIA
BARBADOS

ST. VINCENT AND
THE GRENADINES St. Vincent

GRENADA

Windward Islands

Lesser Antilles

Aruba
Netherlands Antilles (Netherlands)
Bonaire Islas Roques
Curacao
La Tortuga

Barranquilla

COLOMBIA

Lake
Maracaibo

Caracas

Valencia

VENEZUELA

Isla de
Margarita

TRINIDAD
AND TOBAGO
Port-of-Spain

Tobago

Trinidad

0   200 miles
0   300 kilometers

C D E F G H I

South America

South America, the world's fourth-largest continent, is a region of contrasts and extremes. The world's longest mountain range, the Andes, stretches along the continent's western coast. Even though the equator crosses South America and four-fifths of the continent is located in the tropics, the tall peaks of the Andes remain cold and snow covered year-round. To the east of the Andes lies the world's largest tropical rain forest. The waters of the mighty Amazon River have their source in the mountains of Peru. The river flows across Peru and into Brazil. The Amazon River Basin is hot, humid and rainy. The Atacama Desert in northern Chile is cold and extremely dry.

South America's broad range of climate and terrain offers ideal conditions for a wide variety of plant and animal life. Colorful birds, giant snakes, monkeys and jaguars are among the many creatures that make their home in the lush rain forest. At the southern tip of the continent, seals, penguins and whales swim in the waters of the Southern Ocean. Animals that are found nowhere else on earth, such as Darwin finches and giant tortoises, can be seen on Ecuador's Galápagos Islands.

A toucan in Brazil

Angel Falls in Venezuela

Continent Facts

AREA:
6,878,000 sq mi (17,814,000 sq km)

NUMBER OF COUNTRIES AND TERRITORIES: 12 countries—Argentina, Bolivia, Brazil, Chile, Colombia, Ecuador, Guyana, Paraguay, Peru, Suriname, Uruguay, Venezuela; three territories— Falkland Islands (U.K.), French Guiana (France) and South Georgia and the South Sandwich Islands (U.K.)

LONGEST RIVER: Amazon River, 4,000 mi (6,400 km)

LONGEST MOUNTAIN RANGE: Andes Mountains, 5,500 mi (8,900 km)

HIGHEST PEAK: Mount Aconcagua in Argentina, 22,834 ft (6,960 m).

Wow Zone!

● At a length of about 2,700 mi (4,345 km) and an average width of 110 mi (177 km), Chile is the world's longest, thinnest country.

● The Atacama Desert in Chile is the driest place in the world. In some parts of the desert, rain has never been recorded!

● Ushuaia (oo-*sway*-yah), at the southern tip of Argentina, is the southernmost city in the world. It is just 745 mi (1,199 km) from Antarctica.

● At 3,212 ft (979 m), Angel Falls (Salto Angel), in Venezuela, is the highest waterfall in the world.

● Lake Titicaca, right, located 12,500 ft (3,810 m) above sea level between Bolivia and Peru, is the largest fresh-water lake in South America. It is also the highest lake in the world in which large ships can navigate.

● The Amazon River Basin is home to a third of the world's plant and animal species.

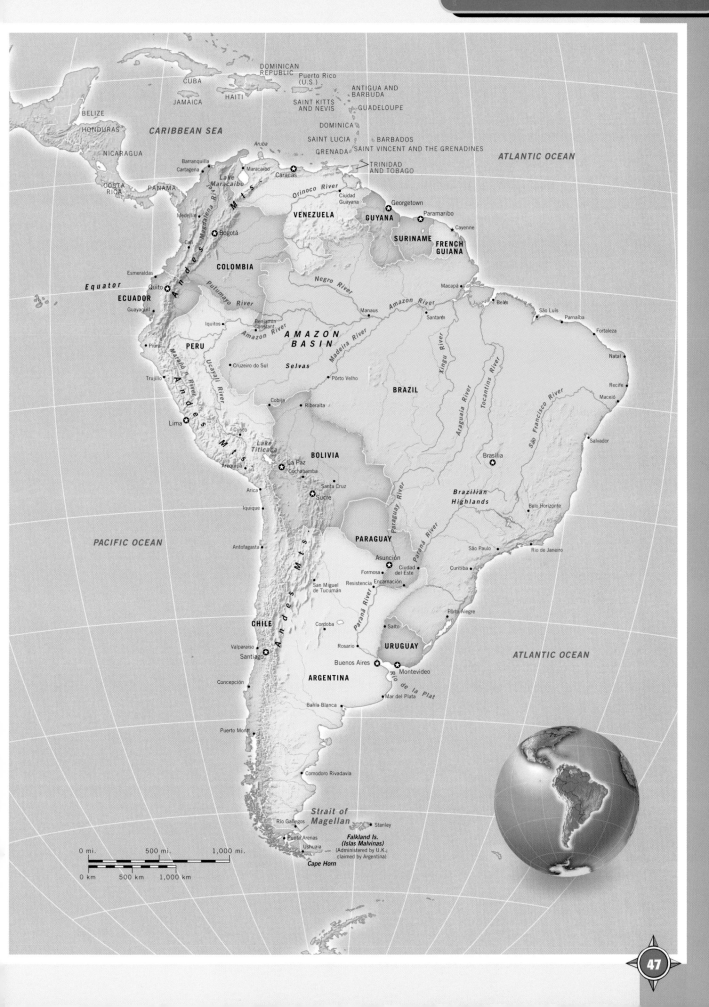

CUBA
JAMAICA
HAITI
DOMINICAN REPUBLIC
Puerto Rico (U.S.)
ANTIGUA AND BARBUDA
SAINT KITTS AND NEVIS
GUADELOUPE
DOMINICA
SAINT LUCIA
BARBADOS
SAINT VINCENT AND THE GRENADINES
GRENADA
TRINIDAD AND TOBAGO

BELIZE
HONDURAS
NICARAGUA
COSTA RICA
PANAMA

CARIBBEAN SEA

ATLANTIC OCEAN

Barranquilla
Cartagena
Maracaibo
Lake Maracaibo
Caracas
Aruba
Orinoco River
Ciudad Guayana
Georgetown
Paramaribo
Cayenne

Medellín
VENEZUELA
GUYANA
SURINAME
FRENCH GUIANA

Magdalena River

Bogotá
Cali
COLOMBIA

Negro River
Macapá

Esmeraldas
Equator
Quito
Putumayo River
Amazon River
Manaus
Amazon River
Santarém
Belém
São Luís
Parnaíba

ECUADOR
Guayaquil
Iquitos
Benjamin Constant
AMAZON BASIN
Fortaleza

Piura
PERU
Marañón River
Amazon River
Selvas
Madeira River
Xingu River
Araguaia River
Tocantins River
Natal

Cruzeiro do Sul
Pôrto Velho
BRAZIL
Recife

Trujillo
Andes Mts.
Ucayali River
Cobija
Riberalta
Maceió

Lima
Cusco
São Francisco River
Salvador

Lake Titicaca
BOLIVIA
La Paz
Cochabamba
Brasília

Arequipa
Santa Cruz
Sucre

Arica
Brazilian Highlands
Belo Horizonte

Iquique
PACIFIC OCEAN
Paraguay River
Paraná River
São Paulo
Rio de Janeiro

Antofagasta
PARAGUAY
Asunción
Ciudad del Este
Curitiba

Formosa
Encarnación
Pôrto Alegre

Resistencia
San Miguel de Tucumán
Paraná River

CHILE
Cordoba
Salto
URUGUAY
ATLANTIC OCEAN

Valparaíso
Rosario
Buenos Aires
Montevideo
Río de la Plata

Santiago
ARGENTINA

Concepción
Bahía Blanca
Mar del Plata

Puerto Montt

Comodoro Rivadavia

Strait of Magellan
Río Gallegos
Stanley
Punta Arenas
Ushuaia
Falkland Is. (Islas Malvinas)
(Administered by U.K.; claimed by Argentina)
Cape Horn

0 mi.   500 mi.   1,000 mi.
0 km   500 km   1,000 km

Northwestern South America

Years before European explorers arrived in what came to be called the New World, a great civilization flourished in Bolivia, Ecuador and Peru. The Inca people built roads and stone cities that stretched for thousands of miles. In 1533, the city of Cuzco, capital of the powerful Inca empire, came under Spain's rule.

Today, Bolivia, Colombia, Ecuador, Peru and Venezuela are a colorful and vibrant blend of Native Indian and Spanish influences. In the region's cities, visitors can find mansions, churches and forts built during Spanish colonial days and museums boasting pre-Columbian treasures. Spanish is spoken and so are native languages.

This region is rich in more than historic treasures. It is marked by an abundance of natural resources and beauty. Venezuela is South America's biggest oil producer. Colombia is famous for its emeralds and coffee. Only Brazil produces more of the world's coffee than Colombia.

The Amazon rain forest covers half of Peru. Millions of plant and animal species live there. Butterflies, pumas, tropical birds and frogs fill the forest with color and sound. Giant tortoises, blue-footed boobies and iguanas enchant visitors to the Galápagos Islands, which lie 650 mi (1,046 km) off Ecuador's coast.

The ancient Incan city of Machu Picchu

Slow and Steady: Giant tortoises at home on the Galápagos Islands

Data Bank

BOLIVIA
AREA: 424,162 sq mi (1,098,580 sq km)
POPULATION: 8,724,156
CAPITAL: La Paz (seat of government), Sucre (legal capital)
LANGUAGES: Spanish, Quechua, Aymara (all official)

COLOMBIA
AREA: 439,733 sq mi (1,138,910 sq km)
POPULATION: 42,310,775
CAPITAL: Bogotá
LANGUAGE: Spanish

ECUADOR
AREA: 109,483 sq mi (283,560 sq km)
POPULATION: 13,971,798
CAPITAL: Quito
LANGUAGES: Spanish (official), native languages

PERU
AREA: 496,223 sq mi (1,285,220 sq km)
POPULATION: 28,863,494
CAPITAL: Lima
LANGUAGES: Spanish, Quechua (both official), Aymara

VENEZUELA
AREA: 352,141 sq mi (912,050 sq km)
POPULATION: 25,017,387
CAPITAL: Caracas
LANGUAGES: Spanish (official), native dialects

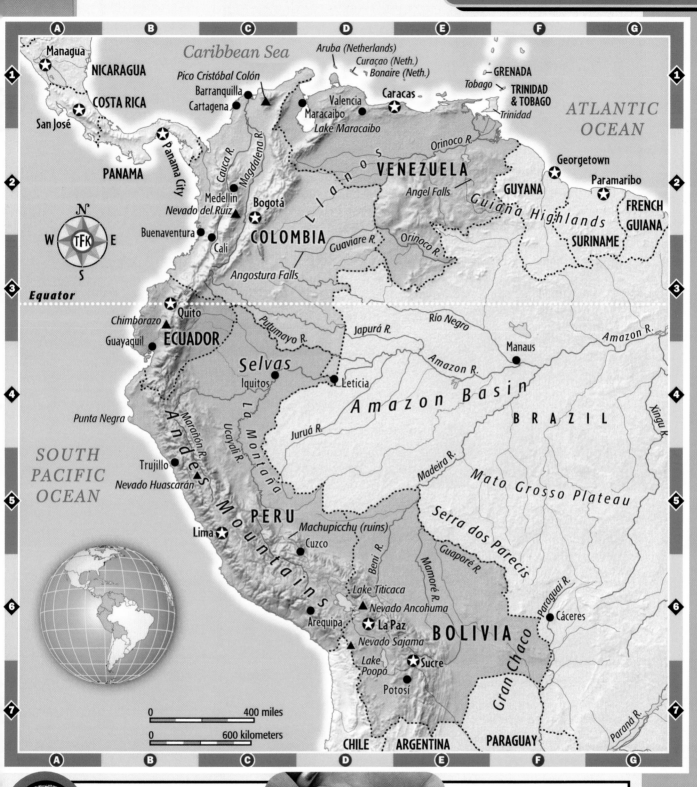

A B C D E F G

1
Managua
NICARAGUA
COSTA RICA
San José
Caribbean Sea
Aruba (Netherlands)
Curaçao (Neth.)
Bonaire (Neth.)
Pico Cristóbal Colón
Barranquilla
Cartagena
Maracaibo
Lake Maracaibo
Valencia
Caracas
GRENADA
Tobago
TRINIDAD
& TOBAGO
Trinidad
ATLANTIC
OCEAN

2
PANAMA
Panama City
Cauca R.
Magdalena R.
Medellín
Nevado del Ruiz
Bogotá
Buenaventura
Cali
COLOMBIA
Llanos
VENEZUELA
Orinoco R.
Angel Falls
Guaviare R.
Orinoco R.
Guiana Highlands
Georgetown
Paramaribo
GUYANA
SURINAME
**FRENCH
GUIANA**

3
Equator
Angostura Falls
Quito
Chimborazo
Guayaquil
ECUADOR
Selvas
Putumayo R.
Japurá R.
Río Negro
Amazon R.

4
Punta Negra
Andes
Marañón R.
La Montaña
Ucayali R.
Iquitos
Leticia
Juruá R.
Amazon R.
Manaus
Amazon Basin
B R A Z I L
Xingu R.

5
SOUTH
PACIFIC
OCEAN
Trujillo
Nevado Huascarán
Mountains
PERU
Machupicchu (ruins)
Lima
Cuzco
Beni R.
Madeira R.
Mato Grosso Plateau
Serra dos Parecis
Guaporé R.

6
N W E S
TFK
Lake Titicaca
Nevado Ancohuma
Arequipa
La Paz
Nevado Sajama
Mamoré R.
BOLIVIA
Gran Chaco
Paraguai R.
Cáceres

7
0 400 miles
0 600 kilometers
Lake
Poopó
Sucre
Potosí
CHILE
ARGENTINA
PARAGUAY
Paraná R.

A B C D E F G

Colombian emeralds
are considered the
world's finest.

Did You Know?

● Colombia is the only country in the Americas that was named after Christopher Columbus.

● The Galápagos giant tortoise, which is found only on Ecuador's Galápagos Islands, can live to be more than 150 years old. A male giant tortoise can weigh as much as 600 lb (270 kg).

● Panama hats are made in Ecuador, not Panama! The straw hats became popular after workers building the Panama Canal in the early 1900s began wearing them.

● The giant blue morpho butterfly is a member of one of 3,700 butterfly species found in Peru.

● Bolivia was named for the South American general and statesman Simón Bolívar.

Peru

¡Hola!

My name is Stefani. I'm in fourth grade, and I live in Villa El Salvador, near Lima. In my country, lunch is the main meal of the day. My favorite food is papa rellena (*pah*-pah rey-*yeh*-nah), a baked potato that is stuffed with meat and then rebaked. I love to sew clothes for my cat, Amimi. Welcome to Peru. Let me show you more!

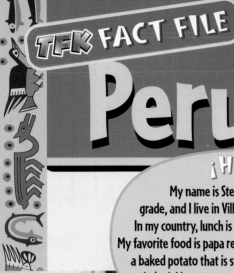

The Peruvian Flag

The flag includes symbols that honor the country's animal, plant and mineral wealth.

The **vicuña** is a small relative of the llama. It is valued for its fine, soft wool.

The **cinchona tree** is found throughout Peru. Its bark is used to make medicine.

A **goat's horn** spills coins of gold and silver, metals that are mined in Peru.

Peru's Ethnic Groups

Three of every four people in Peru have Native Indian heritage. Many Peruvians are descendants of the Incas.

- Mestizo (mixed Native Indian and white) **37%**
- Native Indian **45%**
- White **15%**
- Black, Japanese, Chinese and other **3%**

The Economy

AGRICULTURE: Sugarcane, potatoes, rice

MANUFACTURING: Processed foods, textiles, leather goods, metal products from zinc, copper and iron ore

MAJOR INDUSTRIES: Food production, fishing, mining, tourism

MAJOR EXPORTS: Gold, copper and copper products, zinc products, fish meal, coffee, petroleum products

MAJOR IMPORTS: Machinery, automobiles and trucks

TRADING PARTNERS: U.S., Japan, Britain, Colombia, Germany

Top 5 Largest Rodents

Peru is home to the biggest rodent on earth, the capybara (ka-pih-*bear*-uh). It is related to the rat and the guinea pig, but it's the size of a sheep!

1. **Capybara** Up to 145 lb (66 kg)
2. **Beaver** Up to 77 lb (35 kg)
3. **Porcupine** Up to 44 lb (20 kg)
4. **Paca** Up to 26 lb (12 kg)
5. **Plains Viscacha** Up to 20 lb (9 kg)

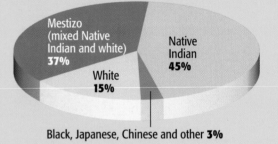

Major Events in Peru's History

7500 B.C.-2500 B.C. The first Native American settlements are built in Peru.

1438 The Inca Empire begins its rise to power. Over the next 300 years, the small tribe grows into the largest empire ever known in the Americas.

1532-1535 Spanish soldiers, led by Francisco Pizarro, defeat the Incas. Pizarro declares Lima as Spain's capital in Peru.

1824 Peru wins its independence from Spain in two decisive battles. It is the last colony in Latin America to do so.

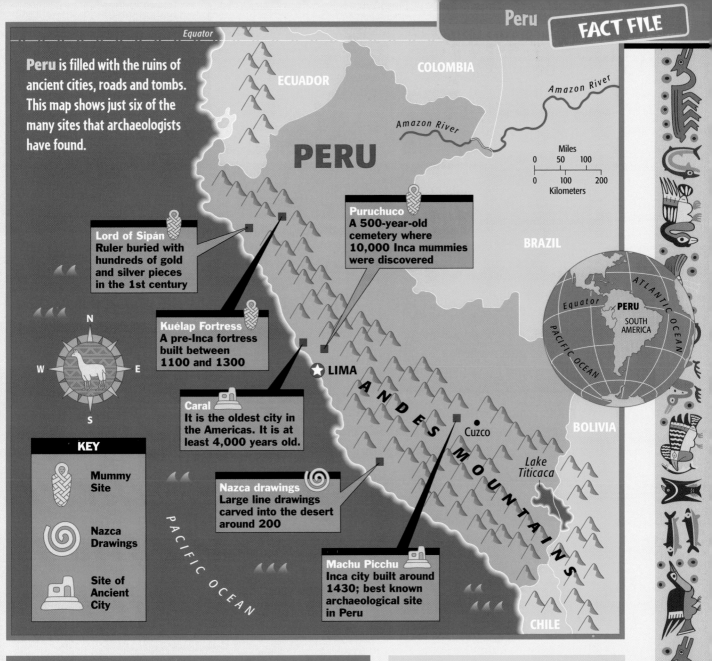

Peru is filled with the ruins of ancient cities, roads and tombs. This map shows just six of the many sites that archaeologists have found.

ECUADOR

COLOMBIA

Equator

Amazon River

Amazon River

PERU

BRAZIL

Puruchuco
A 500-year-old cemetery where 10,000 Inca mummies were discovered

Miles
0 50 100
0 100 200
Kilometers

Lord of Sipán
Ruler buried with hundreds of gold and silver pieces in the 1st century

Equator   **PERU**
SOUTH
AMERICA
ATLANTIC OCEAN
PACIFIC OCEAN

Kuélap Fortress
A pre-Inca fortress built between 1100 and 1300

LIMA

Caral
It is the oldest city in the Americas. It is at least 4,000 years old.

Cuzco

BOLIVIA

Lake Titicaca

ANDES MOUNTAINS

N
W   E
S

KEY

🔹 **Mummy Site**

🌀 **Nazca Drawings**

🏛 **Site of Ancient City**

Nazca drawings
Large line drawings carved into the desert around 200

PACIFIC OCEAN

Machu Picchu
Inca city built around 1430; best known archaeological site in Peru

CHILE

PERU
Is Known for ...

Seviche (suh-*vee*-chay) This spicy dish includes raw fish, hot pepper, onions and lime juice. It is served cold.

Potatoes Peru grows more than 3,000 different kinds of potatoes. Potatoes are eaten at almost every meal.

Surfing Famous worldwide for its waves, Peru has 1,500 mi (2,414 km) of coastline.

Cuy (*coo*-wee) Guinea pig is a popular Peruvian food when roasted on a spit.

Spanish nicknames These are often used to describe a person's size or looks. If you are small and thin, you might be called *flaquita* (fla-*kee*-ta), or "little thin one."

Say It in Quechua

Quechua (*keh*-chuh-wuh) is the language of the Incas. You may already know a few Quechua words: *cocoa*, *lima* (bean), *condor* and *llama*.

Hello ⟶ Napaykullayki (nah-pie-*coo*-*yah*-key)

Please ⟶ Allichu (ah-*yee*-chew)

Father ⟶ Tayta (*tie*-ta)

Mother ⟶ Mama (mah-*mah*)

Yes ⟶ Ari (ah-*ree*)

No ⟶ Mana (mah-*nah*)

My name is ⟶ Noga kani (neeoh-*ha*-cha-*nee*)

Napaykullayki

1911 On July 24, Machu Picchu is discovered by U.S. archaeologist Hiram Bingham.

1980 After years of unstable leadership, a new constitution ensures that a freely elected president and legislature will govern Peru.

1998 Peru signs a treaty with neighbor Ecuador to peacefully resolve a 57-year border dispute.

2001 Alejandro Toledo is elected president. He is Peru's first president of Native Indian descent.

go To learn more about Peru, go to timeforkids.com/gpperu.

Northeastern South America

Sugarloaf Mountain looms over the bay in Rio de Janeiro, Brazil.

Every spring, the people of Rio de Janeiro, in Brazil, throw the world's biggest party, called carnival. It is a four-day extravaganza that brings together people from all backgrounds and cultures. Brazil is the fifth-most-populous nation on earth and South America's biggest country. But more than 75% of Brazil's people are crowded into six large cities. Brazil is one of the world's top producers of steel, iron ore, tin, gold, emeralds, motor vehicles, coffee and sugar.

Much of Brazil is untamed wilderness. The Amazon jungle is home to millions of rare plants and animals, including 1,600 kinds of birds. Sadly, in the past 100 years, about 13% of the original forest has been destroyed.

Brazil shares a border with every nation in South America except Chile and Ecuador. To Brazil's north are the small countries of Suriname and Guyana and the territory of French Guiana. Guyana, the only English-speaking nation on the continent, gained its independence from Britain in 1966. Nine years later, neighboring Suriname gained its independence from the Netherlands. Most of French Guiana, which is a department of France, is unsettled wilderness.

Data Bank

BRAZIL
AREA: 3,286,470 sq mi (8,511,965 sq km)
POPULATION: 184,101,109
CAPITAL: Brasília
LANGUAGES: Portuguese (official), Spanish, English, French

FRENCH GUIANA (Department of France)
AREA: 35,135 sq mi (91,000 sq km)
POPULATION: 186,917
CAPITAL: Cayenne
LANGUAGE: French

GUYANA
AREA: 83,000 sq mi (214,970 sq km)
POPULATION: 705,803
CAPITAL: Georgetown
LANGUAGES: English, Amerindian dialects, Creole, Hindi, Urdu

SURINAME
AREA: 63,039 sq mi (163,270 sq km)
POPULATION: 436,935
CAPITAL: Paramaribo
LANGUAGES: Dutch (official), Surinamese, English

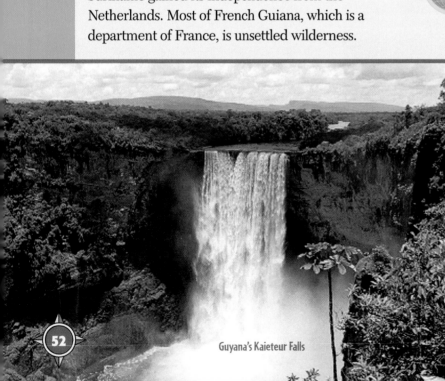

Guyana's Kaieteur Falls

A · B · C · D · E · F · G

1 · 2 · 3 · 4 · 5 · 6 · 7

Orinoco R.

VENEZUELA

GUYANA · Georgetown · SURINAME · Paramaribo · FRENCH GUIANA

Kaieteur Fall · Cayenne

COLOMBIA

Guiana Highlands

Lethem

Equator · Pico da Neblina · Canal do Norte · Canal do Sul-Perigoso

Japurá R. · Río Negro · Marajó I. · São Luis

A m a z o n   B a s i n · Amazon R. · Belém · Fortaleza

Amazon R. · Manaus

Benjamin Constant · Borba · Tapajós R. · Xingu R.

Juruá R. · S e l v a s · Madeira R. · Tocantins R. · Catingas

Porto Velho · B R A Z I L · São Francisco R. · Recife

La Montaña · Serra dos Parecis · Araguaia R. · C a m p o s

Guaporé R.

PERU · A n d e s · Salvador

Lake Titicaca · Mato Grosso Plateau · Brasília · Brazilian Highlands

BOLIVIA

La Paz · Campo Grande · Serra de Amambaí · Belo Horizonte

Lake Poopó · Pico da Bandeira

Sucre · Paraíba R.

Gran Chaco · São Paulo · Serra do Mar

PACIFIC OCEAN · Paraná R. · Rio de Janeiro

CHILE · PARAGUAY · Iguazú Falls

Asunción · Curitiba

ARGENTINA · ATLANTIC OCEAN

Paraná R. · Uruguay R.

Pôrto Alegre

N · W · TFK · E · S

URUGUAY

0 — 500 miles
0 — 750 kilometers

Did You Know?

- **Brazil was originally called Pau Brasil by Europeans. Pau Brasil is a wood, found only in Brazil's forests, that is used to make a red dye.**

- **Nearly a third of Brazilians are kids.**

- **More than 80 kinds of monkeys live in the Amazon jungle. Brazil has more primate species than any other country.**

- **Until 1938, France sent prisoners to colonies in French Guiana. Devil's Island, in the Atlantic Ocean, housed the most notorious prison.**

- **The Potaro River in Guyana comes to a sheer 741-ft (226-m) drop at Kaieteur Falls.**

One of Brazil's endangered golden lion tamarins

Brazil

Oi!

I'm Lizzie, and I'm 11 years old. I go to school in Rio de Janeiro. Sometimes, on the weekends, I go to the beach. I like to swim and play volleyball. Let me show you my beautiful country!

The Brazilian Flag

The flag's colors and symbols represent Brazil's history and culture. Here is what they mean.

Green stands for the lush fields and forests.

Yellow is for the gold that can be found in many areas.

The blue sphere is the night sky.

27 stars are for the capital city of Brazil, Brasília, and the nation's 26 federal states

The Motto is *Ordem E Progresso* (Order and Progress)

A Cultural Rainbow

Brazil's first settlers arrived from Portugal some 500 years ago. Today the country's culture and language are still rooted in Portuguese tradition.

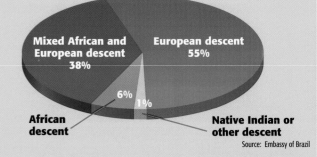

- Mixed African and European descent **38%**
- European descent **55%**
- African descent **6%**
- Native Indian or other descent **1%**

Source: Embassy of Brazil

The Economy

AGRICULTURE: Coffee (leading grower in the world), sugarcane, cocoa beans, rice, oranges, bananas

MANUFACTURING: Cars, cement, chemicals, rubber, electrical equipment, machinery, paper

MINING: Diamonds, crystals, gold, iron ore, chrome, tin

FOREST PRODUCTS: Brazil nuts, cashews, waxes, latex, timber

MAJOR EXPORTS: Iron ore, steel, aluminum, soybeans, orange juice, shoes, coffee, sugar

MAJOR IMPORTS: Oil, machinery, chemical products

TRADING PARTNERS: U.S., Argentina, the Netherlands, Germany, Italy

Top 5 Nations with the Biggest Rain Forests

Millions of rare plants and animals call the rain forest home. Here are the world's largest—and lushest—jungles...

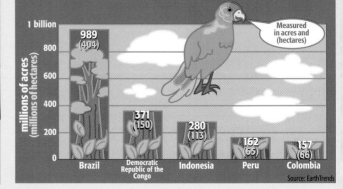

Measured in acres and (hectares)

millions of acres (millions of hectares)

- Brazil: 989 (404)
- Democratic Republic of the Congo: 371 (150)
- Indonesia: 280 (113)
- Peru: 162 (65)
- Colombia: 157 (66)

Source: EarthTrends

Major Events in Brazil's History

1500 While looking for India, Portuguese explorer Pedro Cabral lands in Brazil. He is the first European to set foot there. He claims it for his country.

1695 Gold is discovered in Brazil's interior. Gold-rush towns crop up.

1822 Brazil's leader Pedro I declares the country's independence from Portugal and establishes the Brazilian empire.

1889 Emperor Pedro II is forced by Brazil's military to give up his throne. Brazil becomes a republic.

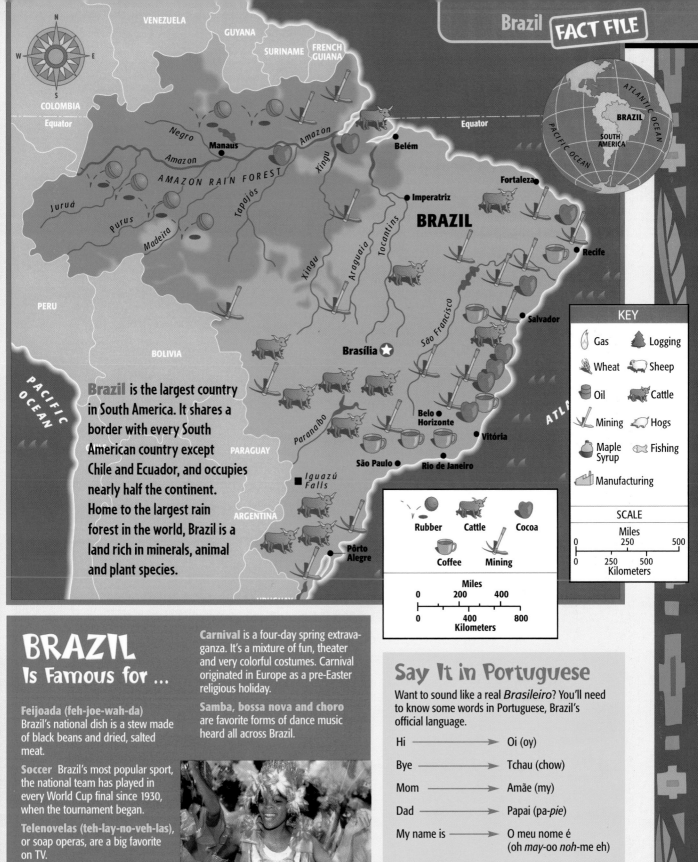

VENEZUELA
GUYANA
SURINAME
FRENCH GUIANA
COLOMBIA
Equator

N
W E
S

Negro
Amazon
Amazon
Manaus
AMAZON RAIN FOREST
Juruá
Purus
Madeira
Tapajós
Xingu

Belém
Imperatriz
Fortaleza

BRAZIL

Xingu
Araguaia
Tocantins
São Francisco
Recife
Salvador

PERU
BOLIVIA

Brasília ★
Paranaíba

Belo Horizonte
Vitória

ATLANTIC OCEAN
Equator
BRAZIL
SOUTH AMERICA
PACIFIC OCEAN
ATLANTIC OCEAN

PACIFIC OCEAN

Brazil is the largest country in South America. It shares a border with every South American country except Chile and Ecuador, and occupies nearly half the continent. Home to the largest rain forest in the world, Brazil is a land rich in minerals, animal and plant species.

PARAGUAY
Iguazú Falls
São Paulo
Rio de Janeiro
ARGENTINA
Pôrto Alegre
URUGUAY

Rubber Cattle Cocoa
Coffee Mining

Miles
0   200   400
0   400   800
Kilometers

KEY

🔥	Gas	🌲	Logging
🌾	Wheat	🐑	Sheep
🛢	Oil	🐄	Cattle
⛏	Mining	🐖	Hogs
🍁	Maple Syrup	🎣	Fishing
🏭	Manufacturing		

SCALE

Miles
0   250   500
0   250   500
Kilometers

BRAZIL Is Famous for ...

Feijoada (feh-joe-wah-da) Brazil's national dish is a stew made of black beans and dried, salted meat.

Soccer Brazil's most popular sport, the national team has played in every World Cup final since 1930, when the tournament began.

Telenovelas (teh-lay-no-veh-las), or soap operas, are a big favorite on TV.

Carnival is a four-day spring extravaganza. It's a mixture of fun, theater and very colorful costumes. Carnival originated in Europe as a pre-Easter religious holiday.

Samba, bossa nova and choro are favorite forms of dance music heard all across Brazil.

Say It in Portuguese

Want to sound like a real *Brasileiro*? You'll need to know some words in Portuguese, Brazil's official language.

Hi ⟶ Oi (oy)

Bye ⟶ Tchau (chow)

Mom ⟶ Amãe (my)

Dad ⟶ Papai (pa-*pie*)

My name is ⟶ O meu nome é (oh *may*-oo *noh*-me eh)

Cool ⟶ Legal (lay-*gahl*)

1890s Farmers rush to southeastern Brazil to grow coffee beans. Coffee becomes Brazil's most important crop.

1938 Brazil is the first Latin American country to send a team to soccer's World Cup.

1960 Brasília, an inland wilderness, is chosen to replace Rio de Janeiro as Brazil's capital.

1992 More than 100 world leaders meet in Rio de Janeiro for the first international Earth Summit, to discuss protecting the environment.

 Find out more about Brazil at *timeforkids.com/gpbrazil*.

Southern South America

Avenida 9 de Julio in Buenos Aires may be the world's widest avenue.

The countries of southern South America—Argentina, Chile, Paraguay and Uruguay—form a long, geographically diverse triangle stretching from Chile's hot, dry Atacama Desert across Argentina's rolling grasslands (called Pampas) to the frigid lands of Tierra del Fuego near Antarctica. Much of the region is abundant in natural resources.

At the center of the triangle is the landlocked country of Paraguay. The people of Paraguay take great pride in their heritage. Many are more comfortable speaking the native language Guarani than Spanish.

Millions of immigrants from Spain, Italy, France and other European nations settled in Argentina, Chile and Uruguay. The wide boulevards of Argentina's capital, Buenos Aires, and the cosmopolitan flair of Uruguay's capital, Montevideo, show a strong European influence.

Perito Moreno Glacier in Argentina

Polynesians were the first inhabitants of Easter Island, which is located in the Pacific Ocean 2,300 mi (3,750 km) west of Chile's capital, Santiago. The remote island is famous for its giant stone statues called *maoi*.

Did You Know?

● The Perito Moreno Glacier, located at the southern tip of Argentina, is 20 mi (32 km) long!

● Argentines call the Falkland Islands the Malvinas. In 1982, Argentina went to war against Britain over ownership of the islands.

● Dinosaur fossils have been found all over Patagonia, in southern Argentina.

● The Andes Mountains separate Argentina from Chile. The mountains cover one-third of Chile.

● Portuñol, which is spoken near the Uruguay-Brazil border, is a language that mixes Portuguese and Spanish.

● Easter Island is one of the most isolated places on earth. It is equidistant from Chile and Tahiti.

Data Bank

ARGENTINA
AREA: 1,068,296 sq mi (2,766,890 sq km)
POPULATION: 39,144,753
CAPITAL: Buenos Aires
LANGUAGES: Spanish (official), English, Italian, German

CHILE
AREA: 292,258 sq mi (756,950 sq km)
POPULATION: 15,827,180
CAPITAL: Santiago
LANGUAGE: Spanish

PARAGUAY
AREA: 157,046 sq mi (406,750 sq km)
POPULATION: 6,191,368
CAPITAL: Asunción
LANGUAGES: Spanish, Guarani (both official)

URUGUAY
AREA: 68,038 sq mi (176,220 sq km)
POPULATION: 3,440,205
CAPITAL: Montevideo
LANGUAGES: Spanish, Portuñol

Easter Island *maoi*

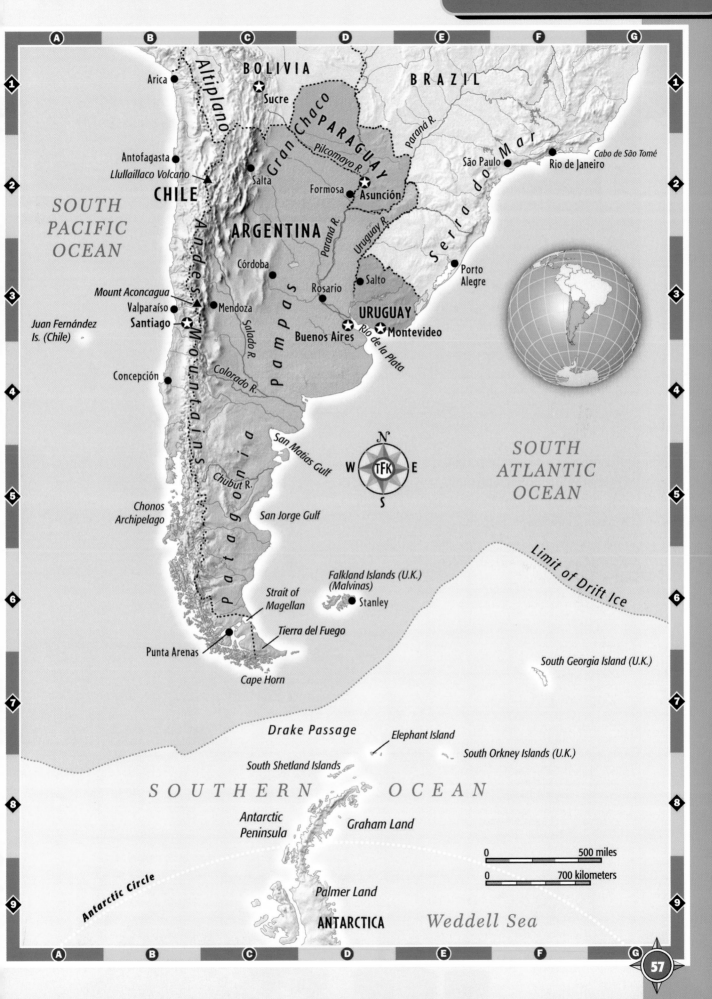

A B C D E F G

1

Arica

BOLIVIA

Sucre

Altiplano

Antofagasta

Gran Chaco

PARAGUAY

Pilcomayo R.

BRAZIL

Paraná R.

São Paulo

Rio de Janeiro

Cabo de São Tomé

2

Llullaillaco Volcano

CHILE

Salta

Formosa

Asunción

Serra do Mar

SOUTH
PACIFIC
OCEAN

ARGENTINA

Paraná R.

Uruguay R.

3

Córdoba

Rosario

Salto

Porto
Alegre

Mount Aconcagua

Valparaíso

Mendoza

Pampas

URUGUAY

Santiago

Buenos Aires

Montevideo

Juan Fernández
Is. (Chile)

Salado R.

Río de la Plata

4

Concepción

Colorado R.

SOUTH
ATLANTIC
OCEAN

Andes Mountains

Patagonia

San Matías Gulf

Chubut R.

N
W E
S

TFK

5

Chonos
Archipelago

San Jorge Gulf

Limit of Drift Ice

6

Strait of
Magellan

Falkland Islands (U.K.)
(Malvinas)

Stanley

Tierra del Fuego

Punta Arenas

South Georgia Island (U.K.)

Cape Horn

7

Drake Passage

Elephant Island

South Orkney Islands (U.K.)

South Shetland Islands

8

SOUTHERN OCEAN

Antarctic
Peninsula

Graham Land

0   500 miles

0   700 kilometers

9

Antarctic Circle

Palmer Land

ANTARCTICA

Weddell Sea

A B C D E F G

Europe

Norway's dazzling Geirangerfjord

Technically, Europe is not really a continent. Most geographers consider Europe to be a part of a larger area called Eurasia. The Ural and the Caucasus mountains separate Europe from Asia. The countries to the west of the mountains are part of Europe, and the countries to the east of the mountains make up Asia. Russia and Turkey are considered part of both Europe and Asia. A tiny portion of Azerbaijan also lies in Europe.

By area, Europe is the second-smallest of the continents. But by population, it is the third largest. It is also one of the richest. Four out of the five wealthiest countries in the world—Luxembourg, Switzerland, Liechtenstein and Norway—are in Europe. (Japan, in Asia, is the only non-European country to make that Top 5 list!)

Europe is also rich in natural resources and beauty. From Scandinavia's frozen fjords to Greece's sun-drenched islands, Europeans enjoy breathtaking surroundings. Large, bustling cities such as Athens, Bonn, London, Paris, Madrid, Rome and Vienna are cultural and industrial centers.

Oia village, on Greece's Santorini Island

Continent Facts

AREA: 3,997,929 sq mi (10,354,636 sq km)

NUMBER OF COUNTRIES: 44 countries—Albania, Andorra, Austria, Belarus, Belgium, Bosnia and Herzegovina, Bulgaria, Croatia, Czech Republic, Denmark, Estonia, Finland, France, Germany, Greece, Hungary, Iceland, Ireland, Italy, Latvia, Liechtenstein, Lithuania, Luxembourg, Macedonia, Malta, Moldova, Monaco, Netherlands, Norway, Poland, Portugal, Romania, Russia, San Marino, Serbia and Montenegro, Slovakia, Slovenia, Spain, Sweden, Switzerland, Turkey, Ukraine, United Kingdom, Vatican City

HIGHEST PEAK: Mount Elbrus, in Russia, 18,481 ft (5,633 m)

LONGEST RIVER: Volga River, in Russia, 2,293 mi (3,689 km)

LARGEST COUNTRY: Russia

SMALLEST COUNTRY: Vatican City (Holy See), .17 sq mi (.44 sq km)

Reykjavik

0 mi.   300 mi.
0 km   300 km   600 km

IREL

GL
JE

ATLANTIC OCEAN

BA
BI

Porto   Bil

Lisbon   PORTUGAL   Madrid

SPAIN

Faro   Seville

Málaga

Gibraltar

MOROCCO

AFRICA

DE ISLANDS
(Denmark)

Torshavn

SHETLAND ISLANDS

ORKNEY ISLANDS

Aberdeen

Edinburgh

UNITED KINGDOM

Leeds

Sheffield

NORTH SEA

NETHERLANDS

Amsterdam

The Hague

Rotterdam

ndon

Calais

Lille

ve

Antwerp

Brussels

BELGIUM

LUXEMBOURG

aris

Luxembourg

ANCE

Dijon

Geneva

Lyon

Turin

Genoa

Marseille

Corsica

ANDORRA

EAN SEA

Arctic Circle

Tromso

Kiruna

Lulea

Umea

Trondheim

NORWAY

Bergen

Oslo

Gävle

Stavanger

SWEDEN

Göteborg

DENMARK

Alborg

Copenhagen

Malmö

Hamburg

Bremen

GERMANY

Berlin

Essen

Dusseldorf

Cologne

Bonn

Frankfurt

Poznan

Wroclaw

Stuttgart

Munich

Strasbourg

LIECHTENSTEIN

Zürich

Bern

Vaduz

SWITZERLAND

Milan

Ljubljana

SLOVENIA

Trieste

Zagreb

CROATIA

SAN MARINO

Florence

Bastia

ITALY

ADRIATIC SEA

Vatican City

Rome

Bari

Sardinia

Naples

Cagliari

Palermo

Messina

Sicily

Valletta

MALTA

Murmansk

Oulu

FINLAND

Tampere

Turku

Helsinki

St. Petersburg

Stockholm

Tallinn

BALTIC SEA

ESTONIA

Riga

LATVIA

LITHUANIA

Vilnius

Kaliningrad

RUSSIA

Gdansk

POLAND

Warsaw

Lodz

Brest

Krakow

CZECH REPUBLIC

Prague

Brno

Bratislava

Vienna

SLOVAKIA

AUSTRIA

HUNGARY

Budapest

Arad

Belgrade

BOSNIA AND HERZEGOVINA

Sarajevo

SERBIA AND MONTENEGRO

Podgorica

Nis

Tirane

Korce

ALBANIA

Kerkira

GREECE

Volos

Athens

Crete

Pechora

Arkhangel'sk

ASIA

RUSSIA

Izhevsk

Nizhniy Novgorod

Kazan

Moscow

Samara

Smolensk

Lipetsk

Saratov

Voronezh

Minsk

BELARUS

Hornyel'

Kiev

Kharkiv

UKRAINE

L'viv

Derazhnya

Voroshilovgrad

Gorlovka

Makeyevka

Zhdanov

Rostov

KAZAKHSTAN

Volgograd

Chisinau

Iasi

MOLDOVA

Odessa

Mykolaiva

Kerch'

Simferopol'

Sevastopol'

ROMANIA

Bucharest

Craiova

Constanta

Sofia

BULGARIA

Varna

BLACK SEA

Groznyy

Skopje

MACEDONIA

Thessaloniki

Istanbul

Izmir

T U R K E Y

SYRIA

IRAQ

IRAN

CYPRUS

LEBANON

Mont Blanc, France

● At 15,771 ft (4,807 m), Mont Blanc in the French Alps is the highest mountain in Western Europe.

● Finland has about 55,000 lakes and nearly 180,000 islands.

● There are no snakes in Ireland. You won't find any snakes in New Zealand or at the North

and South Poles either!

● With a population of 32,270 and an area of .75 sq mi (1.95 sq km), Monaco has the highest population density of any country in the world.

● Amsterdam, in the Netherlands, has about 1,300 bridges.

United Kingdom and Ireland

The Emerald Isle: A green pasture in Ireland

reland is often called the Emerald Isle. The English sing of "England's green and pleasant land." Both lands have a wet, temperate climate, which makes the soil fertile—and green! Over the centuries, these lands have been cultivated and mined for coal and minerals. The lush farms, gardens and forests of the region continue to impress visitors.

Britain, Northern Ireland and several smaller islands are all part of a nation called the United Kingdom, which is also referred to as Britain. England, Scotland and Wales are located on the island of Britain, which is the eighth-largest island in the world. Ireland is a separate island. While England, Scotland, Wales and Northern Ireland are all governed by one democratic system, the southern part of Ireland, called the Republic of Ireland, is a separate nation.

Huge stone structures like Stonehenge, barrows (burial mounds), ruined castles and crumbling stone walls tell some of the area's history. The islands were first inhabited 7,000 years ago. Ancient peoples, including Druids and Celts, built mysterious stone circles that fascinate us today. Roman Emperor Julius Caesar invaded the region in 54 A.D., and the Romans ruled until 410 A.D. They too built lasting structures. Then came the Middle Ages, the time of knights and castles. Dozens of little kingdoms fought one another, forming and breaking alliances. It was not until 1707 that England, Scotland and Wales joined together to form the United Kingdom. By the 19th century, a huge British Empire circled the globe. Today, that empire is nearly gone. But the United Kingdom and Ireland are each part of the European Union, which is made up of 25 countries.

London's Tower Bridge was completed in 1894.

Data Bank

UNITED KINGDOM
AREA: 94,525 sq mi (244,820 sq km)
POPULATION: 60,270,708
CAPITAL: London
LANGUAGES: English, Welsh, Gaelic

IRELAND
AREA: 27,136 sq mi (70,280 sq km)
POPULATION: 3,969,558
CAPITAL: Dublin
LANGUAGES: English, Irish (Gaelic)

United Kingdom and Ireland

Shetland Is.

Fair Isle

Orkney Is.

NORWAY

Stavanger

Isle of Lewis

Ben Hope

Outer Hebrides

Inner Hebrides

Moray Firth

Loch Ness

Spey R.

Aberdeen

Ben Nevis

Grampian Mtns.

Dundee

Islay

Glasgow

Clyde R.

Edinburgh

North Channel

NORTHERN IRELAND (U.K.)

SCOTLAND

Tyne R.

UNITED KINGDOM

Donegal Bay

Lake Neagh

Belfast

Isle of Man

Central Plain

Galway

REPUBLIC OF IRELAND

Shannon R.

Dublin

Irish Sea

Liverpool

Leeds

Manchester

Eastern Plain

The Wash

Aran Is.

Limerick

Blackwater R.

Waterford

Cambrian Mtns.

Trent R.

Midland Plain

Norwich

Amsterdam

NETHERLANDS

Carrantuohill

Cork

St. George's Channel

WALES

Severn R.

Birmingham

ENGLAND

London

Cardiff

Swansea

Bristol

Bristol Channel

Thames R.

Southampton

Dover

Strait of Dover

Calais

BELGIUM

Brussels

Land's End

Plymouth

English Channel

FRANCE

Is. of Scilly

Channel Islands (U.K.)

Guernsey

Jersey

Cherbourg

Seine R.

ATLANTIC OCEAN

North Sea

ATLANTIC OCEAN

0   150 miles

0   200 kilometers

N W E S TFK

A B C D E F G
1 2 3 4 5 6 7

Did You Know?

● At its height in the 19th century, the British Empire included one-fourth of the earth's surface.

● One out of every eight residents of the United Kingdom lives in London.

● The Royal Observatory in Greenwich, England, is the home of Greenwich Mean Time (GMT) and the Prime Meridian of the world—a line of longitude that separates the eastern and western hemispheres of the earth. That means that Greenwich is at longitude 0 degrees.

● At 4,407 ft (1,343 m), Ben Nevis, in Scotland, and at 3,560 ft (1,085 m), Mount Snowdon, in Snowdonia National Park in Wales, are the highest points in Britain.

● Bagpipes were actually brought to Scotland by the Romans, who discovered them in the Middle East.

Scandinavia

In the far north of Europe are the seafaring nations of Denmark, Sweden, Norway, Iceland and Finland. All five share a similar history, culture and climate. Only Norway and Sweden form the Scandinavian Peninsula, but all five countries are often grouped under the headings Scandinavia or Nordic nations.

The midnight sun shines over Norway's Vesteralen Islands.

Though winters are harsh where Scandinavia overlaps the Arctic Circle, the climate in the rest of the region is less severe. Surrounding waters keep temperatures from becoming bitterly cold. Because Scandinavia is so far north, summers in the region can have daylight almost around the clock. In winter, darkness often falls after only a few hours of twilight.

Although each of the Scandinavian countries has its own history and language, all of Scandinavia shares the legacy of the Vikings. Beginning in about 800 A.D., these warrior-sailors from Denmark, Sweden and Norway built open sailing ships that ventured as far as what is known today as North America. They also visited Finland and laid claim to some of its islands. As the Vikings traveled the seas, they conquered and claimed other lands, including Iceland, Greenland, Britain, France, Russia, Belgium and Holland. Gradually, the Vikings became part of the communities they conquered.

The Nobel Prize is the top award for scientists and scholars.

Today, all the Scandinavian nations are members of the European Union, and all enjoy a high standard of living. Cities such as Oslo, Copenhagen and Stockholm are international cultural centers.

Data Bank

DENMARK
AREA: 16,639 sq mi (43,094 sq km)
POPULATION: 5,413,392
CAPITAL: Copenhagen
LANGUAGES: Danish, Faroese, Greenlandic, German

FINLAND
AREA: 130,127 sq mi (337,030 sq km)
POPULATION: 5,214,512
CAPITAL: Helsinki
LANGUAGES: Finnish, Swedish (both official)

ICELAND
AREA: 39,768 sq mi (103,000 sq km)
POPULATION: 282,151
CAPITAL: Reykjavik
LANGUAGES: Icelandic, English, Nordic languages, German

NORWAY
AREA: 125,181 sq mi (324,220 sq km)
POPULATION: 4,574,560
CAPITAL: Oslo
LANGUAGE: Norwegian

SWEDEN
AREA: 173,731 sq mi (449,964 sq km)
POPULATION: 8,986,400
CAPITAL: Stockholm
LANGUAGE: Swedish

Reindeer Games: A Lapp father and son care for their animal.

Iceland inset map

A B C D E F G

Horn
Húna Bay
Grimsey I.
Arctic Circle
Fontur
Akureyri
Hvítá R.
ICELAND
Vatnajökull
Faxa Bay
Keflavik
Reykjavík
Hvannadalshnúkur
Hekla (volcano)
Surtsey I.
100 miles

Main map

North Cape
Hammerfest
Barents Sea
Tana
Norwegian Sea
Tromso
Finnmark Plateau
Lake Inari
Murmansk
Mt. Haltia
Narvik
Muonio R.
L A P L A N D
Vest Fjord
Mt. Kebnekaise
Arctic Circle
Kemi R.
ATLANTIC OCEAN
Kölen Mts.
Lule R.
Lulea
Oulu
Faroe Is.
(Denmark)
Trondheim Fjord
Angerman R.
Skelleftea
Oulu R.
N
W TFK E
S
Alesund
Trondheim
S W E D E N
Östersund
F I N L A N D
Shetland Is. (U.K.)
N O R W A Y
Vaasa
Lake Saimaa
Glittertind Peak
Gulf of Bothnia
Tampere
Lake Ladoga
Bergen
Klar R.
Turku
Helsinki
St. Petersburg
Drammen
Oslo
Dal R.
Gulf of Finland
Hardanger Fjord
Karlstad
Uppsala
Tallinn
North Sea
Stavanger
Otra R.
Lake Vänern
Aland Is.
Stockholm
ESTONIA
RUSSIA
SCOTLAND
Arendal
Lake Vättern
Norrköping
Kristiansand
Skagerrak
Kattegat
Göteborg
Baltic Sea
Gulf of Riga
Alborg
Gotland
LATVIA
Riga
D E N M A R K
Öland
LITHUANIA
Esbjerg
Odense
Malmö
Bornholm (Denmark)
Vilnius
BELARUS
Kiel
Copenhagen
Kaliningrad
RUSSIA
300 miles
Gdansk
450 kilometers
ENGLAND
GERMANY
POLAND

A B C D E F G

63

Did You Know?

- The Lapp, or Sami, people live in northern Norway, Sweden, Finland and Russia.

- Reykjavik, the capital of Iceland, is the northernmost national capital in the world.

- In his will, Swedish inventor and businessman Alfred Nobel established the Nobel Prizes. They were first awarded in 1901. The prizes reward leaders in the fields of physics, chemistry, medicine, literature, economics and peace.

- Danish storyteller Hans Christian Andersen wrote "The Little Mermaid." A statue of the mermaid watches over the harbor of the Danish capital, Copenhagen.

- Sweden is famous for the smorgasbord, a buffet including all kinds of foods, such as pickled and smoked fish.

The Iberian Peninsula

Poets and writers have often likened Spain to a fortress. The snowcapped Pyrenees Mountains have protected Spain as well as its smaller neighbors on Europe's Iberian Peninsula—Portugal and Andorra. But the mountains have also separated the countries from the rest of the European continent.

The geography of the peninsula, which ranges from high plateaus and mountains to Mediterranean and Atlantic coastlines, presents varying climates. The north is the wettest; the central region, home to Spain's capital and largest city, Madrid, is dry and, in the winter, cold. The coasts experience mild winter temperatures. Summer is hot almost everywhere. The sunny beaches and resorts are popular tourist destinations.

At the peninsula's southern tip is the British territory of Gibraltar. It is only about eight miles from Africa. The influence of Moors from North Africa, who conquered the Iberian Peninsula in the 8th century, is reflected in some of the region's architecture. Throughout the area, great works of art adorn magnificent cathedrals and museums.

Fiestas occur at intervals all year. The lively celebrations, which honor everything from saints to the changing seasons, often include parades and fireworks. Spain is also known for flamenco dancing and bullfighting, one of the country's most popular sporting events.

Spanish architect Antoni Gaudí designed La Sagrada Familia church in Barcelona, Spain.

Olé: Flamenco dancers in Seville, Spain

Moors built the Alhambra palace.

Data Bank

ANDORRA
AREA: 181 sq mi (468 sq km)
POPULATION: 69,865
CAPITAL: Andorra la Vella
LANGUAGES: Catalan (official), French, Castilian, Portuguese

PORTUGAL
AREA: 35,672 sq mi (92,391 sq km)
POPULATION: 10,119,250
CAPITAL: Lisbon
LANGUAGE: Portuguese

SPAIN
AREA: 194,896 sq mi (504,782 sq km)
POPULATION: 40,280,780
CAPITAL: Madrid
LANGUAGES: Castilian Spanish, Catalan, Galician, Basque

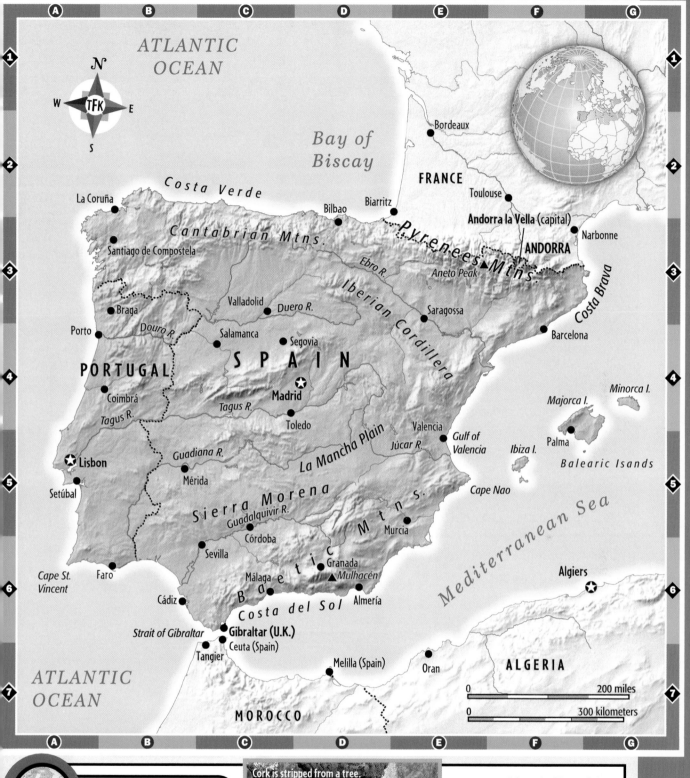

ATLANTIC OCEAN

N
W · E
S
TFK

Bay of Biscay

FRANCE

Bordeaux

Toulouse

Biarritz

Andorra la Vella (capital)

ANDORRA

Narbonne

Costa Verde

La Coruña

Bilbao

Cantabrian Mtns.

Santiago de Compostela

Ebro R.

Pyrenees Mtns.

Aneto Peak

Costa Brava

Valladolid

Duero R.

Saragossa

Iberian Cordillera

Braga

Porto

Douro R.

Salamanca

Segovia

Barcelona

PORTUGAL

SPAIN

Coimbrá

Madrid

Tagus R.

Tagus R.

Toledo

La Mancha Plain

Valencia

Gulf of Valencia

Minorca I.

Majorca I.

Júcar R.

Palma

Ibiza I.

Balearic Isands

Lisbon

Guadiana R.

Mérida

Setúbal

Sierra Morena

Guadalquivir R.

Baetic Mtns.

Murcia

Cape Nao

Mediterranean Sea

Córdoba

Granada

Mulhacén

Algiers

Cape St. Vincent

Faro

Sevilla

Málaga

Almería

Cádiz

Costa del Sol

Strait of Gibraltar

Gibraltar (U.K.)

Ceuta (Spain)

Tangier

Melilla (Spain)

Oran

ALGERIA

ATLANTIC OCEAN

MOROCCO

0   200 miles

0   300 kilometers

Did You Know?

- About one-third of the world's cork oak trees grow in Portugal. The country produces about half the world's cork.

- *Don Quixote*, written by Spanish author Miguel de Cervantes in the early 1600s, is considered to be the first modern novel.

- At midnight on New Year's Eve, Spaniards eat

Cork is stripped from a tree.

one grape with each chime of the clock. The grapes are said to bring luck for the next 12 months.

- Spain is the world's leading olive-oil producer. In 2003, 865,000 metric tons of it were made.

- Spanish-born Pablo Picasso is considered the founder of modern art.

- Spain, under the Terms of the Treaty of Utrecht of 1713, ceded Gibraltar to Britain in perpetuity.

France and Monaco

France is a feast for the senses. The sights, scents and flavors of Western Europe's largest country have been celebrated for hundreds of years. The French are proud of their nation's history and culture. They treasure their artistic and architectural accomplishments and savor their country's fine cuisine and flair for fashion.

Paris, the City of Light, is France's capital and cultural center. The city sits on the banks of the Seine River and is a magnet for writers and artists. It is considered to be one of the world's most romantic cities and an ideal place to people-watch at a sidewalk café.

Most of France's 60 million residents live in cities or towns, but much of the country is fertile farmland. Grapes of all varieties are among the country's main products. France is one of the world's leading wine producers.

In southern France, the resort towns of Nice and Cannes grace the French Riviera. Monaco, the world's second-smallest country, hugs the border with Italy. Monaco is known for its casinos.

Tourists flock to the Eiffel Tower in Paris.

Monte Carlo, in Monaco, is packed with resorts and hotels.

Data Bank

FRANCE
AREA: 211,208 sq mi (547,030 sq km)
POPULATION: 60,424,213
CAPITAL: Paris
LANGUAGE: French

MONACO
AREA: .75 sq mi (1.95 sq km)
POPULATION: 32,270
CAPITAL: Monaco
LANGUAGES: French (official), English, Italian, Monégasque

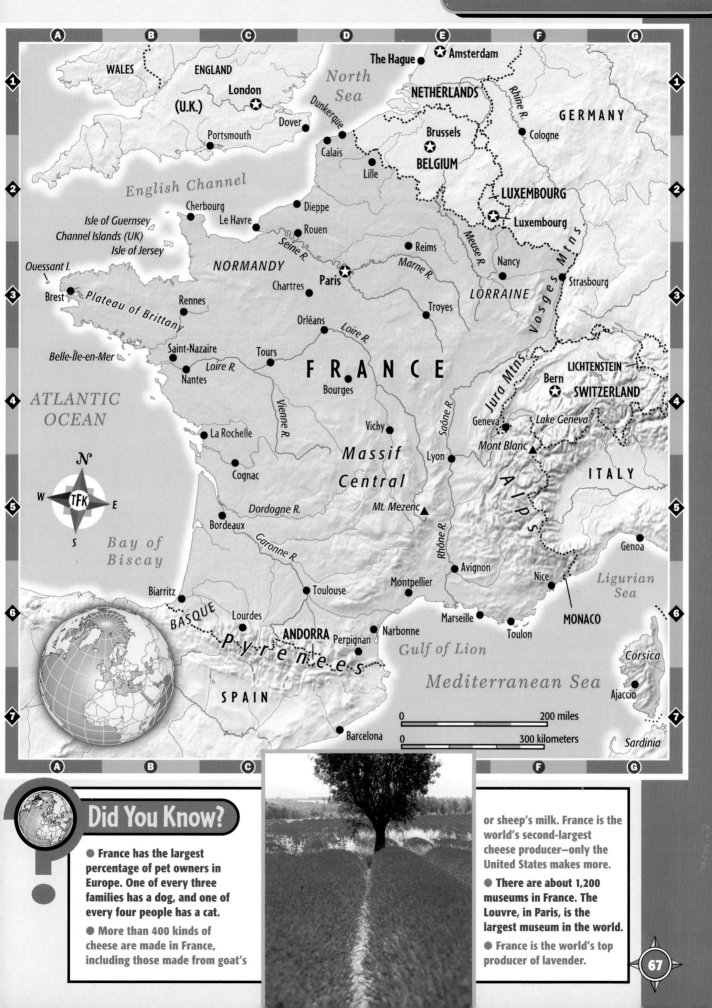

A B C D E F G

WALES ENGLAND

North Sea

The Hague ★ Amsterdam

London ✪

(U.K.) Dover Dunkerque NETHERLANDS Rhine R. GERMANY

Portsmouth Calais Brussels ✪ Cologne

English Channel Lille BELGIUM

Cherbourg Dieppe LUXEMBOURG

Isle of Guernsey Le Havre Rouen Luxembourg ✪

Channel Islands (UK) Seine R. Meuse R. Nancy Vosges Mtns.

Isle of Jersey NORMANDY Reims Strasbourg

Ouessant I. Chartres Paris ✪ Marne R. LORRAINE

Brest *Plateau of Brittany* Troyes

Rennes Orléans Loire R.

Saint-Nazaire Tours LICHTENSTEIN

Belle-Île-en-Mer *Loire R.* **F R A N C E** Jura Mtns. Bern ✪ SWITZERLAND

Nantes Bourges Vienne R.

ATLANTIC OCEAN Geneva Lake Geneva

La Rochelle Vichy Saône R. Mont Blanc ▲ ITALY

Cognac *Massif Central* Lyon *Alps*

Dordogne R. Mt. Mezenc ▲ Genoa

Bay of Biscay Bordeaux Rhône R. Nice *Ligurian Sea*

Garonne R. Avignon MONACO

Biarritz Montpellier

BASQUE Toulouse Marseille Toulon

Lourdes Narbonne Corsica

ANDORRA Perpignan *Gulf of Lion*

Pyrenees *Mediterranean Sea* Ajaccio

S P A I N Barcelona *Sardinia*

N W E S TFK

0 ——— 200 miles

0 ——— 300 kilometers

Did You Know?

● **France has the largest percentage of pet owners in Europe. One of every three families has a dog, and one of every four people has a cat.**

● **More than 400 kinds of cheese are made in France, including those made from goat's** or sheep's milk. France is the world's second-largest cheese producer—only the United States makes more.

● **There are about 1,200 museums in France. The Louvre, in Paris, is the largest museum in the world.**

● **France is the world's top producer of lavender.**

France

Bonjour!

My name is Matthieu. I am 8 years old and live in Senlis, near Paris, with my parents and my little sister. My school day is very long–eight hours! After school, I take karate lessons and often stop to pick up a baguette, or bread, from the bread truck. My favorite dinner is lamb chops and couscous. I like to ride my bike and skateboard. Let me show you France!

The French Flag

The French call their flag the Tricolore (tree-cooh-*luhr*) because of its three colors. It was created in 1790, during the French Revolution, when citizens rebelled against the king in favor of a representative government.

Blue and **red** are the ancient colors of the city of Paris, where the revolution began.

White symbolizes the king.

France's Population

France has an aging population. Fewer children are born each year, and adults are living longer. The number of people age 80 and older is expected to nearly double by 2030.

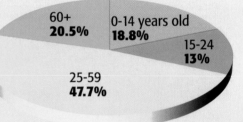

60+ **20.5%**
0-14 years old **18.8%**
15-24 **13%**
25-59 **47.7%**

The Economy

AGRICULTURE: Wheat, grapes, sugar beets, corn, barley, apples, sunflower seeds

MANUFACTURING: Motor vehicles, aircraft, radios and televisions, pharmaceuticals, printing and publishing

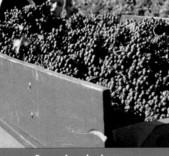
France: A worker harvests grapes.

MAJOR INDUSTRIES: Tourism, food and wine production, fashion, transportation equipment

MAJOR EXPORTS: Cars, trucks, aircraft, chemical products, cheese, wine and food products, plastic goods

MAJOR IMPORTS: Machinery, chemicals, oil and gas

TRADING PARTNERS: Germany, Italy, Britain, U.S., Spain

Top 5 Tourist Destinations

France gets more visitors than any other nation. Here are the countries most popular with international tourists in 2001.

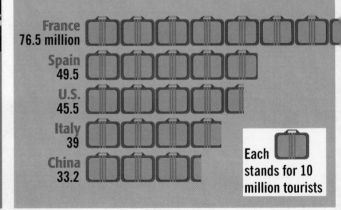

France 76.5 million
Spain 49.5
U.S. 45.5
Italy 39
China 33.2

Each 🧳 stands for 10 million tourists

Major Events in France's History

58 B.C.–51 B.C. Roman Emperor Julius Caesar conquers Gaul, which is now France.

486 A.D.–511 A.D. A tribe called the Franks rules the region. The land is named for them.

1643–1715 Louis XIV, the Sun King, reigns longer than any other French ruler. In this era, France gains influence throughout Europe.

1789 On July 14, citizens storm the Bastille, a Paris prison. The French Revolution begins.

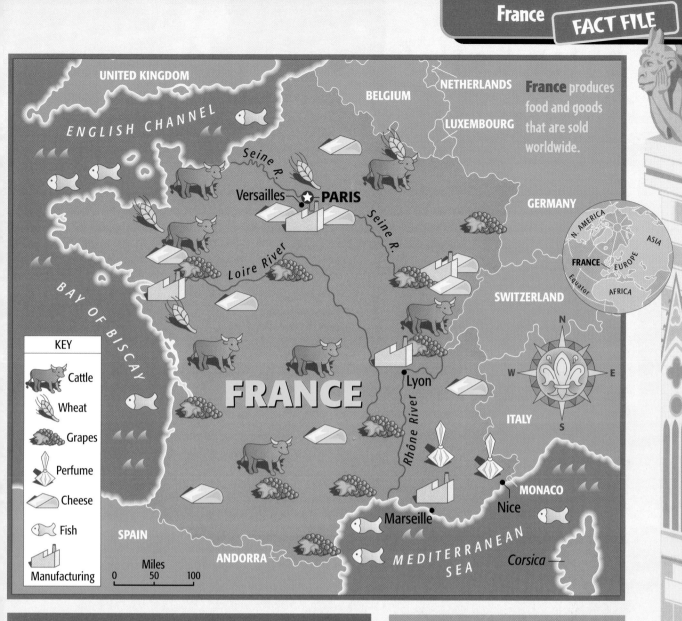

France produces food and goods that are sold worldwide.

KEY

- Cattle
- Wheat
- Grapes
- Perfume
- Cheese
- Fish
- Manufacturing

Miles
0   50   100

UNITED KINGDOM

ENGLISH CHANNEL

BELGIUM
NETHERLANDS
LUXEMBOURG

Seine R.
Versailles ★ **PARIS**
Seine R.

GERMANY

Loire River

BAY OF BISCAY

FRANCE

SWITZERLAND

Lyon

Rhône River

ITALY

MONACO
Nice

Marseille

MEDITERRANEAN SEA

Corsica

SPAIN

ANDORRA

N. AMERICA
ASIA
FRANCE EUROPE
Equator
AFRICA

FRANCE Is Famous for ...

Food Every meal is important to the French. The world's first restaurant opened in Paris in about 1765. More than 400 kinds of cheese are made in France.

Museums The giant Louvre in Paris

and other museums attract millions of people each year. There are about 1,200 museums in the country!

Fashion One of the most important industries in France is fashion. Paris is considered the fashion capital of the world.

The Tour de France This bicycle race is the world's most famous. Each summer, cyclists race over a 2,051-mile route for three weeks.

Pets France has the highest percentage of pet owners in Europe. One out of three families has a dog. One out of four people has at least one cat.

Say It in French

Parlez-vous français? (Par-lay-*voo* frahn-*say*?) That means, "Do you speak French?" You can do it. Just check out these French words!

Hello ⟶ Bonjour (bohn-*zhoor*)

Thank you ⟶ Merci (mehr-*see*)

That's life! ⟶ C'est la vie! (say lah *vee*)

How are you? ⟶ Comment allez-vous? (koh-mahnt ah-lay-*voo*)

Please ⟶ S'il vous plait (see voo *pleh*)

My name is ⟶ Je m'appelle (zhe mah-*pell*)

 Find out more about France at *timeforkids.com/gpfrance*.

1804 Military hero Napoleon Bonaparte crowns himself emperor after leading France to victory over Europe's strongest nations. In 1815, Napoleon is finally defeated at Waterloo, in Belgium.

1914-1918 France battles Germany in World War I.

1940 Germany invades France during World War II. In 1945, Britain, France, the U.S. and other allies defeat Germany, Japan and Italy.

1994 The Channel Tunnel opens, connecting Britain and France under the English Channel.

The Low Countries

Waterway: Amsterdam, in the Netherlands, has more than 150 canals.

Belgium, the Netherlands and Luxembourg are often called the Low Countries. It is a fitting name for this densely populated region, as much of its land lies either below, or just slightly above, sea level. The terrain seems endlessly flat, which is perfect for bicycling, a favorite activity and popular mode of local transportation. Travel by boat is also essential. Thousands of rivers and canals connect gabled cities, quaint villages and bountiful farmland throughout the region.

Flower Power: Tulips bloom across the Dutch landscape.

The Low Countries produce some of the world's finest flowers, cheeses and chocolates. The Netherlands (commonly called Holland) is the world's flower hub. It is host to flower festivals and auctions, and exports more blossoms than any other nation. Belgium's capital, Brussels, is called the capital of Europe. A uniquely multicultural city, it houses the headquarters of the European Union (E.U.) as well as NATO (the North Atlantic Treaty Organization).

Luxembourg, one of the world's smallest countries, is tucked just below Belgium. Despite its size—998 sq mi (2,586 sq km)—it is an important worldwide banking center. Luxembourg also houses the E.U.'s financial headquarters.

Many of the world's most famous painters came from the Low Countries. Hieronymus Bosch, Rembrandt van Rijn, Johannes Vermeer and Vincent van Gogh were all from the Netherlands; Jan van Eyck, Pieter Brueghel the Elder and Peter Paul Rubens were all from Belgium.

Say Cheese: Holland is famous for its delicious butter and cheese.

Data Bank

BELGIUM
AREA: 11,781 sq mi (30,510 sq km)
POPULATION: 10,348,276
CAPITAL: Brussels
LANGUAGES: Dutch, French, German (all official)

LUXEMBOURG
AREA: 998 sq mi (2,586 sq km)
POPULATION: 462,690
CAPITAL: Luxembourg
LANGUAGES: Luxembourgish, German, French

NETHERLANDS
AREA: 16,033 sq mi (41,526 sq km)
POPULATION: 16,318,199
CAPITAL: Amsterdam
LANGUAGES: Dutch, Frisian (both official)

The Low Countries map showing:

England, **Germany**, **Netherlands**, **Belgium**, **Luxembourg**, **France**

North Sea

West Frisian Islands — Terschelling I., Ameland I., Vlieland I., Texel I.

East Frisian Islands

Waddenzee

Leeuwarden, Dike, Groningen, Bremen

Ijsselmeer Dam, Ijsselmeer

NORTHEAST POLDER, EASTERN FLEVOLAND

Haarlem, Amsterdam, The Hague, Leiden, Utrecht, Arnhem

Teutoburg Forest

Goeree, Delft, Rotterdam, Rhine R., Ruhr Valley, Essen

Brouwers Dam, Schouwen, Oosterschelde Dam, Walcheren

Maas R., Ruhr R.

Tilburg, 's-Hertogenbosch, Eindhoven, Rhine R., Düsseldorf

Dover, Strait of Dover, Ostend, Bruges, Ghent, Antwerp, Scheldt R., Lys R.

FLANDERS, BELGIUM

Dunkerque, Calais, Boulogne, Lille

Maastricht, Vaalser Hill, Cologne, Bonn

Brussels, Waterloo, Liège, Botrange

Mons, Namur, Meuse R., Spa, Koblenz

Charleroi, Mosel R.

Frankfurt am Main, Weisbaden

Somme R., Oise R., Ardennes, Eifel, Hunsrück

Buurgplaatz, LUXEMBOURG

FRANCE, Aisne R., LORRAINE, Luxembourg, Esch-sur-Alzette

Seine R., Rhine R.

N W E S — TFK

0 — 80 miles
0 — 120 kilometers

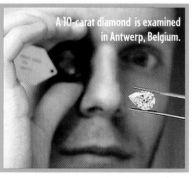

Germany

Although Germany is mainly urban, the country has a wide range of natural landscapes. Mountains covered by lush forests dominate the south. Along the edges of the North Sea and the Baltic Sea, low-lying coastal land gives way to a central region of hills and river valleys. Germany is blessed with a temperate climate and fertile soil.

Because of the numerous rivers and canals that stretch across the country, Germany developed into a major transportation hub. Centrally located in Europe, it has historically been a crossroads for ideas, cultures—and armies. The country's long history includes the devastating rule of Adolf Hitler, whose actions sparked World War II. The war tore the country apart—Germany was divided into East and West zones—and the economy was destroyed. West Germany rebounded to become a major industrial power, while East Germany allied itself with the Soviet Union. In 1989, the fall of the Berlin Wall, which had separated East and West Berlin, helped bring democracy to the newly reunited country. In 1991, Germany's capital was moved from Bonn to Berlin.

Europe's most populous nation is divided into 16 states. Bavaria is the largest state, and its landscape is graced by numerous castles. The elaborate Neuschwanstein Castle, in the Bavarian Alps, was built for King Louis II, called "Mad Ludwig."

The lavish Neuschwanstein Castle in Bavaria

Germany is known for world-class cars, such as the BMW

Dividing Line: The Berlin Wall once separated East and West Berlin.

Data Bank

GERMANY
AREA: 137,846 sq mi (357,021 sq km)
POPULATION: 82,424,609
CAPITAL: Berlin
LANGUAGE: German

A B C D E F G

1

DENMARK

☆ Copenhagen

Baltic Sea

Kiel Bay

North Frisian Is.

Rügen

North Sea

West Frisian Is.

East Frisian Is.

Nord Ostsee Canal

Kiel

Fehmarn I.

Mecklenburg Bay

Pomeranian Bay

Rostock

2

Hamburg

Elbe R.

Lake Müritz

N
W E
TFK
S

Oder R.

Weser R.

3

North German Plain

☆ Amsterdam

NETHERLANDS

Rhine R.

Bremen

Teutoburg Forest

Hannover

Mittelland Canal

Magdeburg

Berlin ☆

POLAND

Oder R.

Münster

Brocken Peak

Harz Mtns.

Leipzig

Ruhr Valley

Rhine R.

Dortmund

4

BELGIUM

☆ Brussels

Dusseldorf

Essen

Cologne

GERMANY

Erfurt

Dresden

Erzegebirge

Liège

Bonn

Eifel

Moselle R.

Wiesbaden

Frankfurt am Main

Main R.

Fichtelberg

☆ Prague

5

Luxembourg

Hunsrück

CZECH REPUBLIC

LUXEMBOURG

Haardt Mtns.

Würzberg

Nürnberg

Bohemian Forest

Heidelberg

Danube R.

6

FRANCE

Rhine R.

Black Forest

Swabian Jura

Stuttgart

Augsburg

Isar R.

Danube R.

Vienna ☆

Ulm

BAVARIA

AUSTRIA

Munich

Salzburg

Lake Constance

Bavarian Alps

Watzmann

0   100 miles

7

LIECHTENSTEIN

Zugspitze

0   150 kilometers

SWITZERLAND

A B C D E F G

Austria, Liechtenstein and Switzerland

The Alps are a huge chain of mountains that stretches across 750 mi (1,207 km), from the Austrian capital of Vienna to southern Italy. The mountains form a barrier between Northern and Southern Europe. But for centuries, passes cut through the Alps have provided Europeans with trade routes.

Switzerland, which contains more of the Alps than any other nation, is renowned for its magnificent landscapes. It is a politically neutral nation, and many international organizations, including the United Nations and the Red Cross, are based there. There is no official Swiss language; instead, the Swiss speak the languages of the countries that surround them: German, French and Italian.

Alpine Racer: A skier hurtles down a mountain.

Austrian cyclists ride past the State Opera House, in Vienna, Austria.

Between Switzerland and Austria lies the tiny nation of Liechtenstein. After World War I, Liechtenstein allied itself with Switzerland. That close connection is still strong, and Switzerland represents Liechtenstein diplomatically. Liechtenstein is a constitutional monarchy. It is governed by a prince, but the people are represented by an elected parliament.

Just east of Switzerland and Liechtenstein is Austria. The Danube, Europe's second-longest river, passes through Austria's capital city, Vienna. More than 40% of Austria is covered in forests and woodlands, which make it attractive to international tourists.

Data Bank

AUSTRIA
AREA: 32,375 sq mi (83,858 sq km)
POPULATION: 8,174,762
CAPITAL: Vienna
LANGUAGE: German

LIECHTENSTEIN
AREA: 62 sq mi (160 sq km)
POPULATION: 33,436
CAPITAL: Vaduz
LANGUAGES: German (official), Alemannic dialect

SWITZERLAND
AREA: 15,942 sq mi (41,290 sq km)
POPULATION: 7,450,867
CAPITAL: Bern
LANGUAGES: German, French, Italian, Romansch (all official)

The Matterhorn towers 14,692 ft (4,478 m) above Zermatt, Switzerland.

C D E F G H I

1

Frankfurt am Main

Main R.

Erzegebirge

Elbe R.

Prague

2

Mannheim

GERMANY

CZECH REPUBLIC

Brno

Bavarian Forest

Bohemian Forest

Sumava Mtns.

SLOVAKIA

3

Danube R.

Augsburg

Krems

Bratislava

Braunau

Linz

Danube R.

Vienna

Haardt Mtns.

Swabian Jura

Munich

Lake Neusiedler

Lake Constance

LIECHTENSTEIN

Bavarian Alps

Salzburg

AUSTRIA

4

St. Gall

Enns R.

rich

Lake Zürich

Inn R.

Salzach R.

Niedere Tauern

Mur R.

Räba R.

HUNGARY

Zug

Vaduz

Innsbruck

Grossglockner

Graz

ITZERLAND

Ötztal Alps

Drau R.

Klagenfurt

Lake Balaton

5

gfrau

Rhaetian Alps

Brenner Pass

Carnic Alps

Maribor

Piz Bernina

Dolomites

Julian Alps

lps

plon

Lake Como

Ljubljana

Zagreb

nel

SLOVENIA

Como

6

Milan

Adige R.

Trieste

Lake Garda

Venice

CROATIA

Padua

Po R.

ITALY

Ferrara

Pula

Adriatic Sea

0 100 miles

Genoa

0 150 kilometers

Ravenna

C D E F G

Did You Know?

● During the late 1800s, Austria was the center of the powerful Austro-Hungarian Empire.

● Salzburg, Austria, is the birthplace of composer Wolfgang Amadeus Mozart.

● Bern, Switzerland's capital, is named for the generations of bears that have lived there in a bear pit. The pit was built in 1513.

● The Spanish Riding School, in Vienna, Austria, was founded in 1572. The first horses used at the riding academy were imported from Spain. Beginning in 1580, the horses were bred in Lipizza, Slovenia.

● Liechtenstein is smaller than Washington, D.C.

● In 218 B.C., Hannibal, a Carthaginian general, used elephants to carry his troops over the Alps. Many of his men and elephants died of the cold.

Vienna's Spanish Riding School

Central Europe

The Blue Danube: Parliament in Budapest, Hungary

The great plains of Poland, the mountains of the Czech Republic and the beautiful landscapes of Hungary and Slovakia add beauty to this region's rich, historical character. Architectural masterpieces are common throughout each country. Prague Castle, in the Czech Republic's capital, is one of the largest castles in the world. More castles decorate the Czech Republic's landscape, illustrating the nation's grand heritage. Museums in Budapest, Hungary, are decorated with ornate details that are symbolic of the country's love of art and design. Slovakia has its share of impressive monuments as well as an array of modern buildings that demonstrate its stature as a growing, vibrant country.

Once a part of the communist bloc of nations, in recent years much of Central Europe has adopted a more progressive, enterprising economy. But some of the advances in manufacturing have led to problems. For example, Poland is struggling with high levels of air and water pollution; its government is looking for new solutions to these challenges.

Each year, more and more tourists visit the region. Some travelers come to hear the captivating folk music of Hungary, others to taste the delicious foods of Warsaw, Poland. As the countries grow more cosmopolitan, each strives to become an integral part of a new, unified Europe while maintaining its own unique character and flavor.

Old Town Square in Prague, Czech Republic

Data Bank

CZECH REPUBLIC
AREA: 30,450 sq mi (78,866 sq km)
POPULATION: 10,246,178
CAPITAL: Prague
LANGUAGE: Czech

HUNGARY
AREA: 35,919 sq mi (93,030 sq km)
POPULATION: 10,032,375
CAPITAL: Budapest
LANGUAGE: Hungarian

POLAND
AREA: 120,727 sq mi (312,685 sq km)
POPULATION: 38,626,349
CAPITAL: Warsaw
LANGUAGE: Polish

SLOVAKIA
AREA: 18,859 sq mi (48,845 sq km)
POPULATION: 5,423,567
CAPITAL: Bratislava
LANGUAGES: Slovak (official), Hungarian

Baltic Sea

LITHUANIA

Vilnius

RUSSIA

Kaliningrad

Vistula Spit

Gdansk

Elblag

Koszalin

Pomeranian Bay

Grodno

Oder-Haff

Szczecin

Oder R.

N o r t h e r n   E u r o p e a n   p l a i n   *Masuria*

Bialystok

BELARUS

Bydgoszcz

Torun

Warta R.

Vistula R.

Narew R.

Bug R.

Berlin

GERMANY

Poznan

Plock

P O L A N D   Warsaw

Elbe R.

Oder R.

Zielona Góra

Kalisz

Lódz

Radom

Lubelska Hills

Lublin

Dresden

Wroclaw

Malopolska Hills

Vistula R.

San R.

Erzegebirge

Sudety Mtns.

Mt. Snezka

Zabrze

Lviv

Elbe R.

Kraków

Dniester R.

Prague

BOHEMIA

Plzen

Katowice

Bug R.

Sumava Mtns.

Bohemian Forest

CZECH REPUBLIC

Ostrava

Morava R.

B e s k i d s

UKRAINE

MORAVIA

Brno

Zlín

Gerlachovsky Peak

Danube R.

Zilina

S L O V A K I A

Carpathian Mtns.

Kosice

Váh R.

Nitra

Miskolc

BAVARIA

Danube R.

Tisza R.

Munich

Vienna

Bratislava

Mount Kékes

The Great Alföld

AUSTRIA

A l p s   A l p s

Gyor

Danube R.

Budapest

Debrecen

Bakony Mtns.

H U N G A R Y

TRANSYLVANIA

Graz

Danube R.

Cluj-Napoca

Lake Balaton

Mecsek Mtns.

Szeged

ROMANIA

I T A L Y

SLOVENIA

Ljubljana

Zagreb

Pécs

Venice

Trieste

CROATIA

0   150 miles

0   200 kilometers

TFK

W E N S

---

his operas and symphonic poems, he was one of the first Czech composers to write in his native tongue. The Czech composer Antonin Dvořák (1841–1904) wrote many classical pieces, including *Symphony No. 9 in E Minor "New World,"* based on American folk music.

● In 1918, a union of Czech and Slovak lands was formed. The nation of Czechoslovakia existed until January 1, 1993, when the Czechoslovakian federation was dissolved.

● The composer and pianist Bedrich Smetana (1824–1884) lived in Prague. Known for

● One of the continent's biggest herds of European bison lives in Poland's Bialowieska Forest.

● Composer Frédéric Chopin was born in Poland.

● Almost 80% of Slovakia sits more than 2,460 ft (750 m) above sea level.

A Slovak girl in traditional dress

77

Italy, Malta, San Marino and Vatican City

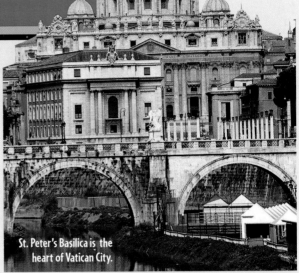

St. Peter's Basilica is the heart of Vatican City.

Although Italy did not become a unified nation until 1861, Italians are understandably proud of their region's ancient history. The city of Rome, which was founded in 625 B.C., was the center of the Roman Empire. At the height of its power, the empire extended across much of Europe and northern Africa and portions of Asia. Roman monuments, aqueducts and amphitheaters can still be found throughout the land.

Italy is as magnificent now as it was in the past. The country is divided into 20 regions, each with its own unique flavor, big cities and attractions. Rome, Italy's capital and largest city, is located in Lazio. Milan, in Lombardy, is a world-famous fashion center. Florence, in Tuscany, is known for its museums and galleries and as the birthplace of the Renaissance, which was a time of great artistic and scientific growth. Many people consider Venice, in the Veneto region, the world's most beautiful city.

Italy is a long, boot-shaped peninsula. At the top of the boot, the Alps form a border that separates Italy from France, Switzerland, Austria and Slovenia. The rest of Italy is surrounded by seas—the Ligurian, Tyrrhenian, Mediterranean, Ionian and Adriatic. The Apennine Mountains form a backbone that extends down the peninsula. Italy includes two large islands, Sardinia and Sicily, and several small islands. Lying between Sicily and Africa is the tiny island nation of Malta. Sharing the Italian peninsula are San Marino and Vatican City or Holy See (*see* means "cathedral town"). The Vatican is the home of the Pope, the head of the Roman Catholic Church.

Data Bank

ITALY
AREA: 116,305 sq mi (301,230 sq km)
POPULATION: 58,057,477
CAPITAL: Rome
LANGUAGES: Italian (official), German, French, Slovene

MALTA
AREA: 122 sq mi (316 sq km)
POPULATION: 403,342
CAPITAL: Valletta
LANGUAGES: Maltese, English (both official)

SAN MARINO
AREA: 24 sq mi (61 sq km)
POPULATION: 28,503
CAPITAL: San Marino
LANGUAGE: Italian

VATICAN CITY (HOLY SEE)
AREA: .17 sq mi (.44 sq km)
POPULATION: 890
CAPITAL: None
LANGUAGES: Latin, Italian, others

The Grand Canal in Venice, Italy

Map labels:

LIECHTENSTEIN
SWITZERLAND
Geneva
Mont Blanc ▲
Mt. Dufour ▲
Lake Como
Piz Bernina ▲
A L P S
Brenner Pass
Dolomites
AUSTRIA
HUNGARY
Danube R.
N E W S — TFK
Milan
Lake Garda
Po R.
Ticino R.
Po R.
Turin
Tanaro R.
FRANCE
ITALY
Venice
Verona
Padua
Reno R.
Piave R.
Trieste
Gulf of Venice
Ljubljana
SLOVENIA
Zagreb
CROATIA
Rijeka (Fiume)
Belgrade
SERBIA AND MONTENEGRO
Genoa
Bologna
Ravenna
SAN MARINO
BOSNIA AND HERZEGOVINA
Sarajevo
Marseille
Nice
MONACO
Ligurian Sea
Pisa
Florence
Arno R.
Ancona
Split
SERBIA
Capri
Elba I.
TUSCANY
Lake Trasimeno
A p e n n i n e s
Pescara
Mt. Corno ▲
Adriatic Sea
Dubrovnik
MONTENEGRO
Corsica (France)
Bastia
Tuscan Archipelago
Tiber R.
Ajaccio
Strait of Bonifacio
Rome ★
VATICAN CITY
Ofanto R.
Bari
Tirana
ALBANIA
Naples
Mt. Vesuvius (volcano) ▲
Ischia
Salerno
PUGLIA
Brindisi
Taranto
Strait of Otranto
Corfu (Greece)
Sardinia
Mount Marmora ▲
Tyrrhenian Sea
Stromboli I.
CALABRIA
Gulf of Taranto
Ionian Sea
Cagliari
Lipari Islands
Catanzaro
Palermo
Messina
Strait of Sicily
Sicily
Mt. Etna (volcano) ▲
Strait of Messina
Catania
Ragusa
Syracuse
Mediterranean Sea
Tunis ★
Pantelleria I. (Italy)
0 — 200 miles
0 — 300 kilometers
TUNISIA
ALGERIA
MALTA
Valletta ★

Did You Know?

● Europe's only active volcanoes are in Italy. Mount Etna is in Sicily, and Mount Vesuvius is near Naples.

● The Colosseum, in Rome, seated 50,000 people.

● According to legend, Rome was founded in 753 B.C. by the twin brothers Romulus and Remus.

● The Vatican Museums make up one of the world's largest museum complexes. The museums' 1,400 rooms are filled with antiquities and works of art.

● In 1508, Pope Julius II asked Michelangelo to paint the ceiling of the Vatican's Sistine Chapel. It took him four years to complete the project.

● The Swiss Guard is the world's smallest army. It consists of 100 men who have sworn allegiance to the Pope. The guards' colorful uniforms, left, have changed very little since the 16th century.

The Balkans

Busy City: Split, Croatia, is a commercial center.

The Balkan Peninsula is a mountainous area in Eastern Europe. Located between Western Europe and Asia are the nations known as the Balkan States. The western Balkan States include Albania, Bosnia and Herzegovina, Croatia, Macedonia, Serbia and Montenegro, and Slovenia. Albanians are descendants of the Illyrians, whose civilization came before that of the Greeks. Split, Croatia, is the site of ancient Roman ruins, as is Butrint, Albania. Slovenia, a nation of mountains and lakes, has close ties to Germany, Austria and other Western European countries.

Because the Balkan Peninsula acts as a land bridge between east and west, it has great strategic value. As a result, it has been the site of frequent wars. Over many centuries, different portions of the Balkans were conquered by the Roman Empire, the Byzantine Empire and the Ottoman Empire. But the people of the region have always been fiercely independent. They are proud of their cultures and languages. During the 19th century, ethnic groups in the Balkans began to declare their independence and fight over territory. In 1912, the Balkan Wars began, and two years later, World War I engulfed the area. In the 1990s, much of the Balkans was again caught up in ethnic strife. Today, a fragile peace exists.

Harvesting salt in Serbia and Montenegro

Tradition: A girl in Serbia and Montenegro

Data Bank

ALBANIA
AREA: 11,000 sq mi (28,748 sq km)
POPULATION: 3,544,808
CAPITAL: Tirana
LANGUAGES: Albanian (Tosk is the official dialect), Greek

BOSNIA AND HERZEGOVINA
AREA: 19,741 sq mi (51,129 sq km)
POPULATION: 4,007,608
CAPITAL: Sarajevo
LANGUAGES: Croatian, Serbian, Bosnian

CROATIA
AREA: 21,829 sq mi (56,542 sq km)
POPULATION: 4,435,960
CAPITAL: Zagreb
LANGUAGE: Croatian

MACEDONIA
AREA: 9,781 sq mi (25,333 sq km)
POPULATION: 2,071,210
CAPITAL: Skopje
LANGUAGES: Macedonian, Albanian, Turkish, Serbo-Croatian

SERBIA AND MONTENEGRO
AREA: 39,517 sq mi (102,350 sq km)
POPULATION: 10,663,022
CAPITAL: Belgrade
LANGUAGES: Serbian, Albanian

SLOVENIA
AREA: 7,827 sq mi (20,273 sq km)
POPULATION: 1,938,282
CAPITAL: Ljubljana
LANGUAGES: Slovenian, Serbo-Croatian

A B C D E F G

1 Grossglockner ▲

AUSTRIA

Graz •

● Budapest

HUNGARY

The Great Alföld

Julian Alps

Drau R.

Maribor •

Lake Balaton

Danube R.

2 Triglav Mtn.

▲ Ljubljana ☆

Kras Plateau

SLOVENIA

Zagorzje Hills

Drava R.

Pécs •

Timisoara •

Trieste •

Zagreb ☆

CROATIA

VOJVODINA

ROMANIA

Venice •

Rijeka •

Sisak •

Sava R.

Osijek •

Novi Sad ☆

Transylvanian Alps

ISTRIA

Banja Luka •

Sava R.

Iron Gate Gorge

3 Pula •

Dinaric Alps

Bosna R.

Brcko •

Drina R.

Belgrade ☆

Craiova •

SAN MARINO

Zadar •

Dalmatia

BOSNIA AND HERZEGOVINA

Tuzla •

Valjevo •

Danube R.

Zenica •

Kragujevac •

Ancona •

Split •

Sarajevo ☆

Cacak •

SERBIA AND MONTENEGRO

SERBIA

Balkan Mtns.

4 Brac I.

Mostar •

Bobotov Kuk ▲

Nis •

Adriatic Sea

Morava R.

Sofia ☆

Dubrovnik •

MONTENEGRO ☆

KOSOVO ☆

BULGARIA

5 Podgorica

North Albanian Alps

Pec •

Pristina •

Lake Scutari

Mount Korab ▲

Skopje ☆

Apennines

MACEDONIA

Vardar R.

ITALY

Bari •

Durres ☆

Lake Ohrid

Bitola •

Thessaloníki •

6 Naples •

Tirana ☆

Brindisi •

ALBANIA

Lake Prespa

GREECE

N
W ☆TFK☆ E
S

Vlore •

Korce •

Pindus Mtns

Tyrrhenian Sea

Strait of Otranto

Butrint •

7 0 ———— 200 miles

Corfu (Greece)

0 ———— 300 kilometers

Ionian Sea

A B C D E

Ancient Ruins: Butrint, Albania

Did You Know?

● *Balkan* means "mountain" in Turkish.

● The ancient city of Butrint, in southern Albania, reflects 3,000 years of history. It has Greek, Roman and Byzantine ruins.

● Bosnia and Herzegovina, Croatia, Macedonia, Serbia and Montenegro, and Slovenia were all part of the larger nation of Yugoslavia. Yugoslavia broke into separate countries in 1991.

● The Balkan Peninsula is surrounded by the Adriatic, Black, Ionian and Aegean Seas.

● The rugged and beautiful Dinaric and Julian Alps in the Balkans are popular with skiers.

● Folk dancing and music are popular throughout the Balkan region. The music of Turkey has had a strong influence on the music of Bosnia and Herzegovina.

Southeastern Europe

Surrounded on three sides by water, Greece is a land of sparkling beauty. Magnificent ruins are framed by deep blue skies and turquoise water. At the center of Greek life is the sea. Much of the country's early power and wealth came from shipping, trading and fishing. Today, the sea is still important to Greece's economy. Millions of people visit the country's sunny beaches and historic sites each year, making tourism Greece's top industry. Visitors especially love to cruise around the country's nearly 2,000 islands, most of which are uninhabited. Athens is the country's capital and largest city. Its most notable structure is the Acropolis, which was built some 2,000 years ago.

Tourism is important for Greece's northeastern neighbors, Bulgaria and Romania. Black Sea resorts boast beautiful sandy beaches and draw many visitors from neighboring countries.

An Ancient Treasure: The Acropolis in Athens, Greece

Festival of Roses: Bulgaria is one of the world's top rose-oil producers.

Data Bank

BULGARIA
AREA: 48,822 sq mi (110,910 sq km)
POPULATION: 7,517,973
CAPITAL: Sofia
LANGUAGE: Bulgarian

GREECE
AREA: 50,942 sq mi (131,940 sq km)
POPULATION: 10,647,529
CAPITAL: Athens
LANGUAGES: Greek (official), English, French

ROMANIA
AREA: 91,700 sq mi (237,500 sq km)
POPULATION: 22,355,551
CAPITAL: Bucharest
LANGUAGES: Romanian (official), Hungarian, German

Did You Know?

Romania's Capital: Bucharest

- Alexander the Great lived from 356 B.C. to 323 B.C. He made Greece a world power by conquering much of the known world.

- Bulgarian rose oil, used in fine perfumes around the world, is produced in the Kazanlak region of Bulgaria.

- Bucharest, Romania's capital, was once known as Little Paris for its wide boulevards and beautiful buildings.

- Transylvania, in Romania, is home to Count Dracula, the fictional character in Bram Stoker's classic tale. The Dracula legend is based on Vlad the Impaler, a Romanian leader who was known for his cruelty.

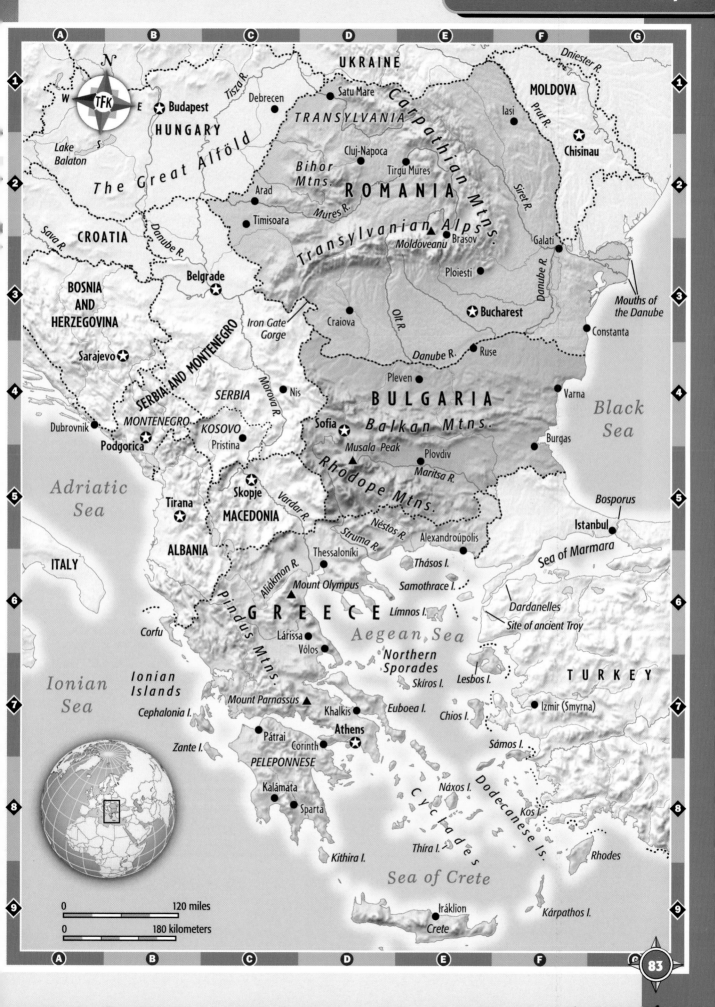

UKRAINE

MOLDOVA

Dniester R.

N
W · TFK · E
S

Budapest

HUNGARY

Debrecen

Satu Mare

TRANSYLVANIA

Carpathian Mtns.

Iasi

Prut R.

Chisinau

The Great Alföld

Lake Balaton

Bihor Mtns.

Cluj-Napoca

Tirgu Mures

ROMANIA

Arad

Timisoara

Mures R.

Transylvanian Alps

Moldoveanu ▲

Brasov

Siret R.

Galati

CROATIA

Sava R.

Danube R.

Belgrade

Ploiesti

Danube R.

Mouths of the Danube

BOSNIA AND HERZEGOVINA

Iron Gate Gorge

Craiova

Olt R.

Bucharest

Constanta

Sarajevo

SERBIA AND MONTENEGRO

Morava R.

SERBIA

Nis

Danube R.

Ruse

Pleven

BULGARIA

Varna

Black Sea

Dubrovnik

MONTENEGRO

Podgorica

KOSOVO

Pristina

Sofia

Balkan Mtns.

Musala Peak ▲

Plovdiv

Maritsa R.

Burgas

Adriatic Sea

Skopje

Vardar R.

Rhodope Mtns.

Bosporus

Tirana

MACEDONIA

Néstos R.

Istanbul

Sea of Marmara

ITALY

ALBANIA

Struma R.

Thessaloníki

Alexandroúpolis

Thásos I.

Samothrace I.

Dardanelles

Aliákmon R.

Mount Olympus ▲

Límnos I.

Site of ancient Troy

Corfu

Pindus Mtns.

G R E E C E

Aegean Sea

TURKEY

Lárissa

Vólos

Northern Sporades

Ionian Sea

Ionian Islands

Skíros I.

Lesbos I.

Izmir (Smyrna)

Cephalonia I.

Mount Parnassus ▲

Khalkis

Euboea I.

Chios I.

Pátrai

Athens

Sámos I.

Zante I.

Corinth

PELEPONNESE

Kalámata

Sparta

Náxos I.

Kos I.

Dodecanese Is.

Cyclades

Thíra I.

Rhodes

Kithira I.

Sea of Crete

Kárpathos I.

Iráklion

Crete

0   120 miles

0   180 kilometers

Greece

Yiassou!

My name is Kosmas, and I'm 12 years old. My friends call me Makis. I live with my parents in Loutraki, a town 50 miles [80 km] south of Athens. I have nine classes at school, including physics and Olympic education. Welcome to Greece!

The Greek Flag

The flag of Greece was designed as a symbol of freedom when the country won its independence from the Ottoman Empire, ending nearly 400 years of occupation.

The **white cross** stands for the Greek Orthodox Church. Greek Orthodoxy is the country's main religion.

The **white stripes** represent Greece's struggle for independence.

The **blue** is for the sea and the sky.

The Moneymakers

With its sunny beaches and impressive ancient sites, Greece attracts many visitors. Tourism is vital to the nation's economy.

Services (including tourism, trade and transportation) **64.4%**

Manufacturing **27.3%**

Agriculture **8.3%**

The Economy

AGRICULTURE: Corn, sugar beets, cotton, tobacco, olives, grapes

MAJOR INDUSTRIES: Food processing, mining, tourism

MAJOR EXPORTS: Cement, clothing, olive oil, petroleum products, prepared fruits, textiles

MAJOR IMPORTS: Chemicals, machinery, meat, petroleum, transportation equipment, manufactured goods

TRADING PARTNERS: Britain, Germany, France, Italy

For Sale: Peppers and olives at a market

Top 5 Olive-Oil Producers

Olive oil is an important ingredient in Greek cuisine. The country produces more than 400,000 metric tons of olive oil each year.

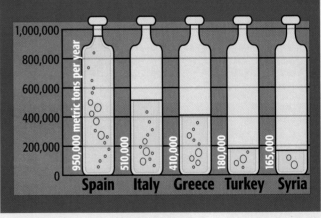

	metric tons per year
Spain	950,000
Italy	510,000
Greece	410,000
Turkey	180,000
Syria	165,000

1,000,000 — 800,000 — 600,000 — 400,000 — 200,000 — 0

Major Events in Greece's History

3000 B.C. The first major civilization in the region begins on the island of Crete.

1550 B.C. The Mycenaean (my-suh-nee-un) culture develops on the Greek mainland. Its people are the first known Greek speakers.

776 B.C. The first games are held at Olympia. The winning athletes receive an olive-branch crown, as a symbol of honor.

336 B.C.–323 B.C. Alexander the Great of Macedonia makes Greece a part of his powerful empire.

MACEDONIA

ALBANIA

Mount Olympus

Dodoni

Oracle of Zeus

GREECE

Corfu

Aegean Sea

Sea of Marmara

ATLANTIC OCEAN EUROPE

GREECE

TURKEY

Delphi

Dionysos

Parthenon

ATHENS

Poseidon

Peloponnese

Delos

Olympia

Argos

Aphaia

Epidaurus

Ionian Sea

Sporades

Rhodes

N

W E

S

Sea of Crete

Lindian Athena

More than 2,500 years ago, the Greeks built one of the greatest civilizations the world has ever seen. Today, the ruins of splendid theaters and marble temples are found throughtout the landscape.

Crete

MEDITERRANEAN SEA

Miles
0   50   100

0   50   100   150
Kilometers

GREECE Is Famous for ...

Ancient Treasures Archaeological sites dot the landscape.

Democracy Greece is known as the birthplace of democracy. Early Greeks believed in government by the people, trial by jury and equality under the law.

Olympic Games Sports-loving ancient Greeks held the first Olympic Games in 776 B.C.

Theater and Literature The tragedies and comedies of early Greek playwrights still keep audiences enthralled.

Great Thinkers Modern science, math and philosophy owe a huge debt to early Greek geniuses like Plato and the mathematician Euclid.

Food Greeks love delicious, simple dishes such as souvlaki, which is made with grilled meat, tomatoes and onions and served on pita bread.

Say It in Greek

To read and write in modern Greek, you have to learn a whole new alphabet. To help you start speaking Greek, try these words and phrases written in our alphabet.

Hello ⟶ Yiassou (*yah*-sue)

Good morning ⟶ Kalimera (kah-lee-*meh*-rah)

How are you? ⟶ Ti kanis? (tee *kah*-nees?)

What is your name? ⟶ Po se lene? (po seh *leh*-neh)

My name is ⟶ Me lene (meh *leh*-neh)

Mother ⟶ Mitera (mee-*teh*-rah)

Father ⟶ Pateras (pa-*teh*-ras)

1453 A.D. The Ottoman (Turkish) Empire takes control of Greece.

1896 The first modern Olympic Games are held in Athens.

1960 Cyprus, an island south of Turkey, gains its independence from Britain.

2004 The Olympic Games are set to return to Athens.

go ⟶ To find out more about Greece, go to *timeforkids.com/gpgreece*.

The Baltic States and Belarus

Medieval Treasure: Tallinn reflects Estonia's rich history.

During the early 1940s, the Soviet Union expanded its borders by invading the surrounding small nations. Estonia, Lithuania, Latvia and Belarus all fell to the armies of dictator Joseph Stalin. These ancient independent states became republics of the Soviet Union. Not until the early 1990s did they regain their independence. Today, each of these states is a sovereign nation with its own government, economy, language and history.

Estonia, Lithuania and Latvia are known as the Baltic States because they are located on the coast of the Baltic Sea. The Baltic Sea connects these nations to Scandinavia and northern Europe. Tallinn, Estonia's capital, is only 40 mi (64 km) from Helsinki, Finland. Since gaining their independence from the Soviet Union, the Baltic States have proudly reclaimed their historic languages and cultures. They have a rich legacy of music, dance, folklore and literature. The region is heavily forested and has a wide range of wildlife, including elk, deer and wild boar.

Belarus, just east of Lithuania, shares the Baltic States' flat landscape and cool climate. Unlike the Baltics, however, Belarus holds its Soviet past in high regard, and much of its culture is connected to that of Russia and the former Soviet Union. Minsk, the capital of Belarus, was largely rebuilt after World War II.

The Baltic States were invited to join NATO and the European Union in 2002. With these alliances, they will become important parts of the global economy. Belarus has continued to maintain its close ties with Russia.

Festival Fun: These Lithuanian girls are dressed in traditional clothes.

Data Bank

BELARUS
AREA: 80,154 sq mi
(207,600 sq km)
POPULATION: 10,310,520
CAPITAL: Minsk
LANGUAGES: Belarusian, Russian

ESTONIA
AREA: 17,462 sq mi
(45,226 sq km)
POPULATION: 1,401,945
CAPITAL: Tallinn
LANGUAGES: Estonian (official),
Russian, Ukrainian, Finnish

LATVIA
AREA: 24,938 sq mi
(64,589 sq km)
POPULATION: 2,332,078
CAPITAL: Riga
LANGUAGES: Latvian (official),
Lithuanian, Russian

LITHUANIA
AREA: 25,174 sq mi
(65,200 sq km)
POPULATION: 3,584,836
CAPITAL: Vilnius
LANGUAGES: Lithuanian (official),
Polish, Russian

Gulf of Bothnia

FINLAND

SWEDEN

Helsinki

Gulf of Finland

Tallinn

St. Petersburg

Stockholm

Narva

E S T O N I A

Narva Reservoir

Hiiumaa I.

Novgorod

Lake Ilmen

Saaremaa I.

Parnu

Tartu

Lake Peipus

Point Kolka

Gulf of Riga

Lake Pskov

Pskov

R U S S I A

Gotland

Velikaya R.

Valdai Hills

LIVONIA

Riga

L A T V I A

Volkhov R.

Baltic Sea

Kurzeme Upland

Liepaja

Daugava R.

Mount Gaizins

Jelgava

Volga R.

Western Dvina R.

Dnieper R.

COURLAND

Siaulai

Daugavpils

Klaipeda

Polatsk

KALININGRAD OBLAST (RUSSIA)

L I T H U A N I A

Polatsk Lowland

Smolensk-Moscow Upland

Gulf of Gdansk

Nemen R.

Neris R.

Vitsyebsk

Smolensk

Kaliningrad

Kaunas

Vilnius

Mahilyow

Gdansk

Alytus

Dzerzhinskaya Mountain

Berezina R.

Dnieper R.

MASURIA

Nemen R.

Belorussian Ridge

Minsk

Sozh R.

P O L A N D

Hrodna

B E L A R U S

Vistula R.

Bug R.

Babruysk

Warsaw

Brest

Pinsk

Pripyat R.

Homyel

Polesye Marshes

0   150 miles

0   200 kilometers

Pripyat Marshes

U K R A I N E

Did You Know?

● Folklore is popular in the Baltic States. *The Bear Slayer*, an epic poem, tells one of Latvia's most famous stories.

● The Baltic States and Belarus are ancient. Many of the buildings and traditions go back almost a thousand years.

● Estonia has some 1,520 islands in the Baltic Sea.

● The Astronomical Observatory (pictured), in Vilnius, Lithuania, was founded in 1753. It was Europe's fourth observatory, and is the oldest in Eastern Europe.

Ukraine, Moldova and the Caucasus Republics

Ukraine, located in northern Europe, stretches across the top of the Black Sea. Its gently rolling countryside, called steppes, is rich in minerals, history and culture. The country has two mountain regions: the Crimean Mountains in the south and the Carpathians in the west. Because of its fertile black soil, Ukraine is sometimes called "the breadbasket of Europe."

The largest country entirely within Europe, Ukraine became part of the Soviet Union in 1922. Under Soviet rule, much of Ukraine's culture disappeared. Its famous painted Easter eggs (*pysanky*), fast-paced folk music, language and religious art were repressed, because they were considered too nationalistic. Since 1991, when Ukraine declared its independence from the Soviet Union, many of its customs and art forms have been revived.

Eggs-traordinary: Ukrainian Easter eggs are works of art.

Armenia, Azerbaijan, Georgia and Moldova also broke away from the Soviet Union. The small republic of Moldova lies to the west of Ukraine. The Caucasus Republics—Armenia, Azerbaijan and Georgia—are considered part of Asia. Beautiful mountain scenery can be found throughout the region. Nearly half of Azerbaijan is covered by mountains. Georgia, which sits on the Black Sea, enjoys a pleasant climate.

Data Bank

ARMENIA
AREA: 11,500 sq mi (29,800 sq km)
POPULATION: 3,325,307
CAPITAL: Yerevan
LANGUAGES: Armenian, Russian

AZERBAIJAN
AREA: 33,400 sq mi (86,000 sq km)
POPULATION: 7,868,385
CAPITAL: Baku
LANGUAGES: Azerbaijani (Azeri), Russian, Armenian

GEORGIA
AREA: 26,911 sq mi (69,700 sq km)
POPULATION: 4,909,633
CAPITAL: Tbilisi
LANGUAGES: Georgian (official), Russian, Armenian, Azeri

MOLDOVA
AREA: 13,067 sq mi (33,843 sq km)
POPULATION: 4,446,455
CAPITAL: Chisinau
LANGUAGES: Moldovan (official), Russian, Gagauz

UKRAINE
AREA: 233,088 sq mi (603,700 sq km)
POPULATION: 47,732,079
CAPITAL: Kiev
LANGUAGES: Ukrainian, Russian, Romanian, Polish, Hungarian

The Monastery of the Caves, in Kiev, Ukraine

C **D** **E** **F** **G** **H** **I**

1

BELARUS

Dnieper R.

ipyat R.

Chernigov

Kursk

Central Russian Upland

Don R.

RUSSIA

Saratov

Volga R.

Ural R.

2

v Reservoir

omyr

Kiev ✪

Dnieper Lowland

Kharkov

Voronezh

Don R.

Yergeni Hills

KAZAKHSTAN

per Upland

innytsya

Dnieper Upland

Poltava

Donets Hills

Donets Basin

Volgograd

Volga R.

3

Southern Bug R.

Dnieper R.

Dnipropetrovsk

Donetsk

Donets R.

Tsimlyansk Reservoir

Volga R.

Astrakhan

U K R A I N E

Zaporizhzhya

Kokhovka Reservoir

Mariupol

Rostov-na-Donu

nau

Odessa

Sea of Azov

Kuban Lowland

4

be R.

tanta

CRIMEA

Sevastopol

Crimean Mtns.

Yalta

Kirch Strait

Krasnodar

Kuban R.

Stavropol

Stavropol Plateau

Caspian Sea

osporus

B l a c k   S e a

Mt. Elbrus ▲

Kuma R.

Grozny

5

Sukhumi

C a u c a s u s   M t n s

ul

Samsun

Kutaisi

Poti

GEORGIA

✪ **Tbilisi**

Quba

AZERBAIJAN

Baku ✪

6

Pontic Mtns.

ARMENIA

Mt. Aragats ▲

Araks R.

Yerevan ✪

Ganca

Kura R.

LakeSevan

Araks R.

Talish Mtns.

✪ **Ankara**

T U R K E Y

Mt. Ararat ▲

AZERBAIJAN

Lake Tuz

Kayseri

Lake Van

0   300 miles

7

Anatolian Plateau

0   400 kilometers

Lake Urmia

I R A N

D **E** **F** **G** **H** **I**

Did You Know?

- Armenia was the first country in the world to proclaim Christianity as its official religion.
- Moldova was once known as Moldavia.
- The bandura (right), a musical instrument with up to 45 strings, is popular in Ukraine.

- Borscht, a beet soup that is often served cold, originated in Ukraine.
- Kiev, Ukraine's capital, was known as the "Mother of Russian Cities."
- The world's worst nuclear-power-plant accident took place in Chernobyl, Ukraine, in 1986.
- In recent years, Ukraine has signed treaties to protect the environment.

Western Russia

The Hermitage museum in Saint Petersburg

Russia is the world's largest country. It spans two continents—Europe in the west and Asia in the east—and 11 time zones! Stretching across 6.6 million sq mi (17 million sq km), it reaches from the Baltic Sea in the west to the Pacific Ocean in the east. Between Russia's coasts lie historic cities, rugged mountain ranges and, in Siberia, some of the coldest places on earth.

At the heart of Russia is Moscow, the nation's capital and largest city. More than 850 years old, the city centers around the imposing Kremlin, a walled fortress that includes elaborate cathedrals, onion-domed churches and government buildings.

Saint Petersburg is Russia's second-largest—and perhaps most European—city. It has been called the "Venice of the North" for its elegant boulevards, lyrical bridges and palace-lined waterways. Saint Petersburg was the Russian capital until 1918. Today, it is still a major cultural and intellectual center.

Did You Know?

● Moscow's Red Square—the site of Saint Basil's Cathedral and Lenin's Mausoleum—was not named for communism or the red bricks of the Kremlin. The word for red also means beautiful in Russian.

● The opulent Hermitage, located in Saint Petersburg, is one of the world's largest museums. Visitors can view some 3 million works of art.

Saint Basil's cathedral

● The Trans-Siberian Railroad is the longest in the world, chugging 5,785 mi (9,310 km) from Moscow to Vladivostok, a distance equal to a quarter of the way around the globe.

● Moscow has more subway riders than any other city, transporting 3.2 billion people each year.

Data Bank

RUSSIA
AREA: 6,592,735 sq mi
(17,075,200 sq km)
POPULATION: 144,112,353
CAPITAL: Moscow
LANGUAGES: Russian, others

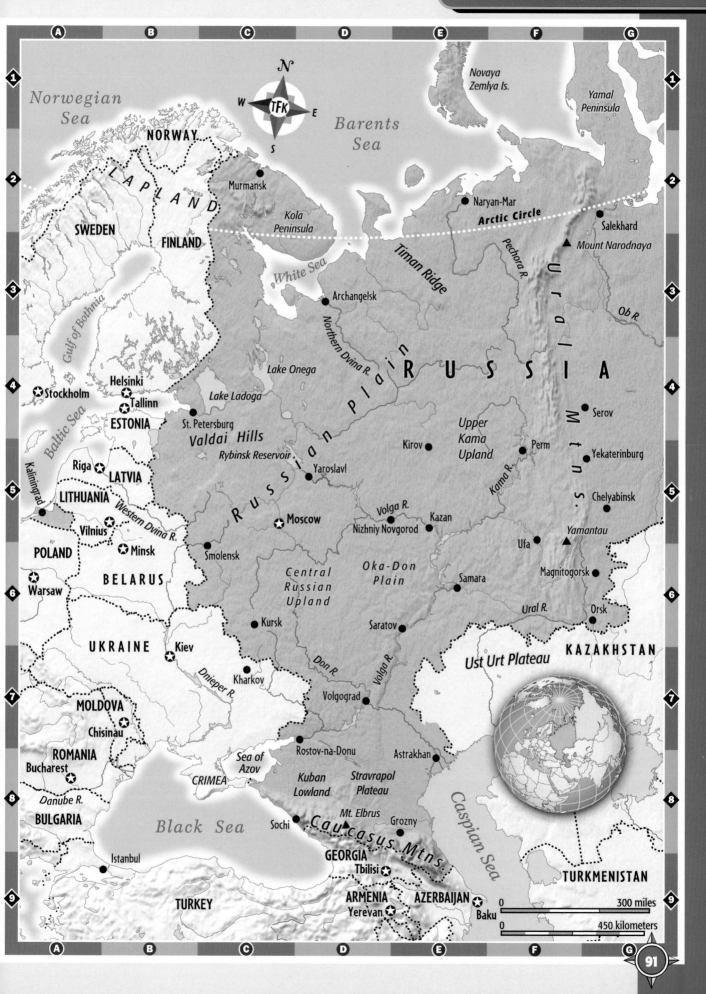

Norwegian Sea

Barents Sea

Novaya Zemlya Is.

Yamal Peninsula

NORWAY

LAPLAND

Murmansk

Kola Peninsula

White Sea

Naryan-Mar

Arctic Circle

Salekhard

▲ Mount Narodnaya

SWEDEN

FINLAND

Timan Ridge

Pechora R.

U r a l

Ob R.

Gulf of Bothnia

Archangelsk

Northern Dvina R.

R U S S I A

Lake Onega

Russian Plain

Helsinki

✪ Stockholm

✪ Tallinn

ESTONIA

St. Petersburg

Lake Ladoga

Valdai Hills

Rybinsk Reservoir

Yaroslavl

Kirov

Upper Kama Upland

Serov

Perm

Kama R.

Yekaterinburg

M t n s.

Baltic Sea

Riga ✪

LATVIA

Kaliningrad

LITHUANIA

Western Dvina R.

Vilnius ✪

✪ Minsk

POLAND

BELARUS

Smolensk

✪ Moscow

Nizhniy Novgorod

Volga R.

Kazan

Oka-Don Plain

Central Russian Upland

Ufa

Yamantau ▲

Chelyabinsk

Magnitogorsk

Samara

Ural R.

Orsk

✪ Warsaw

UKRAINE

Kursk

✪ Kiev

Kharkov

Dnieper R.

Don R.

Saratov

Volga R.

Volgograd

KAZAKHSTAN

Ust Urt Plateau

MOLDOVA

Chisinau ✪

ROMANIA

Bucharest

Danube R.

BULGARIA

Rostov-na-Donu

Sea of Azov

CRIMEA

Kuban Lowland

Stravrapol Plateau

Astrakhan

Caspian Sea

Black Sea

Sochi

Mt. Elbrus ▲

Caucasus Mtns.

Grozny

TURKMENISTAN

Istanbul

GEORGIA

Tbilisi ✪

TURKEY

ARMENIA

Yerevan ✪

AZERBAIJAN

Baku ✪

0 ——————— 300 miles

0 ——————— 450 kilometers

Russia

Privet!

My name is Anastasia, but I'm called Nastya. I'm 8 years old, and I live with my parents, sister and many pets in Abramtsevo, a suburb of Moscow. My family raises borzois, a type of dog, and we have more than 60 animals! My favorite activities are reading and drawing. Enjoy Russia!

The Russian Flag

In 1699, Czar Peter I chose red, white and blue for the Russian flag. In 1991, after the U.S.S.R. broke apart, Russia returned to Peter I's flag.

White represents peace and purity.

Blue is a sign of commitment, faith, dedication and loyalty.

Red stands for the blood lost in fighting to protect Russia.

Russia's Climate

Around Moscow, air from the Atlantic Ocean keeps winters milder than they are in frigid Yakutsk, Siberia.

MOSCOW

YAKUTSK

2002

Average Monthly Temperatures (°F)

The Economy

AGRICULTURE: Wheat, potatoes and sugar beets are vital to Russia's domestic economy.

MANUFACTURING: Steel, cement, fertilizer, plastics, cardboard, linen and wool fabrics, cigarettes, household machinery

Russian caviar, or fish eggs.

MAJOR INDUSTRIES: Fishing, oil and gas production, manufacturing

MAJOR EXPORTS: Oil and gas, metals, lumber and paper goods

MAJOR IMPORTS: Machinery, transportation equipment, food, textiles, clothing

TRADING PARTNERS: Germany, Ukraine, China, Belarus, Italy

Top 5 Largest Countries

Russia is nearly twice the size of the United States. It covers one-eighth of the world's surface!

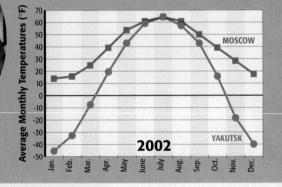

1. **Russia**
   6.59 million sq mi
   (17.08 million sq km)
2. **Canada**
   3.86 million
   (9.98 million)
3. **United States**
   3.72 million
   (9.63 million)
4. **China**
   3.71 million
   (9.60 million)
5. **Brazil**
   3.29 million
   (8.51 milion)

Eastern Hemisphere

Western Hemisphere

Major Events in Russia's History

800–900
Scandinavian Vikings establish forts at Kiev and Novgorod.

1547 Ivan IV, also known as Ivan the Terrible, is crowned the first czar, or emperor, of Russia.

1689–1725 Czar Peter I, known as Peter the Great, builds a modern navy, organizes a new army and lays the foundation for the Russian Empire.

1917 The Russian Revolution begins. The workers' Bolshevik Party, led by Vladimir Lenin (above) and Leon Trotsky, takes control of the government. In 1918, Czar Nicholas II and his family are executed.

Russia stretches across parts of Europe and Asia. It is rich in natural resources.

RUSSIA / ASIA

ARCTIC OCEAN

RUSSIA

WRANGEL ISLAND

Alaska

FRANZ JOSEF LAND

SEVERNAYA ZEMLYA

NEW SIBERIAN ISLANDS

BERING SEA

NORWAY

SWEDEN

NOVAYA ZEMLYA

BARENTS SEA

FINLAND

Kaliningrad

Saint Petersburg

Novgorod

ESTONIA
LATVIA
LITHUANIA

BELARUS

★ MOSCOW

Volga River

Ural Mountains

Ob River

Yenisey River

S I B E R I A

Yakutsk

Lena River

SEA OF OKHOTSK

SAKHALIN ISLAND

Amur River

JAPAN

SEA OF JAPAN

GEORGIA

ARMENIA

AZERBAIJAN

Caucasus Mts.

CASPIAN SEA

UKRAINE

KAZAKHSTAN

Novosibirsk

LAKE BAIKAL

MONGOLIA

CHINA

NORTH KOREA

Vladivostok

KEY

- 🦐 Corn
- 🐟 Fishing
- 🧥 Furs
- 🌾 Grain
- ⛏ Mining
- 🔥 Natural gas
- 🛢 Oil
- 🌲 Timber

Miles
0   500

0   500
Kilometers

RUSSIA Is Famous for ...

Borscht A soup made with beets that is eaten hot or cold.

Matryoshka (mat-*roosh*-kah) These nesting dolls fit one inside the other.

Winter sports Hockey, skating and cross-country skiing are popular.

Ballet Since the early 1900s, Russia has been famous for its talented dancers. Two of its ballet companies, the Bolshoi, in Moscow, and the Kirov, in Saint Petersburg, are among the best in the world.

Fabergé eggs (fab-er-*zhay*) Jeweler Peter Carl Fabergé made the first of his jeweled eggs in 1884 for Russia's royal family. The eggs hold tiny treasures.

Say It in Russian

Russian uses the Cyrillic (suh-*rih*-lik) alphabet, based on Greek letters. Try saying these Russian words written in the English alphabet.

Hi ⟶ Privet (pre-*vyet*)

Bye ⟶ Paka (pah-*kah*)

Yes ⟶ Da (dah)

No ⟶ Nyet (nyet)

Please ⟶ Pozhaluysta (pah-*zhah*-loo-stah)

Thank you ⟶ Spasibo (spah-*see*-bah)

School ⟶ Shkola (*shko*-lah)

I love you ⟶ Ya tebya lyublyu (yah tie-*bya* lyoo-*blyoo*)

go To learn more about Russia, go to *timeforkids.com/gprussia*.

1922 Russia becomes part of the Union of Soviet Socialist Republics (U.S.S.R.).

1924-1953 The brutal leader Joseph Stalin turns the U.S.S.R. into an industrial and military power. During World War II, the U.S.S.R. first sides with Germany but later joins the U.S. and Britain.

1948 The Cold War begins. Relations between the U.S. and the U.S.S.R. are tense. The U.S. believes that the Soviets' communist government and control of eastern Europe are threats to U.S. security.

1985-1991 Mikhail Gorbachev rises to power and begins to restructure the Communist party and the government. His reforms lead to the collapse of the U.S.S.R. Fifteen of the republics, including Russia, declare their independence.

Asia

Peak Season: Ama Dablam in the Himalayas

Asia is the world's largest continent. It includes one third of the land on earth. Asia stretches all the way from the Arctic Circle in the north to the Indian Ocean in the Southern Hemisphere. To the east are the Mediterranean Sea and Red Sea, and to the west are the Ural Mountains. Because the continents of Asia and Europe meet at the Ural Mountains, many geographers consider Asia and Europe to be one enormous land mass called Eurasia.

Asia's terrain is vast and varied. It includes lakes and deserts; rain forests and glaciers; wide, flat plateaus and the highest mountain range on earth. The Middle East, which lies just east of Europe and north of Africa, is the home of one of earth's oldest civilizations. Most of the Middle East is flat and dry, though some areas are green and lush. Central Asia includes nations such as Uzbekistan and Turkmenistan, which were part of a large country called the Soviet Union until 1991. East Asia includes China, the most populous nation in the world. Southeast Asia is home to dense rain forests and jungles in countries such as Singapore, Vietnam and Thailand. Southern Asia, including Nepal, India and Pakistan, is the location of Mount Everest, the world's tallest mountain.

Asia is home to about 3.4 billion people—three-fifths of the world's population. Most of these people live clustered in southern and Southeast Asia. Others parts of the continent, such as Mongolia and Siberia, are sparsely inhabited. Some Asian nations, including Cambodia and Afghanistan, are among the poorest in the world. Others, such as Saudi Arabia, Japan and Singapore, are among the wealthiest and most modern.

Continent Facts

AREA: 7,212,000 sq mi (44,579,000 sq km)

NUMBER OF COUNTRIES: 48 countries— Afghanistan, Armenia, Azerbaijan, Bahrain, Bangladesh, Bhutan, Brunei, Burma (Myanmar), Cambodia, China, Cyprus, East Timor, Georgia, India, Indonesia, Iran, Iraq, Israel, Japan, Jordan, Kazakhstan, Kuwait, Kyrgyzstan, Laos, Lebanon, Malaysia, Maldives, Mongolia, Nepal, North Korea, Oman, Pakistan, Philippines, Qatar, Russia, Saudi Arabia, Singapore, South Korea, Sri Lanka, Syria, Taiwan (not recognized internationally as a free and independent nation; it is instead considered to be part of China), Tajikistan, Thailand, Turkey, Turkmenistan, United Arab Emirates, Uzbekistan, Vietnam, Yemen.

LONGEST RIVER: The Yangtze is the longest river in Asia and the fourth-largest river in the world. It flows for 3,400 mi (5,470 km).

LONGEST MOUNTAIN RANGE: The Himalayas are more than 1,550 mi (2,500 km) long.

HIGHEST PEAK: The world's tallest mountain is Mount Everest in Nepal, at 29,035 ft (8,850 m).

Hang Tight: An orangutan in Malaysia

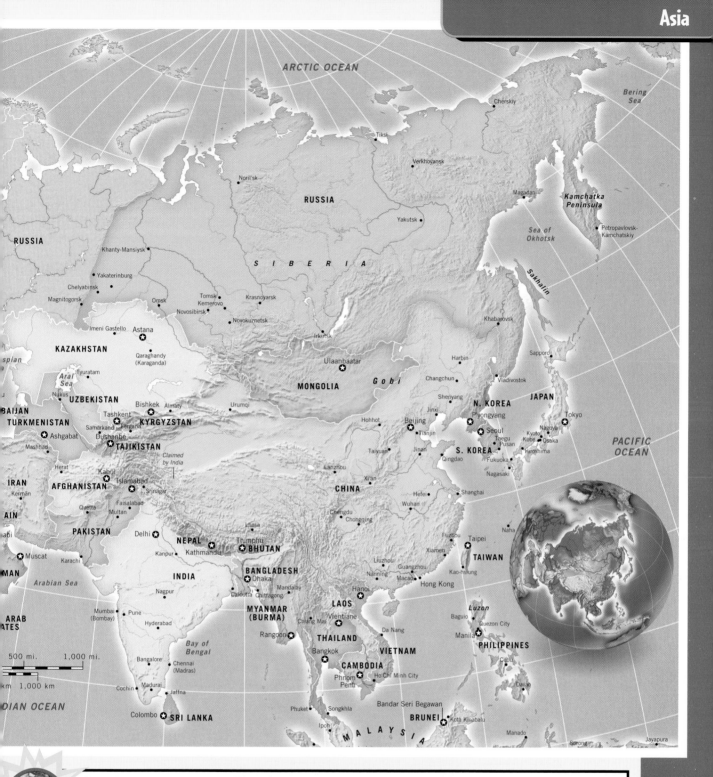

ARCTIC OCEAN

Bering Sea

Cherskiy

RUSSIA

Tiksi

Verkhoyansk

Noril'sk

Kamchatka Peninsula

Magadan

RUSSIA

Yakutsk

Petropavlovsk-Kamchatskiy

Khanty-Mansiysk

S I B E R I A

Sea of Okhotsk

Yakaterinburg

Chelyabinsk

Magnitogorsk

Omsk

Tomsk
Kemerovo

Krasnoyarsk

Novosibirsk

Novokuznetsk

Khabarovsk

Imeni Gastello

Irkutsk

Sakhalin

KAZAKHSTAN

Astana

Qaraghandy
(Karaganda)

Ulaanbaatar

Harbin

Sapporo

Tyuratam

Aral Sea

MONGOLIA

G o b i

Changchun

Vladivostok

spian

Nukus

UZBEKISTAN

Bishkek   Almaty

Urumqi

Hohhot

Shenyang

N. KOREA

JAPAN

BAIJAN

Tashkent

KYRGYZSTAN

Jinxi

Pyongyang

Tokyo

TURKMENISTAN

Samarkand   Fergana

Beijing

Seoul

Nagoya
Kyoto

Ashgabat

Dushanbe

Tianjin

Taegu
Pusan

Kobe Osaka

PACIFIC OCEAN

Mashhad

TAJIKISTAN

Taiyuan

Jinan

S. KOREA

Hiroshima

Herat

Claimed by India

Lanzhou

Qingdao

Fukuoka

IRAN

Kabul

Nagasaki

Kerman

AFGHANISTAN

Islamabad

Xi'an

CHINA

Srinagar

Hefei

Shanghai

abi

Quetta

Faisalabad

Multan

Chengdu

Wuhan

Chongqing

PAKISTAN

Delhi

Lhasa

NEPAL

Thimphu

Fuzhou

Taipei

Muscat

Kanpur

Kathmandu

BHUTAN

Xiamen

TAIWAN

Karachi

Liuzhou

Guangzhou

Kao-hsiung

MAN

Arabian Sea

INDIA

BANGLADESH

Nanning

Macao

Dhaka

Mandalay

Hanoi

Hong Kong

Nagpur

Calcutta Chittagong

Luzon

Mumbai
(Bombay)

Pune

MYANMAR
(BURMA)

LAOS

Baguio

Quezon City

ARAB
ATES

Hyderabad

Chiang Mai

Vientiane

Da Nang

Manila

PHILIPPINES

Rangoon

THAILAND

VIETNAM

Cebu

500 mi.   1,000 mi.

Bay of Bengal

Bangalore

Chennai
(Madras)

Bangkok

CAMBODIA

km   1,000 km

Cochin

Madurai

Jaffna

Phnom Penh

Ho Chi Minh City

Davao

DIAN OCEAN

Colombo

SRI LANKA

Phuket

Songkhla

Bandar Seri Begawan

BRUNEI

Kota Kinabalu

Ipoh

M A L A Y S I A

Manado

Sorong

Jayapura

Mongolia's Gobi Desert

Wow Zone!

● The Dead Sea, which lies between Israel and Jordan, is the lowest point on earth. Its water is 10 times saltier than seawater.

● The Gobi Desert's terrain is mostly rocky, not sandy. The word "gobi" means waterless place in Mongolian.

● Turkey, Azerbaijan and Russia are located in Asia and in Europe.

● The world's most populous countries, China and India, are located in Asia.

● Indonesia, which includes more than 17,000 islands, is the largest archipelago, or string of islands, in the world. It stretches for almost 742,000 sq mi (2 million sq km).

Eastern Russia

All Aboard: The Trans-Siberian Railroad

East of the Ural Mountains lies Eastern Russia, an enormous territory that stretches more than 5 million sq mi (13 million sq km). Commonly called Siberia, the region covers the entire northern part of Asia. It makes up 75% of Russia, the largest country in the world, although fewer than 25% of Russia's people live there. Siberia alone is bigger than all of Canada.

Parts of Siberia can be forbiddingly cold. Two-thirds of the region is covered by permafrost, ground that is frozen year-round. The town of Verkhoyansk, in northeastern Russia, sits in the coldest part of the Northern Hemisphere. Though the average January temperature there is –58°F (–50°C), the temperature has dropped as low as –90°F (–68°C)! Most of Eastern Russia's population lives in the southern and western parts of the region, where the temperatures are milder. Novosibirsk, a chief city in Siberia and the third-largest city in Russia, has an average temperature of 3°F (–16°C) in winter and about 68°F (20°C) in summer.

Sleigh Ride: A man and his reindeer race to the finish line.

Though Siberia has few people, it has tremendous natural resources and wildlife. Siberia is Russia's leading producer of gold and diamonds and is rich in coal, oil and gas. Eastern Russia is also the home of the only viable population of wild Siberian tigers.

Endangered: There are fewer than 500 Siberian tigers left in the wild.

Novaya Zemlya Is.
Naryan Mar
Salekhard
Ural Mtns.
West Siberian Plain
Khanty-Mansiysk
Ob R.
Surgut
Nizhnevartovsk
Vasyuga Swam
Kurgan
Irtysh R.
Tor
Astana
Omsk
Novosibirsk
The Steppes
KAZAKHSTAN
Kazakh Uplands
Irtysh R.
Lake Balkhash
Almaty
Tian Mtns.
Urum
Taklimakan Desert
CHINA

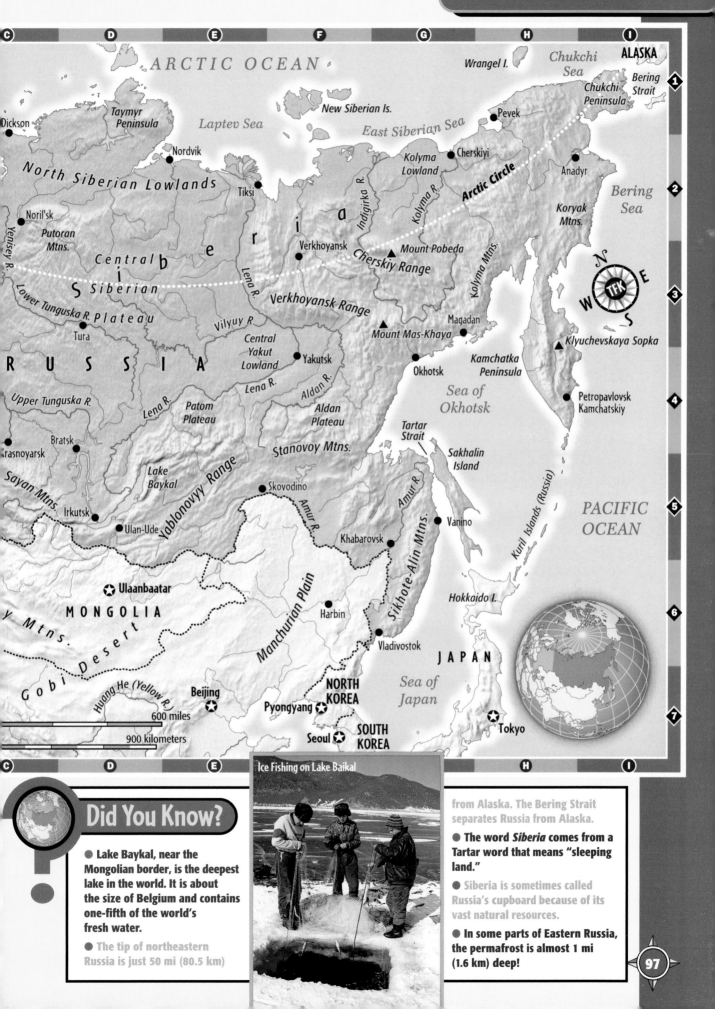

ARCTIC OCEAN

Wrangel I.

Chukchi Sea

ALASKA

Bering Strait

Dickson

Taymyr Peninsula

Laptev Sea

New Siberian Is.

East Siberian Sea

Chukchi Peninsula

Nordvik

North Siberian Lowlands

Tiksi

Pevek

Cherskiyi

Arctic Circle

Anadyr

Bering Sea

Noril'sk

Kolyma Lowland

Kolyma R.

Putoran Mtns.

S i b e r i a

Koryak Mtns.

Yenisey R.

Lower Tunguska R.

C e n t r a l

Verkhoyansk

Indigirka R.

Cherskiy Range

Mount Pobeda

Kolyma Mtns.

N

Siberian

Lena R.

Verkhoyansk Range

W TFK E

Tura

P l a t e a u

Vilyuy R.

Central Yakut Lowland

Mount Mas-Khaya

Magadan

Klyuchevskaya Sopka

S

R U S S I A

Yakutsk

Aldan R.

Lena R.

Okhotsk

Kamchatka Peninsula

Petropavlovsk Kamchatskiy

Upper Tunguska R.

Lena R.

Patom Plateau

Aldan Plateau

Sea of Okhotsk

Krasnoyarsk

Bratsk

Stanovoy Mtns.

Tartar Strait

Sakhalin Island

Sayan Mtns.

Lake Baykal

Yablonovyy Range

Skovodino

Amur R.

Irkutsk

Ulan-Ude

Amur R.

Khabarovsk

Vanino

Sikhote-Alin Mtns.

Kuril Islands (Russia)

PACIFIC OCEAN

Ulaanbaatar

M O N G O L I A

Manchurian Plain

Harbin

Hokkaido I.

Mtns.

Gobi Desert

Vladivostok

J A P A N

Huang He (Yellow R.)

Beijing

NORTH KOREA

Pyongyang

Sea of Japan

600 miles

900 kilometers

Seoul

SOUTH KOREA

Tokyo

Ice Fishing on Lake Baikal

Did You Know?

● Lake Baykal, near the Mongolian border, is the deepest lake in the world. It is about the size of Belgium and contains one-fifth of the world's fresh water.

● The tip of northeastern Russia is just 50 mi (80.5 km) from Alaska. The Bering Strait separates Russia from Alaska.

● The word *Siberia* comes from a Tartar word that means "sleeping land."

● Siberia is sometimes called Russia's cupboard because of its vast natural resources.

● In some parts of Eastern Russia, the permafrost is almost 1 mi (1.6 km) deep!

Turkey and Cyprus

Turkey, a nation about the size of the state of Texas, straddles the border between Europe and Asia. On its western border sit Greece and Bulgaria; to the east and south are Syria, Iraq, Iran, Azerbaijan, Armenia and Georgia. Turkey's unique location means that it is both European and Asian. For more than 4,000 years, it has served as a bridge between the two continents and many different civilizations. Its art, architecture and customs reflect its complicated past.

Turkish Delight: A man sells bread in Antalya.

Up until 1923, Turkey was a Muslim territory under the Ottoman Empire. It was a preindustrial region, with few ties to the modern world. Then Kemal Atatürk, a Turkish soldier who had led a revolution to overthrow the Ottomans, became the leader of the Turkish nation. Atatürk changed many aspects of Turkish culture, including its alphabet, clothing styles, calendar and relationship to the West.

Cyprus, an island off the coast of Turkey and Greece, has been fought over for centuries. In 1960, it became an independent nation whose government included both Turks and Greeks. Tension between the two nationalities grew until 1974, when conflict split the island into two parts. The Greek-led nation of Cyprus, not the Turkish Republic of Northern Cyprus, is considered to be the official government.

Turkey and Cyprus have a warm, dry climate and rely for income on farming, although both countries are becoming more industrialized.

Data Bank

CYPRUS
AREA: 3,572 sq mi (9,250 sq km)
POPULATION: 775,927
CAPITAL: Nicosia
LANGUAGES: Greek, Turkish, English

TURKEY
AREA: 301,381 sq mi (780,580 sq km)
POPULATION: 68,893,918
CAPITAL: Ankara
LANGUAGES: Turkish (official), Kurdish, Arabic, Armenian, Greek

The Blue Mosque in Istanbul, Turkey

Map labels
ROMANIA
Danube R.
Constanta
BULGARIA
Varna
Bosp
Edirne
Istanbul
Gallipoli
Sea of Marmara
Dardanelles
Burs
Bergama
Khios I.
Gediz R.
Izmir
Kucukmenderes R.
Deniz
G R E E C E
Kizla Peak
Rhodes (Greece)

UKRAINE

Sea of Azov

CRIMEA

Krasnodar

RUSSIA

N
W · E
S
TFK

Caspian Sea

Black Sea

Mt. Elbrus ▲

Grozny

Gagra

C a u c a s u s   M t n s.

Poti

Kutaisi

Sinop

GEORGIA   Tbilisi ☆

AZERBAIJAN

Samsun

Mount Kackar

Trabzon

ARMENIA

Koroglu Mtns.

Amasya

P o n t i c   M t n s.   ▲

Kumayri

Mt. Aragats ▲

Gyandzhe

Kura R.

Kizil R.

Kelkit R.

Coruh R.

Yerevan ☆

Lake Sevan

Araks R.

Ankara ☆

T U R K E Y

Aras R.

Sivas

Erzurum

Mt. Ararat ▲

Dagi

A n a t o l i a n   P l a t e a u

AZERBAIJAN

Egridir

Mount Erciyas ▲

Kayseri

Lake Van

Tuz Lake

Seyhan R.

Malatya

Murat R.

Tabriz

eyeshir Lake

Konya

Ceyhan R.

E a s t e r n   T a u r u s   M t n s.

Batman

Uludoruk Peak ▲

Lake Urmia

I R A N

T a u r u s   M t n s.

Adana

Gaziantep

Diyarbakir

Tigris R.

1

Antakya

Aleppo

Euphrates R

Mosul

TURKISH SECTOR

Latakia

PRUS

Nicosia ✪

Hamah

Z a g r . . .   M t n s.

Larnaca

S Y R I A

I R A Q

REEK
CTOR

Limassol

LEBANON

Beirut ☆

Baghdad ☆

Tig

editerranean Sea

Damascus ☆

Syrian Desert

ISRAEL

JORDAN

0   200 miles

0   300 kilometers

Homes were built into the rocks in Cappadocia.

Did You Know?

● **Istanbul**, the largest city in Turkey, is the only city in the world to straddle two continents. Istanbul has been called Byzantium and Constantinople, and was at one time the capital of the Ottoman Empire.

● Kemal Atatürk outlawed the fez, a traditional Turkish hat, because he thought it made Turks look too old-fashioned.

● **Cappadocia** is a district of Turkey famous for its strange and beautiful rock formations. Created by volcanic activity and erosion, they were decorated with frescoes and other works of art.

● Cyprus has been inhabited for about 9,000 years. No wonder it's a favorite spot for archaeologists!

● **Turkish coffee** is dark, thick and sweet, and is served at almost every meal. A famous Turkish dish is shish kebob—meat or seafood and vegetables cut into small chunks, threaded onto a skewer and grilled.

Israel, Jordan, Lebanon and Syria

City of Gold: A view of old Jerusalem from the Mount of Olives

Israel, Jordan, Lebanon and Syria are Middle Eastern lands of ancient cultures and archaeological treasures. Stretching from the banks of the Tigris River to the Gulf of Aqaba, the region has long been a crossroads of conquerors and Crusaders. Because the land is sacred to Judaism, Christianity and Islam, it has also been at the center of centuries-old religious conflicts and political disputes.

Many of the world's holiest sites are found in Israel. Jews pray at the 2,000-year-old Western Wall in Jerusalem. Muslims pray at the golden Dome of the Rock mosque. Christians pray at the Church of the Holy Sepulchre, site of the tomb of Jesus.

The kingdom of Jordan is also known for its religious and archaeological sites. Petra, the best-known of them, is an ancient city of elaborate temples and tombs carved completely from sandstone. Two thousand years ago, the city was a crossroads for the spice trade. Syria, which is to the north of Jordan, has one of the oldest recorded histories in the world. The country's capital, Damascus, has been inhabited since prehistoric times! Lebanon lies between Israel and Syria. From 1975 to 1990, a civil war raged in Lebanon, and the country is still recovering from it.

Syrian Soda:
A boy in Damascus sells soft drinks.

Data Bank

ISRAEL
AREA: 8,020 sq mi (20,770 sq km)
POPULATION: 6,199,008
CAPITAL: Jerusalem
LANGUAGES: Hebrew, Arabic (both official), English

JORDAN
AREA: 35,637 sq mi ((92,300 sq km)
POPULATION: 5,611,202
CAPITAL: Amman
LANGUAGES: Arabic (official), English

LEBANON
AREA: 4,015 sq mi (10,400 sq km)
POPULATION: 3,777,218
CAPITAL: Beirut
LANGUAGES: Arabic (official), French, English, Armenian

SYRIA
AREA: 71,498 sq mi (185,180 sq km)
POPULATION: 18,016,874
CAPITAL: Damascus
LANGUAGES: Arabic (official), French, English

City of Stone: The Treasury at Petra, Jordan

A **B** **C** **D** **E** **F** **G**

N W E S TFK

Taurus Mtns.

Seyhan R. Ceyhan R.

Adana

T U R K E Y

Euphrates R.

Tigris R.

al-Qamishi

al-Hasakah

Antakya

Aleppo

Lake al-Assad

Euphrates R.

Khabur R.

TURKISH SECTOR

Nicosia

CYPRUS

Mt. Olympus

Larnaca

Limassol

GREEK SECTOR

Latakia

Orontes R.

S Y R I A

ar Raqqah

Dayr az-Zawr

Tartus

Hamah

Abu Rujmayn Mtns.

Euphrates R.

Tripoli

Homs

Tadmur

Lebanon Mtns.

Qurnat as-Sawda

Juniyah

Beirut

Bekaa Valley

LEBANON

Damascus

Mediterranean Sea

Tyre

Mt. Hermon

S y r i a n

Acre

Golan Heights

Haifa

Lake Tiberias (Sea of Galilee)

D e s e r t

I R A Q

ISRAEL

Mount ad Duruz

Tel Aviv-Jaffa

West Bank

Irbid

Wadi Hauran

Jordan R.

az-Zarqa

Jebel Aneiza

Jerusalem

Amman

Gaza Strip

Hebron

Madaba

Port Said

Dead Sea

SAUDI ARABIA

Beersheba

Negev

J O R D A N

Suez Canal

Araba R.

Great Rift Valley

Petra

Ma'an

el Jafr Depression

an-Nafud Desert

EGYPT

Suez

Sinai Peninsula

Esh Shera

Elat

Aqaba

Mount Ramm

Gulf of Suez

Gulf of Aqaba

0 — 150 miles
0 — 200 kilometers

A **B** **C** **D** **E** **F** **G**

Today, cedars are found only in protected areas.

Did You Know?

- The ancient, walled city of Jerusalem is divided into quarters: Jewish, Christian, Muslim and Armenian.

- The cedar tree is the national symbol of Lebanon. In biblical times, cedar trees covered the countryside.

- The city of Petra takes its name from a Greek word meaning rock.

- Beirut, the Lebanese capital, was once known as "the Paris of the Middle East."

- The Dead Sea, located between Israel and Jordan, is so salty, bathers float easily on top of the water!

The Arabian Peninsula

Pilgrimage: Muslims gather at the Great Mosque in Mecca, Saudi Arabia.

Windblown desert sands cover much of the Arabian Peninsula. The area's climate is generally hot and dry, and the vegetation is sparse. The Arabian Desert, which takes up a large part of Saudi Arabia, Kuwait, Qatar, the United Arab Emirates and Oman, is the largest subtropical desert in the world. Only the Sahara Desert is larger.

Beneath the desert sands lies a treasure—oil. The countries in this region are highly dependent on the petroleum industry. It has made many of them rich. Saudi Arabia, the largest country in the region, has one-third of the world's known oil reserves. Oil has been both a blessing and a curse for Kuwait. In 1990, in a bid to gain control of Kuwait's lucrative oil fields, Iraq invaded its tiny neighbor. The United States and its allies intervened, and in January 1991, they used bombs and ground forces to set Kuwait free. In 2003, the U.S. again went to war against Iraq. Iraq's leader, Saddam Hussein, was ousted and later captured.

At the tip of the Arabian Peninsula are Yemen and Oman. Although Yemen does not have the oil riches of its neighbors, its location—at the southern entrance to the Red Sea—is strategic. Qatar, Bahrain and the United Arab Emirates lie on the Persian Gulf, along the west coast of Saudi Arabia. Bahrain is made up of a group of small islands, and the United Arab Emirates is a union of seven kingdoms..

Data Bank

BAHRAIN
AREA: 257 sq mi (665 sq km)
POPULATION: 667,886
CAPITAL: Manama
LANGUAGES: Arabic, English, Farsi, Urdu

IRAQ
AREA: 168,753 sq mi (437,072 sq km)
POPULATION: 25,374,691
CAPITAL: Baghdad
LANGUAGES: Arabic, Kurdish, Assyrian, Armenian

KUWAIT
AREA: 6,880 sq mi (17,820 sq km)
POPULATION: 2,257,549
CAPITAL: Kuwait
LANGUAGES: Arabic (official), English

OMAN
AREA: 82,030 sq mi (212,460 sq km)
POPULATION: 2,903,165
CAPITAL: Muscat
LANGUAGES: Arabic (official), English, Indian languages

QATAR
AREA: 4,416 sq mi (11,437 sq km)
POPULATION: 840,290
CAPITAL: Doha
LANGUAGES: Arabic (official), English

SAUDI ARABIA
AREA: 756,981 sq mi (1,960,582 sq km)
POPULATION: 25,100,425
CAPITAL: Riyadh
LANGUAGE: Arabic

UNITED ARAB EMIRATES
AREA: 32,000 sq mi (82,880 sq km)
POPULATION: 2,523,915
CAPITAL: Abu Dhabi
LANGUAGES: Arabic (official), Persian, English, Hindi, Urdu

YEMEN
AREA: 203,848 sq mi (527,970 sq km)
POPULATION: 20,024,867
CAPITAL: Sanaa
LANGUAGE: Arabic

Gleaming Skyline: Dubai, in the United Arab Emirates

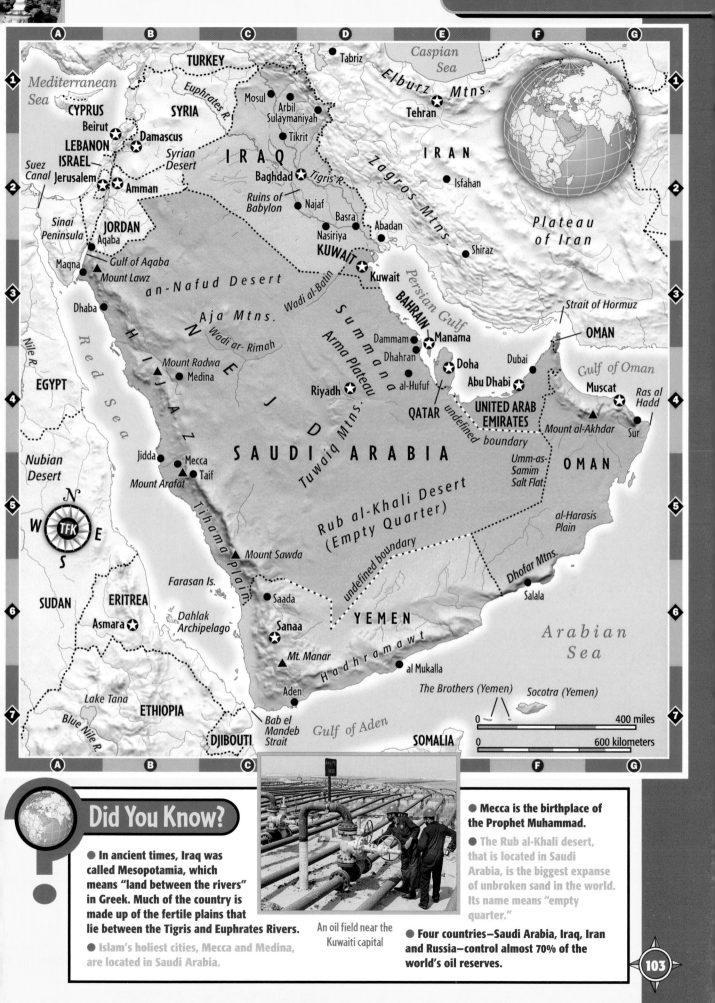

The map shows:

Mediterranean Sea

TURKEY

CYPRUS
Beirut
LEBANON
ISRAEL
Jerusalem

SYRIA
Damascus
Syrian Desert
Amman

JORDAN
Aqaba
Gulf of Aqaba
Magna
Mount Lawz

Suez Canal

Sinai Peninsula

Dhaba

EGYPT

Nile R.

Red Sea

Nubian Desert

an-Nafud Desert

Aja Mtns.
Wadi ar-Rimah

HIJAZ

Mount Radwa
Medina

NEJD

Euphrates R.

Mosul
Arbil
Sulaymaniyah
Tikrit

IRAQ

Baghdad
Tigris R.
Ruins of Babylon
Najaf
Basra
Nasiriya
Abadan

KUWAIT
Kuwait

Wadi al-Batin

Summan

Arma Plateau

Dammam
Dhahran
al-Hufuf

Tabriz

Caspian Sea

Elburz Mtns.

Tehran

IRAN

Isfahan

Zagros Mtns.

Shiraz

Plateau of Iran

Persian Gulf

BAHRAIN
Manama

Strait of Hormuz

OMAN

Doha
Dubai
Abu Dhabi

Muscat
Ras al Hadd

Gulf of Oman

QATAR

UNITED ARAB EMIRATES

undefined boundary

Mount al-Akhdar
Sur

OMAN

Jidda
Mecca
Taif
Mount Arafat

Riyadh

Tuwaiq Mtns.

SAUDI ARABIA

Rub al-Khali Desert (Empty Quarter)

undefined boundary

Umm-as-Samim Salt Flat

al-Harasis Plain

Mount Sawda

Tihama plain

Farasan Is.

Nubian Desert

SUDAN

ERITREA
Asmara

Dahlak Archipelago

Saada

YEMEN

Sanaa

Mt. Manar

Hadhramawt

al Mukalla

Dhofar Mtns.
Salala

Arabian Sea

Lake Tana
Blue Nile R.

ETHIOPIA

Aden

Bab el Mandeb Strait

Gulf of Aden

DJIBOUTI

SOMALIA

The Brothers (Yemen)

Socotra (Yemen)

| 0 | 400 miles |
| 0 | 600 kilometers |

N W E S — TFK

Did You Know?

● In ancient times, Iraq was called Mesopotamia, which means "land between the rivers" in Greek. Much of the country is made up of the fertile plains that lie between the Tigris and Euphrates Rivers.

● Islam's holiest cities, Mecca and Medina, are located in Saudi Arabia.

An oil field near the Kuwaiti capital

● Mecca is the birthplace of the Prophet Muhammad.

● The Rub al-Khali desert, that is located in Saudi Arabia, is the biggest expanse of unbroken sand in the world. Its name means "empty quarter."

● Four countries—Saudi Arabia, Iraq, Iran and Russia—control almost 70% of the world's oil reserves.

Central Asia

Central Asia, which includes the nations of Kazakhstan, Turkmenistan, Uzbekistan, Tajikistan and Kyrgyzstan, stretches from Russia and the Ural Mountains all the way to China. To the south, Central Asia borders Iran and Afghanistan. All the nations of Central Asia were once part of the Soviet Union. While the people here are very different from one another, many share a belief in Buddhism or Islam. Many are also nomads, traveling from place to place. The yurt, which is similar to a tent, is the traditional dwelling of these nomadic people.

Hunting with an eagle is a Kazakh tradition.

Kazakhstan is the largest Central Asian nation. To the west are the Ural Mountains and their foothills. The remainder of the country includes deserts and vast plains called steppes. Kazakhstan is the most modernized of the Central Asian nations. Turkmenistan, the second-largest nation in the region, is almost entirely covered by dry, grassy steppes and the huge Kara-Kum Desert. Uzbekistan, like neighboring Turkmenistan, is largely desert and steppes.

The Pamir Mountains in Tajikistan are among the highest in the world. Two Central Asian mountain systems, the Tian Shan and the Pamirs, meet in Kyrgyzstan. As a result, it is a nation of peaks and valleys. Since Kyrgyzstan gained its independence in 1991, its economy has grown. Today, it is a major exporter of energy to other Central Asian nations.

Data Bank

KAZAKHSTAN
AREA: 1,049,150 sq mi (2,717,300 sq km)
POPULATION: 16,798,552
CAPITAL: Astana
LANGUAGES: Russian (official), Kazakh

KYRGYZSTAN
AREA: 76,641 sq mi (198,500 sq km)
POPULATION: 4,965,081
CAPITAL: Bishkek
LANGUAGES: Kyrgyz, Russian (both official)

TAJIKISTAN
AREA: 55,251 sq mi (143,100 sq km)
POPULATION: 7,011,556
CAPITAL: Dushanbe
LANGUAGES: Tajik (official), Russian

TURKMENISTAN
AREA: 188,455 sq mi (488,100 sq km)
POPULATION: 4,863,169
CAPITAL: Ashgabat
LANGUAGES: Turkmen, Russian, Uzbek, others

UZBEKISTAN
AREA: 172,740 sq mi (447,400 sq km)
POPULATION: 26,410,416
CAPITAL: Tashkent
LANGUAGES: Uzbek, Russian, Tajik, others

Life in a Yurt: Views of the inside and outside of a nomadic home

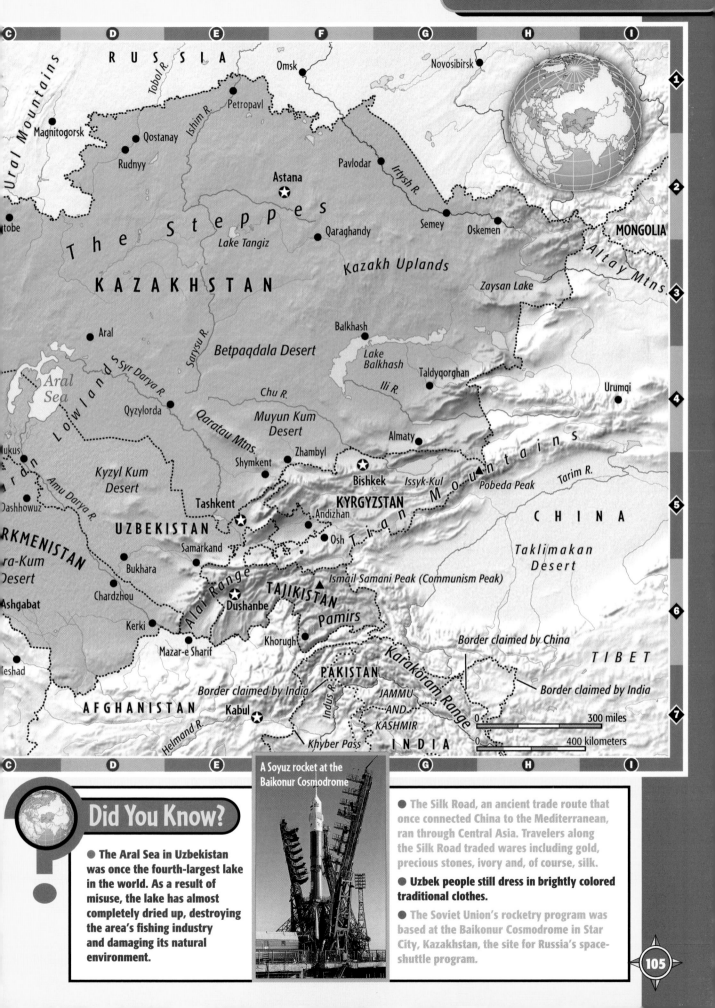

RUSSIA

Ural Mountains

Magnitogorsk

...tobe

Omsk

Tobol R.

Petropavl

Qostanay

Rudnyy

Ishim R.

Novosibirsk

Astana

Pavlodar

Irtysh R.

Semey

Oskemen

MONGOLIA

The Steppes

Lake Tangiz

Qaraghandy

Kazakh Uplands

Zaysan Lake

Altay Mtns.

KAZAKHSTAN

Aral

Syr Darya R.

Sarysu R.

Betpaqdala Desert

Balkhash

Lake Balkhash

Ili R.

Taldyqorghan

Urumqi

Aral Sea

...ran Lowland

Qyzylorda

Qaratau Mtns.

Chu R.

Muyun Kum Desert

Almaty

Amu Darya R.

Kyzyl Kum Desert

Shymkent

Zhambyl

Bishkek

Issyk-Kul

Pobeda Peak

Tarim R.

CHINA

Dashhowuz

Tashkent

KYRGYZSTAN

Tian Mountains

Taklimakan Desert

...RKMENISTAN

UZBEKISTAN

Samarkand

Andizhan

Osh

...ra-Kum Desert

Bukhara

Ismail Samani Peak (Communism Peak)

Chardzhou

Alai Range

TAJIKISTAN

Pamirs

Ashgabat

Kerki

Dushanbe

Border claimed by China

TIBET

Khorugh

Karakoram Range

Border claimed by India

Mazar-e Sharif

PAKISTAN

JAMMU AND KASHMIR

...eshad

AFGHANISTAN

Border claimed by India

Indus R.

Kabul

Helmand R.

Khyber Pass

INDIA

0 — 300 miles

0 — 400 kilometers

A Soyuz rocket at the Baikonur Cosmodrome

Did You Know?

● The Aral Sea in Uzbekistan was once the fourth-largest lake in the world. As a result of misuse, the lake has almost completely dried up, destroying the area's fishing industry and damaging its natural environment.

● The Silk Road, an ancient trade route that once connected China to the Mediterranean, ran through Central Asia. Travelers along the Silk Road traded wares including gold, precious stones, ivory and, of course, silk.

● Uzbek people still dress in brightly colored traditional clothes.

● The Soviet Union's rocketry program was based at the Baikonur Cosmodrome in Star City, Kazakhstan, the site for Russia's space-shuttle program.

Afghanistan, Iran and Pakistan

More than 2,000 years ago, the region now called Iran was the center of the Persian Empire. In 518 B.C., Darius I built an immense palace complex called Persepolis. Today, its ruins are an important archaeological site.

Ancient Splendor: Tourists visit Persepolis in Iran.

Rugged landscapes mark this part of the world. Much of Iran, Afghanistan and Pakistan is covered by deserts or mountains, although Pakistan also has rich wetlands. An 800-mi (1,287-km) desert covers a large portion of Iran. The Hindu Kush, the world's second-highest mountain range, reaches across landlocked Afghanistan into Pakistan. Iran, which lies west of Afghanistan and Pakistan, has a coast on the Caspian Sea to the north and on the Persian Gulf and Arabian Sea to the south. Pakistan, too, has a coast on the Arabian Sea.

All three countries are lands of diverse ethnic and religious groups. The different cultures and beliefs have often been a source of tension. The region has struggled with civil unrest and acts of violence. In 2001, the United States went to war with Afghanistan's Taliban government in an effort to combat terrorism. Since then, the Afghan people have made strides toward a democratic, more inclusive system of government. The new government lifted a ban on education for girls age 10 and older.

Data Bank

AFGHANISTAN
AREA: 249,999 sq mi (647,500 sq km)
POPULATION: 29,547,078
CAPITAL: Kabul
LANGUAGES: Pashtu, Afghan Persian (Dari), other Turkic languages

IRAN
AREA: 636,293 sq mi (1,648,000 sq km)
POPULATION: 69,018,924
CAPITAL: Tehran
LANGUAGES: Persian, Turkic, Kurdish

PAKISTAN
AREA: 310,400 sq mi (803,940 sq km)
POPULATION: 153,705,278
CAPITAL: Islamabad
LANGUAGES: Urdu (official), Punjabi, Sindhi, Siraiki, Pashtu, others

School Days: Girls in Afghanistan

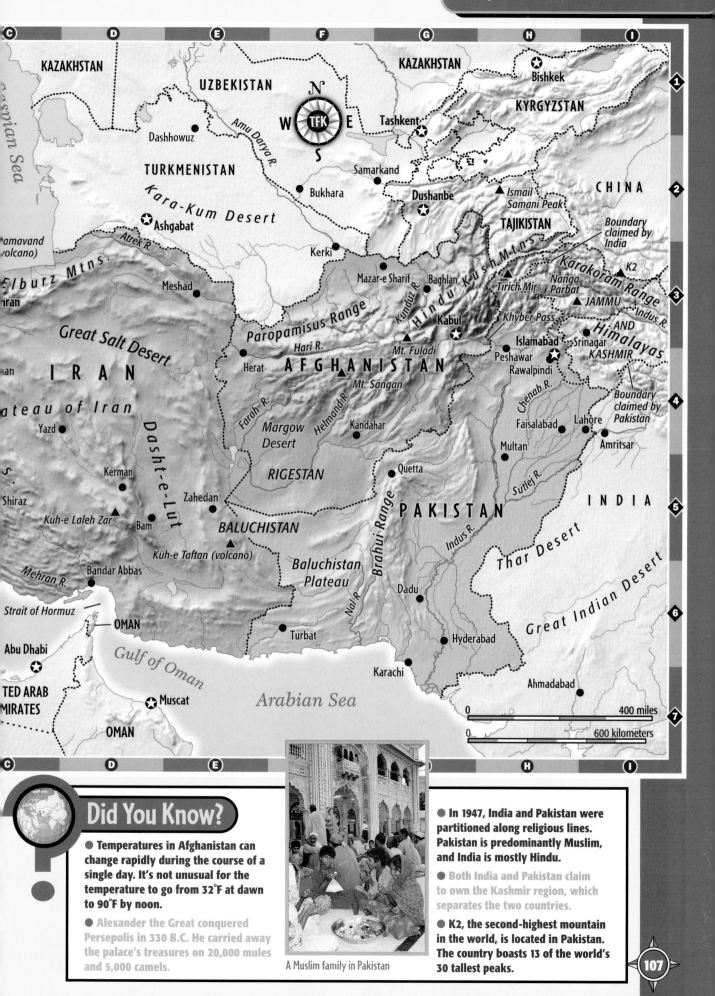

KAZAKHSTAN

KAZAKHSTAN

UZBEKISTAN

Dashhowuz

TURKMENISTAN

Kara-Kum Desert

Ashgabat

Amu Darya R.

Bukhara

Samarkand

Bishkek

Tashkent

KYRGYZSTAN

Dushanbe

CHINA

Ismail Samani Peak

TAJIKISTAN

Boundary claimed by India

Karakoram Range

K2

amavand (volcano)

Elburz Mtns.

Atrek R.

Meshad

hran

Kerki

Mazar-e Sharif

Kunduz R.

Baghlan

Hindu Kush Mtns.

Tirich Mir

Nanga Parbat

JAMMU

Indus R.

AND

Himalayas

Great Salt Desert

Paropamisus Range

Hari R.

Kabul

Khyber Pass

Srinagar

KASHMIR

I R A N

Herat

Mt. Fuladi

Islamabad

Peshawar

Rawalpindi

ateau of Iran

Mt. Sangan

AFGHANISTAN

Boundary claimed by Pakistan

Yazd

Farah R.

Margow Desert

Helmand R.

Kandahar

Chenab R.

Faisalabad

Lahore

Kerman

Dasht-e-Lut

RIGESTAN

Multan

Amritsar

S.

Zahedan

Quetta

Sutlej R.

Shiraz

Kuh-e Laleh Zar

Bam

BALUCHISTAN

Brahui Range

P A K I S T A N

I N D I A

Kuh-e Taftan (volcano)

Baluchistan Plateau

Indus R.

Thar Desert

Mehran R.

Bandar Abbas

Strait of Hormuz

OMAN

Nai R.

Dadu

Great Indian Desert

Abu Dhabi

Turbat

Hyderabad

TED ARAB MIRATES

Gulf of Oman

Muscat

Karachi

Ahmadabad

Arabian Sea

OMAN

0   400 miles

0   600 kilometers

Did You Know?

● **Temperatures in Afghanistan can change rapidly during the course of a single day. It's not unusual for the temperature to go from 32°F at dawn to 90°F by noon.**

● Alexander the Great conquered Persepolis in 330 B.C. He carried away the palace's treasures on 20,000 mules and 5,000 camels.

A Muslim family in Pakistan

● **In 1947, India and Pakistan were partitioned along religious lines. Pakistan is predominantly Muslim, and India is mostly Hindu.**

● Both India and Pakistan claim to own the Kashmir region, which separates the two countries.

● **K2, the second-highest mountain in the world, is located in Pakistan. The country boasts 13 of the world's 30 tallest peaks.**

Indian Subcontinent

The Taj Mahal, in Agra, India, is one of the world's most magnificent buildings.

Chattering monkeys, brightly painted elephants, high-tech computer whizzes and glamorous movie stars are all found in India. The world's seventh-largest country is a vast and diverse land. From snowcapped mountains to leafy jungles to bustling cities, India offers a wealth of sights, smells and sounds. India, which is predominantly Hindu, has on its northeast border the small, Muslim country of Bangladesh.

The Himalayas, the world's tallest mountains, form India's northern border. Nestled at the foot of the mountains' mammoth peaks are the tiny Buddhist kingdoms of Nepal and Bhutan. Despite their rugged setting, the two countries have much to offer. More than 9,500 species of birds can be found in Nepal. The majority of the people in Nepal and Bhutan work in the fields, raising crops or tending livestock. Tourism is an important industry. Nepal's Sherpas are famous for guiding mountain climbers up the steep slopes of Mount Everest and other forbidding peaks.

To India's south, in the Indian Ocean, sits the pearl-shaped island nation of Sri Lanka. Although ethnic conflict has festered in the country for years, Sri Lanka's natural beauty beckons visitors. Sri Lanka is known for its lovely beaches, exotic wildlife and large tea plantations.

Data Bank

BANGLADESH
AREA: 55,598 sq mi (144,000 sq km)
POPULATION: 141,340,476
CAPITAL: Dhaka
LANGUAGES: Bangla (official), English

BHUTAN
AREA: 18,147 sq mi (47,000 sq km)
POPULATION: 2,185,569
CAPITAL: Thimphu
LANGAGES: Dzongkha (official)

INDIA
AREA: 1,269,338 sq mi (3,287,590 sq km)
POPULATION: 1,065,070,607
CAPITAL: New Delhi
LANGUAGES: Hindi (official), English, native languages

NEPAL
AREA: 54,363 sq mi (140,800 sq km)
POPULATION: 27,070,666
CAPTIAL: Kathmandu
LANGUAGES: Nepali (official), English

The Pinnawala elephant orphanage in Sri Lanka

SRI LANKA
AREA: 23,332 sq mi (65,610 sq km)
POPULATION: 19,905,165
CAPITAL: Colombo
LANGUAGES: Sinhala (official), Tamil, English

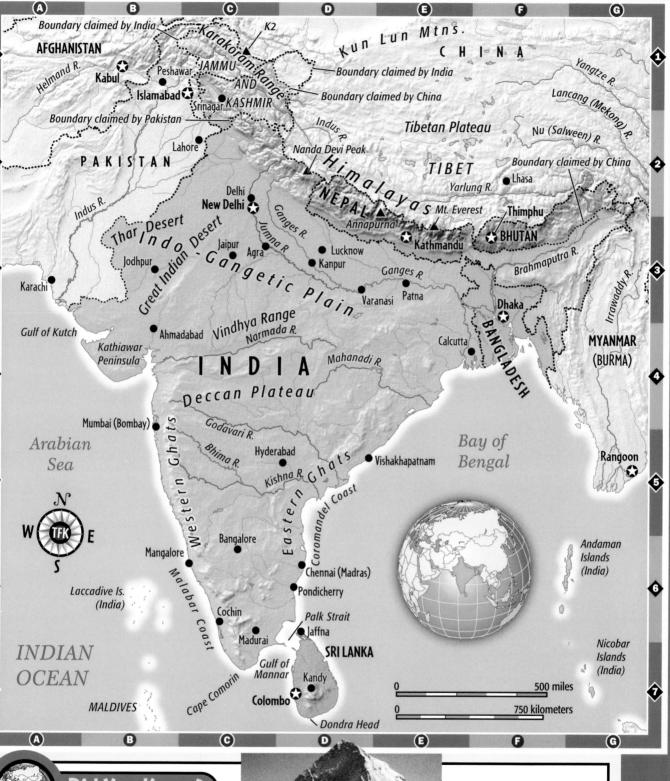

Boundary claimed by India

AFGHANISTAN

Helmand R.

☆ **Kabul**

Peshawar

Karakoram Range

K2

Kun Lun Mtns.

C H I N A

Yangtze R.

JAMMU

Boundary claimed by India

Lancang (Mekong) R.

☆ **Islamabad**

AND

Srinagar

KASHMIR

Boundary claimed by China

Tibetan Plateau

Nu (Salween) R.

Boundary claimed by Pakistan

Indus R.

Nanda Devi Peak

TIBET

Boundary claimed by China

P A K I S T A N

Lahore

H i m a l a y a s

Yarlung R.

• Lhasa

Indus R.

Delhi

New Delhi ☆

NEPAL

Mt. Everest ▲

Thimphu

☆ **BHUTAN**

Thar Desert

Ganges R.

Jumna R.

Annapurna ▲

☆ Kathmandu

Indo-Gangetic Plain

Great Indian Desert

Jaipur

Agra

Lucknow

Ganges R.

Brahmaputra R.

Jodhpur

Kanpur

Irrawaddy R.

Karachi

Varanasi

Patna

Dhaka ☆

Gulf of Kutch

Ahmadabad

Vindhya Range

Narmada R.

Mahanadi R.

Calcutta

BANGLADESH

MYANMAR (BURMA)

Kathiawar Peninsula

I N D I A

Deccan Plateau

Arabian Sea

Mumbai (Bombay)

Godavari R.

Western Ghats

Bhima R.

Hyderabad

Kishna R.

Eastern Ghats

Vishakhapatnam

Bay of Bengal

Rangoon ☆

Bangalore

Coromandel Coast

Mangalore

Malabar Coast

Chennai (Madras)

Pondicherry

Andaman Islands (India)

Laccadive Is. (India)

N
W — TFK — E
S

Cochin

Madurai

Palk Strait

Jaffna

SRI LANKA

Gulf of Mannar

Kandy

INDIAN OCEAN

Cape Comorin

☆ **Colombo**

Dondra Head

MALDIVES

Nicobar Islands (India)

| 0 | | 500 miles |
| 0 | | 750 kilometers |

Did You Know?

● The people of Bhutan call their land Druk Yul, "land of the thunder dragon."

● India is the world's largest democracy. In the past 10,000 years, it has never invaded another country.

● Emperor Shah Jahan built the Taj Mahal in memory of his second wife, Mumtaz Mahal. It took more than 20 years to build the monument.

● Mount Everest is named after Sir George Everest, the British surveyor-general of India, who was the first to record the mountain's height and location.

● Until 1972, Sri Lanka was known as Ceylon.

109

India

Namaste!

My name is Neha, and I'm 11 years old. I live in New Delhi, which is India's capital and a very exciting city. It has markets, monuments, museums–and a lot of people. Take a journey with me to India!

The Indian Flag

The flag of India was designed as a symbol of freedom from the British in 1947.

Orange represents the spirit of courage and sacrifice.

White is for peace, simplicity and truth.

Green stands for fertility in agriculture.

The **wheel**, or "chakra," in the center represents progress. It has 24 spokes, one for each hour of the day.

India's Religious Mix

India has a rich heritage of religious belief. The Hindu, Buddhist, Jain and Sikh religions all originated in India.

- Hindu 82.6%
- Muslim 11.3%
- Christian 2.4%
- Sikh 2%
- Buddhist .71%
- Jain .48%
- Parsi, Jewish, other .51%

The Economy

A worker picks tea leaves.

NATURAL RESOURCES: Coal, iron, copper, gold, crude oil, natural gas, diamonds

MAJOR INDUSTRIES: Mining, agriculture, entertainment. India cranks out more movies per year than any other nation.

MAJOR EXPORTS: Tea, coffee, fish, iron and steel, leather, textiles, clothing, polished diamonds, handmade carpets

MAJOR IMPORTS: Machinery, mineral fuels, pearls, precious and semiprecious stones, chemicals, vehicles

TRADING PARTNERS: U.S., Russia, Britain, Germany

Top 5 Most-Populated Countries

India is a crowded place: There are 857 people per sq mi in India (331 per sq km)! Compare that to Texas, in the U.S., with about 80 people per sq mi (31 per sq km).

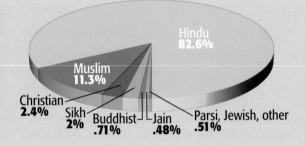

Country	Population
CHINA	1.26 billion
INDIA	1.01 billion
UNITED STATES	276 million
INDONESIA	225 million
BRAZIL	173 million

= 100 million

Major Events in India's History

1526 The rule of the Mughal Empire begins, unifying much of southern India with northern India for the first time.

1600s Eager to gain access to India's spices, tea and jewels, The Netherlands, Britain and France establish trading posts in India.

1858 The British overthrow the Mughals and take control of India.

1915 Mohandas Gandhi (called Mahatma, meaning "great soul") launches a nonviolent campaign against British rule.

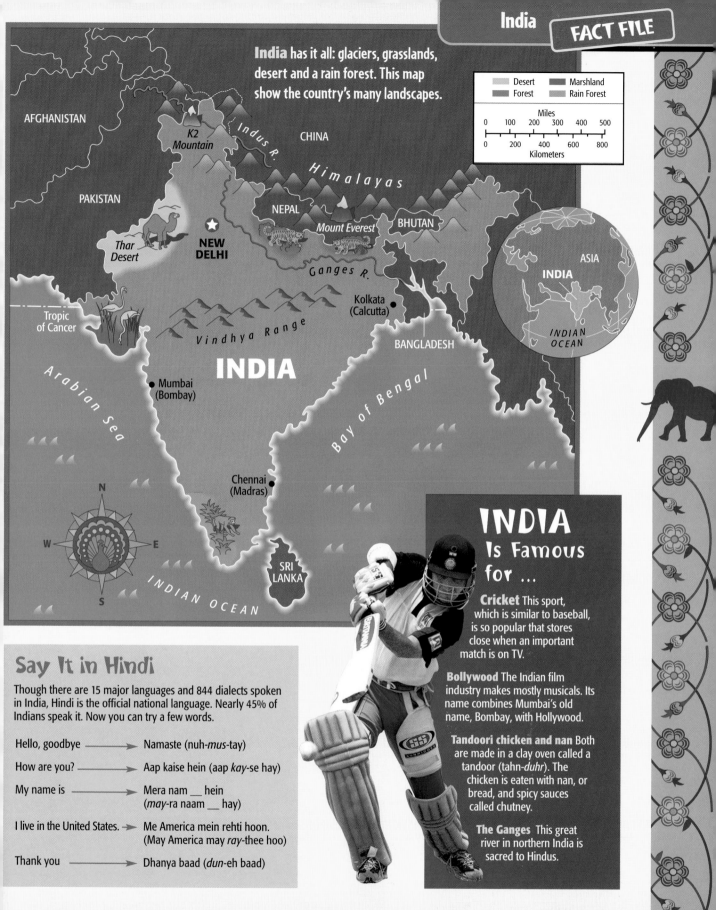

India has it all: glaciers, grasslands, desert and a rain forest. This map show the country's many landscapes.

Desert	Marshland
Forest	Rain Forest

Miles
0 100 200 300 400 500

0 200 400 600 800
Kilometers

AFGHANISTAN

CHINA

K2 Mountain

Indus R.

Himalayas

PAKISTAN

NEPAL

Mount Everest

BHUTAN

Thar Desert

NEW DELHI

Ganges R.

Kolkata (Calcutta)

Tropic of Cancer

Vindhya Range

BANGLADESH

INDIA

ASIA

INDIA

INDIAN OCEAN

Arabian Sea

Mumbai (Bombay)

Bay of Bengal

Chennai (Madras)

N
W   E
S

SRI LANKA

INDIAN OCEAN

Say It in Hindi

Though there are 15 major languages and 844 dialects spoken in India, Hindi is the official national language. Nearly 45% of Indians speak it. Now you can try a few words.

Hello, goodbye ⟶ Namaste (nuh-*mus*-tay)

How are you? ⟶ Aap kaise hein (aap *kay*-se hay)

My name is ⟶ Mera nam __ hein (*may*-ra naam __ hay)

I live in the United States. ⟶ Me America mein rehti hoon. (May America may *ray*-thee hoo)

Thank you ⟶ Dhanya baad (*dun*-eh baad)

INDIA Is Famous for ...

Cricket This sport, which is similar to baseball, is so popular that stores close when an important match is on TV.

Bollywood The Indian film industry makes mostly musicals. Its name combines Mumbai's old name, Bombay, with Hollywood.

Tandoori chicken and nan Both are made in a clay oven called a tandoor (tahn-*duhr*). The chicken is eaten with nan, or bread, and spicy sauces called chutney.

The Ganges This great river in northern India is sacred to Hindus.

1947 India gains independence from Britain and is divided into two countries, India and Muslim-controlled Pakistan.

1948 Mahatma Gandhi is assassinated.

1966 Indira Gandhi becomes prime minister and one of the first women elected to lead a large nation.

2000 India's population exceeds 1 billion.

 To learn more about India, go to *timeforkids.com/gpindia*.

China and Mongolia

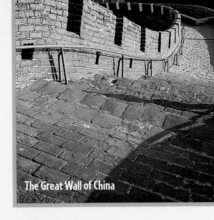
The Great Wall of China

Chhina is a country of giant land mass and giant population. It has more people than any country. One in every five people on the planet is Chinese. The country's varied landscapes include towering mountains, barren deserts and lush valleys. China is also a land of busy cities and gleaming skyscrapers.

Through 2,200 years of recorded history, the Chinese have developed rich traditions in food, festivals, art and medicine. China has seen the rise and fall of eight great dynasties, or ruling families. In 1949, the country embraced a form of government called communism. China insists that the island of Taiwan is not a separate country but belongs to the mainland.

The Gobi Desert, a huge expanse of rocks and dry grasslands, extends north from China into Mongolia. The landlocked nation, which gained its independence from China in 1921, is a place of harsh winters and little vegetation. It is one of Asia's most sparsely populated countries.

Hong Kong's sparkling skyline

Data Bank

CHINA
AREA: 3,705,386 sq mi (9,596,960 sq km)
POPULATION: 1,294,629,555
CAPITAL: Beijing
LANGUAGES: Chinese (Mandarin), local dialects

MONGOLIA
AREA: 604,250 sq mi (1,565,000 sq km)
POPULATION: 2,751,314
CAPITAL: Ulaanbaatar
LANGUAGES: Khalkha Mongol, Turkic, Russian

TAIWAN
AREA: 13,892 sq mi (35,980 sq km)
POPULATION: 22,749,838
CAPITAL: Taipei
LANGUAGES: Chinese (Mandarin), Taiwanese, Hakka dialects

RUSSIA
Lake Baykal
Yenisey R.
Irkutsk
Amur R.
Lake Uvs
Hangayn Mtns
Darhan
Selenga R.
Harbin
Songhua R.
Ulaanbaatar
Kerulen R.
Choybalsan
Lake Khanka
MONGOLIA
MANCHURIA
Urumqi
Vladivostok
Altay Mtns.
XINJIANG
Gobi Desert
Shenyang
NORTH KOREA
tun Mtns.
Yumen
Huang He
Baotou
Hohhot
The Great Wall
Yalu R.
Pyongyang
Sea of Japan
Beijing
Mus Us Desert
Tianjin
Bo Hai
Seoul
SOUTH KOREA
JAPAN
Qinghai Lake
North China Plain
Huang He (Yellow R.)
Jinan
Qingdao
Yellow Sea
tns.
Xining
Lanzhou
Wei R.
Zhengzhou
Hongze Hu
teau
Yangtze R.
CHINA
Xian
Lancang (Mekong) R.
Nanjing
Shanghai
BET
Nu (Salween) R.
Yangtze R.
Wuhan
Tai Hu
East China Sea
Lhasa
Chengdu
Hangzhou
Thimphu
Yarlung R.
Chongqing
Yuan R.
Gongga Peak
Changsha
BHUTAN
Gan R.
Ryukyu Islands (Japan)
Border claimed by China
Dalou Mtns.
Fuzhou
ka
Kunming
Guilin
Wuyi Mtns.
Taipei
PACIFIC OCEAN
Hongshui R.
Guangzhou
Taiwan Strait
TAIWAN
MYANMAR (BURMA)
Red R.
Nanning
Hong Kong
Special Administrative Regions
Macau
N
VIETNAM
Hanoi
W — E
DESH
Haikou
South China Sea
S
ay of
LAOS
Gulf of Tonkin
Hainan I.
500 miles
ngal
THAILAND
Vientiane
0   750 kilometers

Did You Know?

● The Great Wall is about 4,000 mi (6,437 km) long. That's about the distance from Miami, Florida, to Rio de Janeiro, Brazil!

● The Grand Canal is the longest and oldest man-made river in the world. Parts of the canal were built almost 2,500 years ago.

A Chinese woman harvests rice.

● The Chinese invented paper, ink, the compass and silk.

● Shanghai, China's biggest city, is home to 17 million people.

● In 1997, the former British colony of Hong Kong became part of China.

● Almost 100 species in China are endangered, including the giant panda, the South China tiger and the crowned crane.

● *Gobi* means "waterless place" in Mongolian.

China

Nín hao!
My name is Yifu. I'm 7 years old, and I live in Beijing. My dad takes me to school on his bicycle. It takes 35 minutes! On Mondays, all students at my school wear a green kerchief. Let me show you China!

The Chinese Flag

China has used this flag since the Communist Party gained power in 1949. China's former flag is now the flag of Taiwan.

The **red background** is a symbol of communism.

The **four smaller stars** represent China's society: farmers, workers, the middle class and business leaders.

The **large star** stands for the Communist Party, China's only political party.

China's Terrain

China's varied terrain makes it difficult to grow enough food for the country's large population.

- Plateaus 26%
- Basins 19%
- Plains 12%
- Hills 10%
- Mountain areas 33%

The Economy

AGRICULTURE: Rice, corn, wheat, sorghum, soybeans, tobacco, cotton

MANUFACTURING: Cement, steel, chemical fertilizer, cotton fabrics, bicycles, household appliances

MAJOR EXPORTS: Clothing and textiles, rubber and metal goods, small electric appliances, food, live animals

Shoemaking is a big industry in China.

MAJOR IMPORTS: Raw materials for manufacturing, manufacturing equipment, transportation equipment

TRADING PARTNERS: Japan, U.S., Taiwan, South Korea, Germany

Top 5 Highest Mountains

All five of the world's highest mountains are in the Himalayas, the snowy mountain range separating China from Nepal and Pakistan.

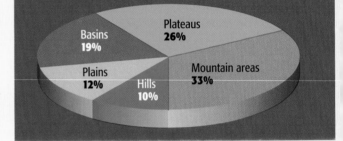

1. **Everest (China/Nepal)** 29,035 ft (8,850 m)
2. **K2 (China/Pakistan)** 28,238 ft (8,607 m)
3. **Kangchenjunga (Nepal/India)** 28,208 ft (8,598 m)
4. **Lhotse (China/Nepal)** 27,923 ft (8,511 m)
5. **Makalu (China/Nepal)** 27,824 ft (8,481 m)

Major Events in China's History

221 B.C. Qin Shi Huangdi unifies China and becomes its first emperor.

105 B.C. The Chinese invent paper. Early paper was made of mulberry-tree bark.

960 A.D.-1279 A.D. The Song family rules China. It is the longest-ruling dynasty in Chinese history.

1368-1644 The Ming dynasty rules China. Landscape painting, calligraphy, porcelain pottery, embroidery and other arts flourish during this period.

China is a land of wonders. Take a look at the country's natural and man-made treasures.

RUSSIA

Aitay Mountains

KYRGYZSTAN

MONGOLIA

Gobi Desert

Takla Makan Desert

Lake Qinghai

Great Wall

★ BEIJING

Plateau of Tibet

Xi'an

Yellow River

Grand Canal

Shanghai

CHINA

ASIA

CHINA

PACIFIC OCEAN

Equator

Himalayas

NEPAL

Mekong River

Yangtze River

EAST CHINA SEA

Mt. Everest

BHUTAN

BANGLADESH

Hongshui River

Guilin

Hong Kong

Taiwan

Tropic of Cancer

INDIA

MYANMAR (BURMA)

LAOS

VIETNAM

SOUTH CHINA SEA

THAILAND

Hainan

SCALE

Miles

0   300   600

KEY
- △ Mountains
- ▢ Desert
- ▢ Plateau
- ▬ Great Wall
- ▬ Grand Canal

CHINA Is Famous for ...

Pandas Giant pandas are found only in the forests of central China. There are fewer than 1,000 pandas in the world!

Rice and noodles These are the basis of the Chinese diet. The Chinese put them in a bowl, hold it with one hand and use chopsticks with the other hand.

Ping-Pong Chinese cities have so few parks and open spaces that kids don't have room to play most sports. But Ping-Pong tables are everywhere.

Tai chi These slow, graceful exercises are designed to shape up the body and mind.

Chinese New Year The New Year, which usually begins in February, is the country's biggest holiday. Every town has a parade with dancers and giant dragons.

Say It in Chinese

Mandarin Chinese is spoken by more than 1 billion people. These words are written in our alphabet. Chat in this 6,000-year-old language.

Hello ⟶ Nin hao (neen how)

Thank you ⟶ Xie xie (syeh syeh)

My name is ⟶ Wo jiao (wah jeeow)

What is your name? ⟶ Nin gui xing? (Neen gway sing)

Goodbye ⟶ Zai jian (dzai jee-an)

1949 Mao Zedong, head of the Communist Party, establishes the People's Republic of China. He forces out Nationalist Party rivals. The Nationalists move to Taiwan, off China's eastern coast.

1958-1961 Mao's plan to change China's economy and agricultural system fails miserably. More than 30 million people starve to death.

April 1989 About 1 million university students protest in Beijing's Tiananmen Square in favor of democracy. The uprising is crushed by Chinese troops.

1997 After 99 years of British rule, China regains control of Hong Kong.

 Hear Mandarin phrases and see more of China at *timeforkids.com/gpchina*.

Japan, North Korea and South Korea

Big City: Tokyo, Japan, is the world's most populous urban area.

Off the southeast coast of Asia, in the North Pacific Ocean, lie the islands of Japan. The country is made up of four main islands and 3,900 smaller islands. Its location in the Ring of Fire makes Japan a hot spot for volcanoes and earthquakes. Most of the country is made up of volcanic mountains.

Japan has been inhabited for over 10,000 years and has a tradition of fine arts. For centuries, artists have painted beautiful portraits and scenes on silks and ceramics. In homes and parks, exquisite gardens feature delicately pruned plants. Japan is also an economic superpower. Tokyo, though sharing a common heritage, Japan's capital and largest city, is one of the world's most important business centers.

Not far to Japan's north, the Korean Peninsula juts off the mainland of Asia. Through war and peace, Japan and Korea have been closely linked. In 1904, the Japanese invaded Korea and, in 1910, made Korea a Japanese territory. In 1945, following World War II, the Allies separated Japan and Korea and split the Korean Peninsula into two separate nations. Today, though sharing a common heritage, North and South Korea remain two distinct and very different countries.

Japan has had a strong influence on the culture of Korea. So, too, has China, which borders North Korea. Yet, the peninsula retains its own language, traditions and cuisine.

Going Mobile: More than 65% of Japan's teens own cell phones.

Standoff: A fence separates North and South Korea.

Data Bank

JAPAN
AREA: 145,882 sq mi (377,835 sq km)
POPULATION: 127,333,002
CAPITAL: Tokyo
LANGUAGE: Japanese

NORTH KOREA
AREA: 46,540 sq mi (120,540 sq km)
POPULATION: 22,697,553
CAPITAL: Pyongyang
LANGUAGE: Korean

SOUTH KOREA
AREA: 38,023 sq mi (98,480 sq km)
POPULATION: 48,598,175
CAPITAL: Seoul
LANGUAGE: Korean

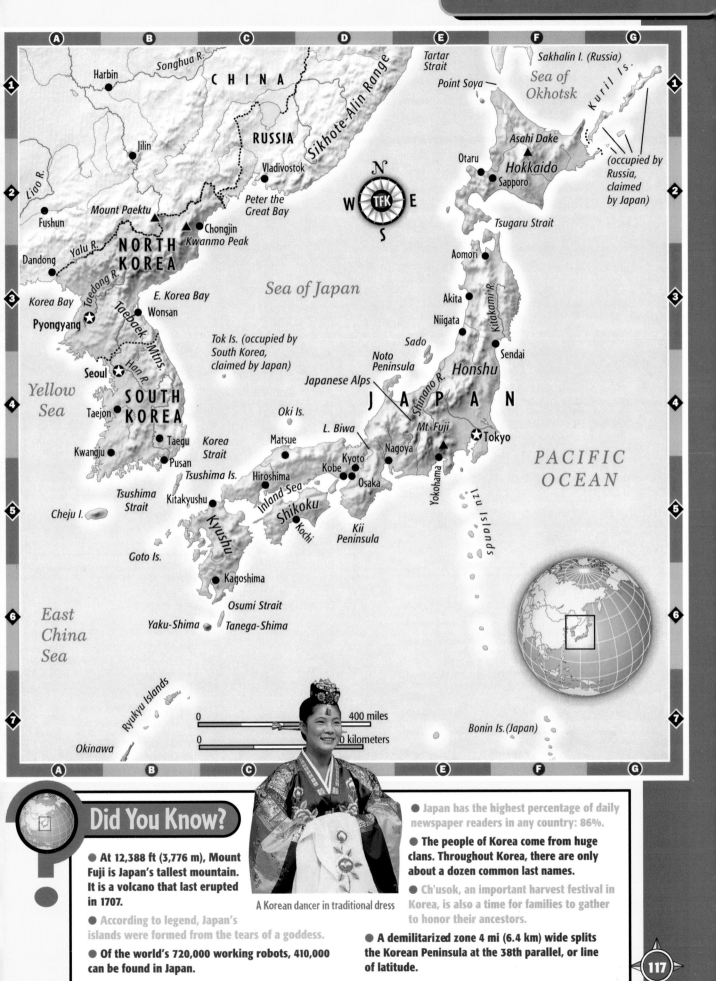

A B C D E F G

1 — CHINA
Harbin
Songhua R.
Sikhote-Alin Range
Tartar Strait
Point Soya
Sakhalin I. (Russia)
Sea of Okhotsk
Kuril Is.

2 — RUSSIA
Jilin
Vladivostok
Peter the Great Bay
Asahi Dake
Hokkaido
Otaru
Sapporo
Tsugaru Strait
(occupied by Russia, claimed by Japan)
Liao R.
Fushun
Mount Paektu
Chongjin
Kwanmo Peak
NORTH KOREA
Yalu R.
Dandong
Taedong R.

3 — Korea Bay
Taebaek Mtns.
E. Korea Bay
Wonsan
Pyongyang
Sea of Japan
Aomori
Akita
Niigata
Sendai
Kitakami R.
Honshu

Tok Is. (occupied by South Korea, claimed by Japan)
Noto Peninsula
Sado
Japanese Alps
Shinano R.

4 — Yellow Sea
Seoul
Han R.
SOUTH KOREA
Taejon
Taegu
Kwangju
Pusan
Korea Strait
Tsushima Is.
Oki Is.
Matsue
L. Biwa
JAPAN
Mt. Fuji
Nagoya
Tokyo
Kyoto
Kobe
Osaka
Yokohama
Hiroshima
Kitakyushu
Inland Sea
Shikoku
PACIFIC OCEAN

5 — Tsushima Strait
Cheju I.
Kyushu
Kochi
Kii Peninsula
Izu Islands

6 — East China Sea
Goto Is.
Kagoshima
Osumi Strait
Yaku-Shima
Tanega-Shima

7 — Ryukyu Islands
Okinawa
0 — 400 miles
0 — kilometers
Bonin Is. (Japan)

A Korean dancer in traditional dress

Did You Know?

● At 12,388 ft (3,776 m), Mount Fuji is Japan's tallest mountain. It is a volcano that last erupted in 1707.

● According to legend, Japan's islands were formed from the tears of a goddess.

● Of the world's 720,000 working robots, 410,000 can be found in Japan.

● Japan has the highest percentage of daily newspaper readers in any country: 86%.

● The people of Korea come from huge clans. Throughout Korea, there are only about a dozen common last names.

● Ch'usok, an important harvest festival in Korea, is also a time for families to gather to honor their ancestors.

● A demilitarized zone 4 mi (6.4 km) wide splits the Korean Peninsula at the 38th parallel, or line of latitude.

117

Southeast Asia

For Sale: Fruits and vegetables in one of Bangkok's floating markets

Southeast Asia is a tropical peninsula covered by thick forests, mighty rivers, fertile plains and tall mountains. For most of its residents, farming is a way of life. Rice is the region's most important crop. It is grown in flooded rice paddies on the plains and on stairlike green terraces on mountain slopes. In the region's cities, exotic sights and smells are everywhere. Bangkok, Thailand, is a teeming commercial center, a mixture of modern skyscrapers and bicycle taxis, ancient temples and brightly colored floating markets.

A busy street in Hanoi, Vietnam

For many older Americans, Vietnam brings to mind images of war. But the country is also a land of spectacular scenery. From the Red River Delta in the north to the Mekong Delta in the south, Vietnam is a patchwork of rushing rivers, sandy coastlines and brilliant-green paddy fields.

Vietnam, Cambodia and Laos have historic ties to France. Myanmar, previously called Burma, was once controlled by Britain. Of the countries in this region, only Thailand was never a European colony. In recent years, Southeast Asia has been plagued by wars and civil unrest. Today, these small countries are slowly rebuilding and reopening to tourists and foreign companies.

Did You Know?

● Most of Laos is covered by forest. The country's nickname is the Land of One Million Elephants.

● Myanmar is known for its rich red rubies, which are mined in the north of the country.

● The world's smallest mammal is the bumblebee bat, found in Thailand.

● Cambodia's Angkor Wat, built in the 12th century, is the world's largest religious structure.

Data Bank

CAMBODIA
AREA: 69,900 sq mi (181,040 sq km)
POPULATION: 13,363,421
CAPITAL: Phnom Penh
LANGUAGES: Khmer (official), French, English

LAOS
AREA: 91,429 sq mi (236,800 sq km)
POPULATION: 6,068,117
CAPITAL: Vientiane
LANGUAGES: Lao (official), French, English, ethnic languages

MYANMAR (BURMA)
AREA: 261,969 sq mi (678,500 sq km)
POPULATION: 42,720,196
CAPITAL: Rangoon
LANGUAGES: Burmese, minority languages

THAILAND
AREA: 198,455 sq mi (514,000 sq km)
POPULATION: 64,865,523
CAPITAL: Bangkok
LANGUAGES: Thai, English

VIETNAM
AREA: 127,243 sq mi (329,560 sq km)
POPULATION: 82,689,518
CAPITAL: Hanoi
LANGUAGES: Vietnamese (official), English, French, Chinese, Khmer, others

Angkor Wat

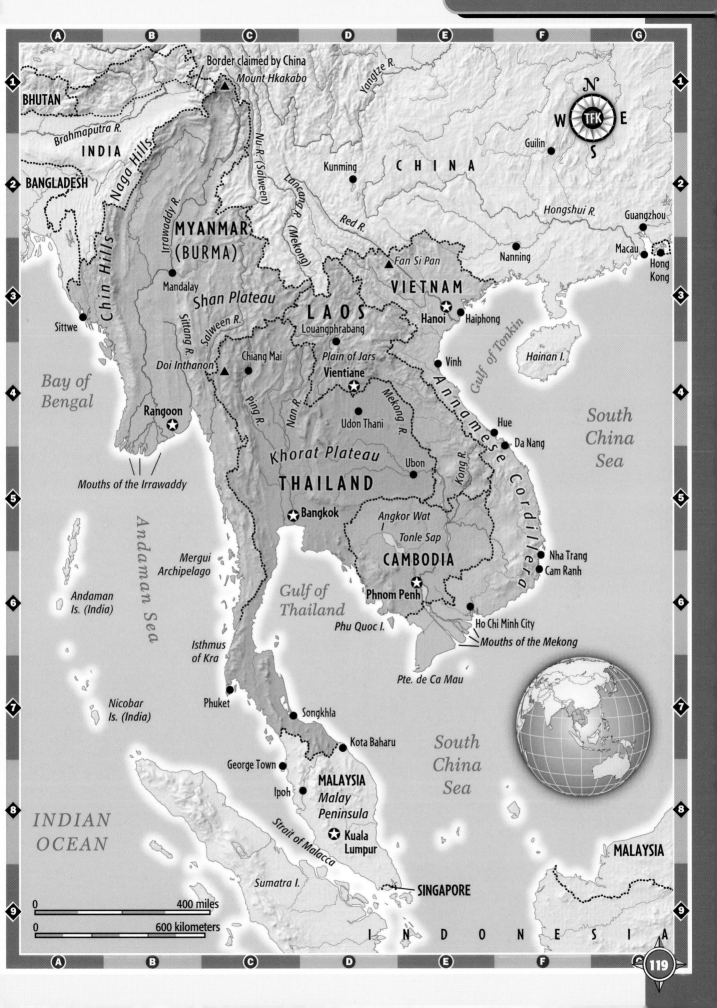

A B C D E F G

1

BHUTAN

Brahmaputra R.

INDIA

Border claimed by China
Mount Hkakabo

Yangtze R.

CHINA

N W S E
TFK

Guilin

2

BANGLADESH

Naga Hills

Nu-R. (Salween)

Irrawaddy R.

Kunming

Red R.

Hongshui R.

Guangzhou

Macau

**MYANMAR
(BURMA)**

Chin Hills

Shan Plateau

Lancang R. (Mekong)

Fan Si Pan

Nanning

**Hong
Kong**

3

Sittwe

Mandalay

Sittang R.

Salween R.

LAOS

Louangphrabang

VIETNAM

Hanoi *Haiphong*

Gulf of Tonkin

Hainan I.

*Bay of
Bengal*

Doi Inthanon

Chiang Mai

Plain of Jars

Vientiane

Vinh

4

Ping R.

Nan R.

Udon Thani

Mekong R.

Hue

Da Nang

*South
China
Sea*

Mouths of the Irrawaddy

Rangoon

Khorat Plateau

THAILAND

Ubon

Kong R.

5

Andaman Sea

*Mergui
Archipelago*

Bangkok

Angkor Wat

Tonle Sap

CAMBODIA

Annamese Cordillera

Nha Trang
Cam Ranh

6

*Andaman
Is. (India)*

*Gulf of
Thailand*

Phnom Penh

Phu Quoc I.

Ho Chi Minh City

Mouths of the Mekong

7

*Nicobar
Is. (India)*

*Isthmus
of Kra*

Phuket

Songkhla

Pte. de Ca Mau

*South
China
Sea*

8

Kota Baharu

George Town

MALAYSIA
*Malay
Peninsula*

Ipoh

**INDIAN
OCEAN**

MALAYSIA

Strait of Malacca

**Kuala
Lumpur**

9

0   400 miles

0   600 kilometers

Sumatra I.

SINGAPORE

I N D O N E S I A

A B C D E F G

TFK FACT FILE
Vietnam

Xin chao!

My name is Son, and I am 11 years old. I live in Hanoi. When I'm not at school, I am usually busy doing homework or helping my mother with chores. I have about two hours of homework every night! Welcome to Vietnam!

The Vietnamese Flag

North Vietnam's flag was adopted throughout the land in 1975.

The **yellow star** represents the communist government of Vietnam.

The **five points of the star** stand for farmers, workers, intellectuals, youths and soldiers.

The **red background** is a symbol of communism.

Rainfall Measures

Every summer, monsoon winds bring heavy rain to Vietnam. Here is the average monthly rainfall for Danang, Vietnam.

35 in (89 cm)
30 (76.2)
25 (63.5)
20 (50.8)
15 (38.1)
10 (25.4)
5 (12.7)
0

Jan. Feb. Mar. April May June July Aug. Sep. Oct. Nov. Dec.

The Economy

AGRICULTURE: Rice, sugarcane, cassava

MAJOR INDUSTRIES: Agriculture, forestry, fishing, mining, food processing, steel

NATURAL RESOURCES: Coal, tin, gold, iron ore, lead, zinc, oil

MAJOR EXPORTS: Rice, coffee, rubber, fish, clothing, textiles

MAJOR IMPORTS: Petroleum products, steel, cotton, chemicals

TRADING PARTNERS: China, Japan, Singapore, South Korea

A Vietnamese farmer plows a rice paddy.

Top 5 Rice Exporters

Rice is a vital part of Vietnam's culture, economy and landscape. Only Thailand and India produce more rice than Vietnam.

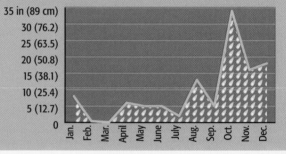

6.36 million metric tons
4.80
3.80
3.79
3.11

Thailand India Vietnam China U.S.

Major Events in Vietnam's History

939 A.D. After more than 1,000 years in power, China withdraws from what is now northern Vietnam. The region becomes an independent kingdom.

1802 Prince Nguyen Anh unites the northern, central and southern regions and calls the country Vietnam.

1883 France takes control of Vietnam.

1940 Japan takes over Vietnam during World War II after its ally Germany defeats the French.

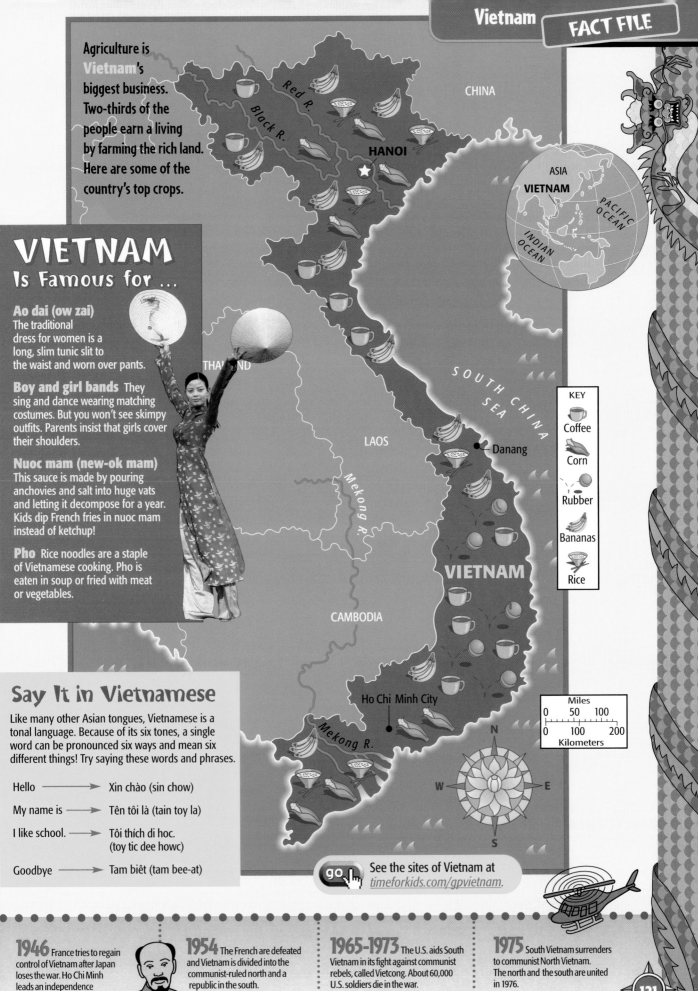

Agriculture is **Vietnam's** biggest business. Two-thirds of the people earn a living by farming the rich land. Here are some of the country's top crops.

VIETNAM Is Famous for ...

Ao dai (ow zai) The traditional dress for women is a long, slim tunic slit to the waist and worn over pants.

Boy and girl bands They sing and dance wearing matching costumes. But you won't see skimpy outfits. Parents insist that girls cover their shoulders.

Nuoc mam (new-ok mam) This sauce is made by pouring anchovies and salt into huge vats and letting it decompose for a year. Kids dip French fries in nuoc mam instead of ketchup!

Pho Rice noodles are a staple of Vietnamese cooking. Pho is eaten in soup or fried with meat or vegetables.

Say It in Vietnamese

Like many other Asian tongues, Vietnamese is a tonal language. Because of its six tones, a single word can be pronounced six ways and mean six different things! Try saying these words and phrases.

Hello ⟶ Xin chào (sin chow)

My name is ⟶ Tên tôi là (tain toy la)

I like school. ⟶ Tôi thích di hoc. (toy tic dee howc)

Goodbye ⟶ Tam biêt (tam bee-at)

CHINA

Red R.

Black R.

HANOI

ASIA

VIETNAM

PACIFIC OCEAN

INDIAN OCEAN

THAILAND

LAOS

Mekong R.

SOUTH CHINA SEA

Danang

KEY

Coffee

Corn

Rubber

Bananas

Rice

VIETNAM

CAMBODIA

Ho Chi Minh City

Mekong R.

Miles
0   50   100

0   100   200
Kilometers

N
W   E
S

go See the sites of Vietnam at *timeforkids.com/gpvietnam*.

1946 France tries to regain control of Vietnam after Japan loses the war. Ho Chi Minh leads an independence movement against the French.

1954 The French are defeated and Vietnam is divided into the communist-ruled north and a republic in the south.

1965-1973 The U.S. aids South Vietnam in its fight against communist rebels, called Vietcong. About 60,000 U.S. soldiers die in the war.

1975 South Vietnam surrenders to communist North Vietnam. The north and the south are united in 1976.

Maritime Southeast Asia

Island Nation: Singapore's stunning skyline

The sea is a major part of this region's geography. Indonesia is the world's largest archipelago, or group of islands. It is made up of about 17,000 islands, with people living on 6,000 of them. The Philippines is made up of more than 7,000 islands. Since the end of World War II, many newly independent nations have emerged in the region. Brunei, Malaysia and Singapore used to be part of the British Empire. The Philippines was ruled by Spain until 1898 when it became a U.S. possession. The nation gained its independence in 1946. Indonesia was once part of the Netherlands. East Timor did not come into existence until 2002.

Much of the region is rain forest, and wildlife is abundant. Malaysia is divided into two areas, one on the Malay Peninsula and the other on the island of Borneo, where elephants, tigers, orangutans and rare Sumatran rhinoceroses can be found. The small nation of Brunei is also located on Borneo. Brunei is made up of two separate areas surrounded by Malaysia and the South China Sea.

Off the tip of the Malay Peninsula lies Singapore. The modern island nation, which gained independence from Malaysia in 1965, boasts one of Asia's best public-transportation systems.

Data Bank

BRUNEI
AREA: 2,228 sq mi (5,770 sq km)
POPULATION: 365,251
CAPITAL: Bandar Seri Begawan
LANGUAGES: Malay (official), English, Chinese

EAST TIMOR
AREA: 5,814 sq mi (15,007 sq km)
POPULATION: 1,019,252
CAPITAL: Dili
LANGUAGES: Tetum, Portuguese (both official), Indonesian, English

INDONESIA
AREA: 741,096 sq mi (1,919,440 sq km)
POPULATION: 238,452,952
CAPITAL: Jakarta
LANGUAGES: Bahasa Indonesian, English, Dutch, local dialects

MALAYSIA
AREA: 127,316 sq mi (329,750 sq km)
POPULATION: 23,522,482
CAPITAL: Kuala Lumpur
LANGUAGES: Bahasa Melayu (official), English, Chinese, Tamil, Telugu, Malayalam

PHILIPPINES
AREA: 115,830 sq mi (300,000 sq km)
POPULATION: 86,241,697
CAPITAL: Manila
LANGUAGES: Filipino, English (both official), Tagalog, other native languages

SINGAPORE
AREA: 267 sq mi (692 sq km)
POPULATION: 4,767,974
CAPITAL: Singapore
LANGUAGES: Malay, Chinese, Tamil, English (all official)

A dancer on the Indonesian island of Bali

THAIL
Bangko
CA
Phno
Gulf of
Thailan

Nicobar Is. (India)
Phuket
George Town
Medan
Mt
Ipoh
Mt. Leuser
Kuala Lumpur
Strait of Malacca
Nias I.
Sumatr
Padang
Mt. Kerin
Mentawai Is.
Bariso
Krakatoa (volc
Sunda

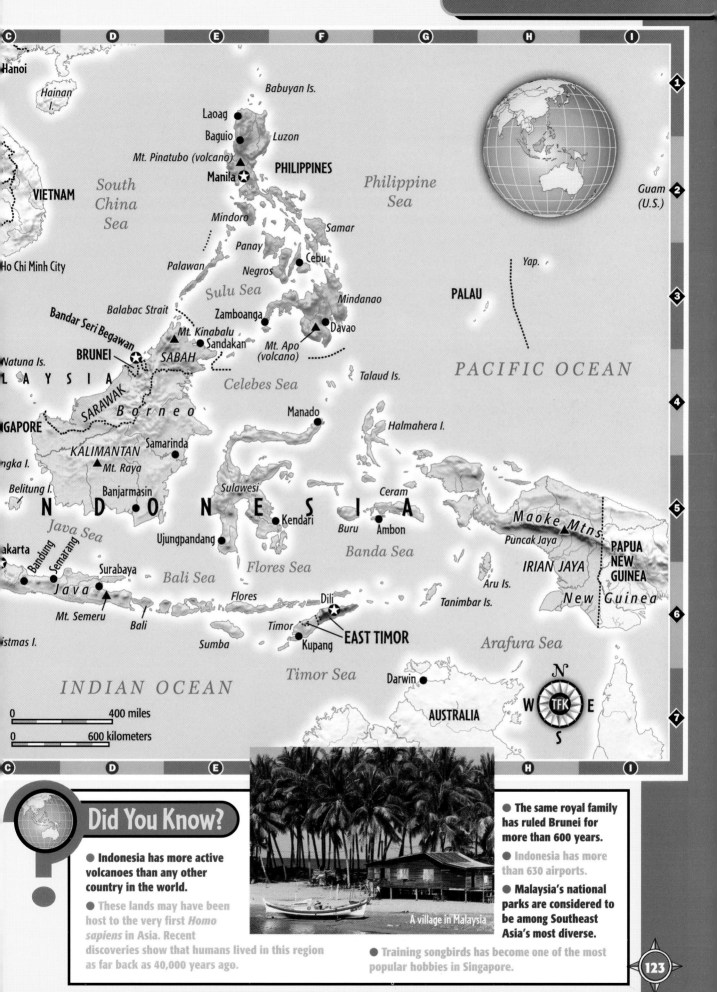

Hanoi

Hainan I.

VIETNAM

South China Sea

Ho Chi Minh City

Babuyan Is.

Laoag

Baguio   Luzon

Mt. Pinatubo (volcano)

Manila   **PHILIPPINES**

Philippine Sea

Mindoro

Panay   Samar

Palawan   Negros   Cebu

Sulu Sea

Balabac Strait   Zamboanga   Mindanao

Bandar Seri Begawan   Mt. Kinabalu   Davao

BRUNEI   **SABAH**   Sandakan   Mt. Apo (volcano)

Natuna Is.

~~LAYSIA~~   **SARAWAK**   *Borneo*

Celebes Sea

Talaud Is.

PALAU

Yap.

PACIFIC OCEAN

~~NGAPORE~~

~~ngka I.~~   **KALIMANTAN**   Samarinda

Mt. Raya

Manado   *Halmahera I.*

Belitung I.   Banjarmasin

~~N~~   ~~D~~   O   N   E   S   I   A

Sulawesi   *Ceram*

Buru   Ambon

M a o k e Mtns

Puncak Jaya

IRIAN JAYA   **PAPUA NEW GUINEA**

Java Sea   Kendari

~~akarta~~   Bandung   Semarang   Surabaya   Ujungpandang

Bali Sea   *Flores Sea*   *Banda Sea*

Aru Is.

New Guinea

J a v a

Mt. Semeru   Bali

Flores   Dili

Timor   **EAST TIMOR**   Tanimbar Is.

~~istmas I.~~   Sumba   Kupang   *Arafura Sea*

Timor Sea   Darwin

INDIAN OCEAN

AUSTRALIA

N W E S TFK

| 0 | 400 miles |
| 0 | 600 kilometers |

Did You Know?

- **Indonesia has more active volcanoes than any other country in the world.**

- These lands may have been host to the very first *Homo sapiens* in Asia. Recent discoveries show that humans lived in this region as far back as 40,000 years ago.

A village in Malaysia

- **The same royal family has ruled Brunei for more than 600 years.**

- Indonesia has more than 630 airports.

- **Malaysia's national parks are considered to be among Southeast Asia's most diverse.**

- Training songbirds has become one of the most popular hobbies in Singapore.

Africa

Mountain gorillas in Rwanda

The world's second-largest continent, Africa, is surrounded by water. To the west of Africa lies the Atlantic Ocean; to the east is the Indian Ocean; to the north is the Mediterranean Sea; and to the northeast is the Red Sea. Many islands and island chains, including Madagascar and the Seychelle Islands, are considered part of the African continent.

The Sahara is the biggest desert in the world.

The central part of Africa is one big, flat plain. There, lying across the warm equator, are Africa's famous rain forests and savannas, or grasslands. Far to the continent's north and south are mountain ranges, deserts and coastal areas. The vast Sahara Desert in North Africa is a dividing line that separates North Africa from the area known as sub-Saharan Africa.

Africa is known for its wide range of amazing wildlife. Though the continent has suffered from environmental damage, it is still home to many creatures. There are camels in the north, penguins in the south, gorillas in the forests and lions and giraffes in the savannas. The island of Madagascar, which separated from the African mainland millions of years ago, is home to many unique species of mammals and amphibians. There are fewer than a billion people in Africa, but they speak more than 2,000 different languages and live in 53 different nations. The African population is growing quickly, and the continent is home to some of the biggest cities in the world. Most people live in rural areas.

Continent Facts

AREA: 11.7 million sq mi (30.3 million sq km)

NUMBER OF COUNTRIES:
53 countries–Algeria, Angola, Benin, Botswana, Burkina Faso, Burundi, Cameroon, Cape Verde, Central African Republic, Chad, Comoros, Congo (Democratic Republic of the), Congo (Republic of the), Côte d'Ivoire, Djibouti, Egypt, Equatorial Guinea, Eritrea, Ethiopia, Gabon, Gambia, Ghana, Guinea, Guinea-Bissau, Kenya, Lesotho, Liberia, Libya, Madagascar, Malawi, Mali, Mauritania, Mauritius, Morocco, Mozambique, Namibia, Niger, Nigeria, Rwanda, São Tomé and Príncipe, Senegal, Seychelles, Sierra Leone, Somalia, South Africa, Sudan, Swaziland, Tanzania, Togo, Tunisia, Uganda, Zambia, Zimbabwe

LONGEST RIVER: The Nile, 4,241 mi (6,825 km)

LONGEST MOUNTAIN RANGE: Atlas Mountain Range in North Africa, about 400 mi (644 km)

HIGHEST PEAK: Mount Kilimanjaro, in Tanzania, 19,340 ft (5,895 m)

LARGEST LAKE: Victoria, 26,828 sq mi (69,485 sq km)

DEEPEST LAKE: Tanganyika, the second-deepest lake in the world, has a maximum

Wow Zone!

● Victoria Falls, on the Zambezi River in Zimbabwe, is 355 ft (108 m) high and 5,500 ft (1,676 m) wide. It is twice as big as Niagara Falls.

● Lake Nyasa (also known as Lake Malawi), in east-central Africa, has more fish species in it than any other lake in the world.

● African elephants are the largest land animals in the world.

● The Goliath beetle, found in equatorial Africa, is the world's largest beetle. It can grow to be 5 in (13 cm) long.

Mount Kilimanjaro looms over the savanna.

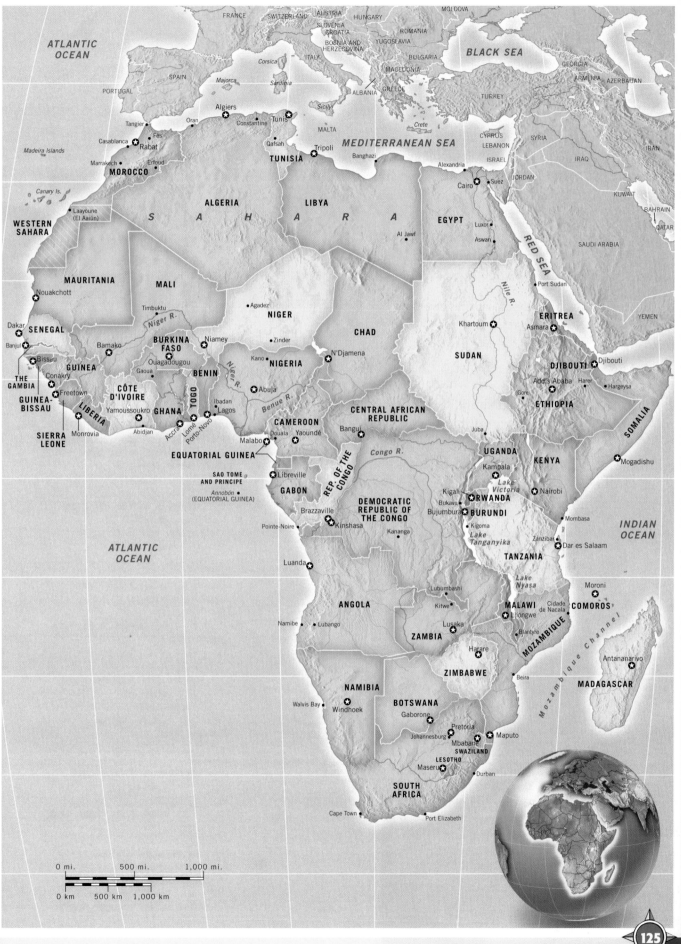

ATLANTIC OCEAN

FRANCE
SWITZERLAND AUSTRIA HUNGARY
SLOVENIA MOLDOVA
CROATIA ROMANIA
BOSNIA AND YUGOSLAVIA
HERZEGOVINA BULGARIA BLACK SEA
ITALY MACEDONIA GEORGIA
Corsica ALBANIA GREECE TURKEY ARMENIA AZERBAIJAN
SPAIN Majorca Sardinia
Sicily MALTA IRAN
Crete CYPRUS SYRIA IRAQ
PORTUGAL Algiers MEDITERRANEAN SEA LEBANON
Tangier Oran Tunis Banghazi ISRAEL JORDAN KUWAIT
Casablanca Fes TUNISIA Tripoli Alexandria BAHRAIN
Madeira Islands Rabat Qafsah Cairo Suez QATAR
Marrakech Erfoud SAUDI ARABIA
MOROCCO Luxor
Canary Is. ALGERIA LIBYA EGYPT Aswan
Laayoune S A H A R A
(El Aaiún) Al Jawf Port Sudan YEMEN
WESTERN Nile R.
SAHARA RED SEA
MAURITANIA MALI Agadez Khartoum ERITREA
Nouakchott Timbuktu Asmara DJIBOUTI Djibouti
NIGER CHAD Hargeysa
Dakar Niger R. Niamey SUDAN Addis Ababa Harer
SENEGAL Bamako BURKINA Zinder N'Djamena Gore
Banjul FASO ETHIOPIA
Bissau GUINEA Ouagadougou Kano NIGERIA Juba SOMALIA
THE Conakry Gaoua BENIN Abuja CENTRAL AFRICAN
GAMBIA CÔTE Ibadan Benue R. REPUBLIC UGANDA Mogadishu
GUINEA- Freetown D'IVOIRE TOGO Lagos Bangui Kampala KENYA
BISSAU Yamoussoukro GHANA Lomé CAMEROON Lake
SIERRA LIBERIA Accra Porto-Novo Douala Yaoundé Congo R. Kigali Victoria Nairobi
LEONE Monrovia Abidjan Malabo REP. OF THE RWANDA
EQUATORIAL GUINEA CONGO Bukavu Mombasa
SAO TOME Bujumbura BURUNDI
AND PRINCIPE Libreville DEMOCRATIC Kigoma
Annobón GABON REPUBLIC Lake INDIAN
(EQUATORIAL GUINEA) OF THE Tanganyika Zanzibar OCEAN
Brazzaville CONGO Dar es Salaam
Pointe-Noire Kinshasa TANZANIA
Kananga
Luanda
Lake
Nyasa Moroni
Lubumbashi
ANGOLA Kitwe MALAWI Cidade COMOROS
Lilongwe de Nacala
Namibe Lubango Lusaka Blantyre
ZAMBIA Antananarivo
ATLANTIC Harare MOZAMBIQUE
OCEAN
ZIMBABWE Beira MADAGASCAR
Walvis Bay NAMIBIA
Windhoek BOTSWANA Mozambique Channel
Gaborone
Pretoria
Johannesburg Maputo
Mbabane
SWAZILAND
Maseru
LESOTHO Durban
SOUTH
AFRICA
Cape Town
Port Elizabeth

0 mi.   500 mi.   1,000 mi.

0 km   500 km   1,000 km

Northeastern Africa

A sailboat on the White Nile in Sudan

Khartoum, the capital of Sudan, stands at the crossroads of the Blue Nile and the White Nile. The two rivers converge to form the Nile, the world's longest river. The life-giving Nile flows through Sudan and Egypt. The river's waters are precious to the area's people, who live and work near its banks. Nearly 95% of Egypt is desert.

Almost 5,000 years ago, Egypt had already established one of the world's most advanced civilizations. Ancient Egyptians mastered a new writing system, unique art forms and grand architecture. In neighboring Nubia, which today is part of Sudan, another great civilization flourished. There, archaeologists have found beautiful ceramic figurines and bowls that date from at least 8,000 B.C. That's 3,000 years older than any known Egyptian objects!

To the east of Sudan lie Eritrea and Ethiopia, which is sub-Saharan Africa's oldest country. In 1993, Ethiopia recognized Eritrea's independence. Until recently, both countries were involved in costly and destructive border clashes.

Harsh weather conditions and drought play important roles in the lives of the people of the region. Djibouti, which lies at the edge of the Red Sea, is mostly desert. Much of Somalia receives less than one quart (one liter) of rain a year.

A woman slices enset— also called false banana— in Ethiopia.

Data Bank

DJIBOUTI
AREA: 8,800 sq mi (23,000 sq km)
POPULATION: 466,900
CAPITAL: Djibouti
LANGUAGES: French, Arabic (both official), Somali, Afar

EGYPT
AREA: 386,660 sq mi (1,001,450 sq km)
POPULATION: 76,117,421
CAPITAL: Cairo
LANGUAGE: Arabic (official)

ERITREA
AREA: 46,842 sq mi (121,320 sq km)
POPULATION: 4,447,307
CAPITAL: Asmara
LANGUAGES: Afar, Amharic, Arabic, Tigre, Kunama, others

ETHIOPIA
AREA: 485,184 sq mi (1,256,634 sq km)
POPULATION: 67,851,281
CAPITAL: Addis Ababa
LANGUAGES: Amharic, Tigrinya, Oromigna, others

SOMALIA
AREA: 246,199 sq mi (637,659 sq km)
POPULATION: 8,304,601
CAPITAL: Mogadishu
LANGUAGES: Somali, Arabic, English, Italian

SUDAN
AREA: 967,493 sq mi (2,505,822 sq km)
POPULATION: 39,148,162
CAPITAL: Khartoum
LANGUAGES: Arabic, Nubian, Nilotic, Nilo-Hamitic, Sudanic languages, English

Mediterranean Sea

Benghazi

A B C D E F G

ISRAEL
Suez Canal
Alexandria
Cairo
Suez
Sinai
Peninsula
JORDAN
Baghdad
IRAQ
IRAN
KUWAIT

Western
Desert
El Faiyum
Gulf
of Suez

E G Y P T

LIBYA
Nile R.

Libyan Desert
Luxor

Kufra
Oasis
Aswan
Lake Nasser
Uweinat Mtn.

Nubian Desert
Red Sea

Mecca
SAUDI ARABIA

BAHRAIN
Riyadh
Persian Gulf
Abu Dhabi
Doha
QATAR
U.A.E.

OMAN

S a h a r a
Nile R.

CHAD
Omdurman
Albara R.
Khartoum
Wad
Medani
ERITREA
Asmara

Port Sudan

S U D A N
Mount Marra
El Obeid
Kosti
Blue Nile R.
Ras Dashan
Gondar

Lake Tana
DJIBOUTI
Djibouti
Berbera
YEMEN
Sanaa
Bab el
Mandeb Strait
Gulf of Aden
Raas
Caseyr
Socotra
(Yemen)

Marra Mtns.
White Nile R.
Choke Mtns.
Dire Dawa
Ahmar Mtns.
Karkar
Mtns.

**CENTRAL
AFRICAN
REPUBLIC**
Lol R.
Malakal
Sudd
Wau
Badigeru
Swamp
Juba
Addis Ababa
Harar
E T H I O P I A
Goba
Shebele R.
Eyl

Ethiopian
Highlands
Great Rift Valley
S O M A L I A
**INDIAN
OCEAN**

**DEMOCRATIC
REPUBLIC OF
THE CONGO**
Congo R.
UGANDA
Lake Turkana
KENYA
Mogadishu

Equator
Kampala
Lake
Victoria
Mount Kenya
Nairobi
Kismaayo

0   400 miles
0   600 kilometers

127

Did You Know?

● Egypt's Suez Canal, which links the
Mediterranean Sea with the Red Sea, was
opened in 1869.

● The Great Sphinx has a human
head and a lion's body. It is 240 ft
(73 m) long and 65 ft (20 m) high.
For centuries, the monument
was buried under sand.

● Ethiopia's royal family claims to be descended
from the Queen of Sheba and King Solomon.

● Sudan, the largest country
on the continent, became
independent on December
15, 1955. Britain and Egypt
had governed Sudan
jointly for almost
60 years.

● Sudan has more
pyramids than Egypt.

Egypt

Ahlan wa sahlan!

My name is Shoruk, and I am 9 years old. I live in Cairo with my mom, dad and older brother. I'm in fourth grade, and my favorite subject is math. After school, I have a late lunch at home. Egyptian food is delicious! Let me show you my country.

The Egyptian Flag

This flag was first used in 1984. Its three bands of color stand for Arab unity.

Red represents Egypt's struggle for independence from Britain.

White stands for the 1952 Revolution, which ended the monarchy without bloodshed.

Black symbolizes the end of unjust rule.

The **national emblem,** a shield and a golden eagle above the official name of Egypt in Arabic script, is at the center.

Egypt's Population

The population is growing quickly. A large part of it is under age 15. Within 30 years, the number of Egyptians is expected to nearly double.

- 15-24 **21%**
- 25-39 **19%**
- 40-59 **17%**
- 60+ **7%**
- 0-14 years old **36%**

The Economy

AGRICULTURE: Cotton, rice, corn, wheat, beans

MAJOR INDUSTRIES: Textiles, food processing, tourism, petroleum, chemicals

MAJOR EXPORTS: Oil and petroleum products, raw cotton and cotton yarn, textiles

MAJOR IMPORTS: Machinery and equipment, food, fertilizers, wood products, household goods

TRADING PARTNERS: U.S., Germany, Italy

Girls pick cotton near the Nile.

Top 5 Longest Rivers in the World

A historian once called Egypt the "gift of the River Nile." The river is the world's longest. Here are the five longest river systems in the world and their main locations.

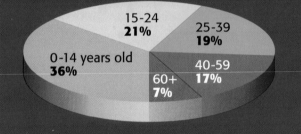

River	Length
Nile, Egypt	**4,132 miles** (6,650 km)
Amazon, Brazil	**4,000 miles** (6,437 km)
Chang (Yangtze), China	**3,915 miles** (6,301 km)
Mississippi, United States	**3,710 miles** (5,971 km)
Yenisey, Russia	**3,440 miles** (5,536 km)

0   1,000   2,000   3,000   4,000   5,000
Length in Miles

Major Events in Egypt's History

3100 B.C.-332 B.C. Ancient Egypt is established when a king named Narmer unifies the Upper and Lower Kingdoms. Egyptians develop hieroglyphic writing. The pyramids and the Sphinxes are built.

332 B.C. Alexander the Great, of Macedonia, conquers Egypt.

30 B.C. Queen Cleopatra dies after romances with Romans Julius Caesar and Mark Antony. Rome takes control of Egypt.

1869 The Suez Canal opens, linking the Mediterranean Sea with the Red Sea.

MEDITERRANEAN SEA

ISRAEL

Alexandria
Giza
CAIRO
Suez Canal
JORDAN

Qattara Depression

Sinai Peninsula

Gulf of Suez

Gulf of Aqaba

SAUDI ARABIA

EGYPT

Nile River

Eastern Desert (Arabian Desert)

RED SEA

The Great Sphinx, pyramids and many of Egypt's temples were built near the banks of the Nile River.

Valley of the Kings
62 pharaohs buried at this site

Luxor

Abu Simbel

Aswan High Dam

Tropic of Cancer

Lake Nasser

Treaty boundary

SUDAN

EUROPE   ASIA

EGYPT

AFRICA   INDIAN OCEAN

Miles
0   50   100
0   50   100
Kilometers

KEY
- Pyramid
- Tomb
- Temple
- Obelisk
- Sphinx

EGYPT Is Famous for ...

History Tutankhamen (too-tong-*kah*-men) ruled Egypt more than 3,300 years ago. His tomb was discovered in 1922. Among its treasures are a gold coffin and a mask.

Music Modern Egyptian music is popular, but classical and folk music is a passion. The music can be heard throughout the country.

Food Most gatherings revolve around food. The main staple is foul (fool), fava beans that are eaten in pita bread with oil, spices and salad. Another dish is koshari (kuh-*shah*-ree), a mix of noodles, rice, black lentils, onions and tomato sauce.

Desert safaris Locals and foreign visitors alike enjoy camping in Egypt's vast deserts. Popular safari spots include the Siwa Oasis near Libya, the Valley of Rayan, which has waterfalls, and the White Desert.

Say It in Arabic

Early Egyptians drew pictures, or hieroglyphs, to represent words. Today, Egyptians use the Arabic alphabet. Try saying these phrases!

Hello	Ahlan wa sahlan (*ah*-lan wa *sah*-lan)
Goodbye	Ma as salama (ma as *sa*-la-mah)
Yes	Aywa (*ay*-wah)
No	La (la-uh)
Where	Fein (feehn)
Thank you	Shukran (*shook*-run)
I, me	Ana (*a*-nah)
My name is	Ismi (*iss*-me)

1914-1922 Britain controls Egypt until a monarchy is established and Fuad I is named king.

1952 The Egyptian army seizes power. Later, Gamal Abdel Nasser becomes president.

1978 Egyptian President Anwar Sadat and Israeli Prime Minister Menachem Begin sign the Camp David Peace Accords.

1981 Sadat is assassinated. Hosni Mubarak succeeds him as president.

 Discover more of Egypt and its history at *timeforkids.com/gpegypt*.

Northwestern Africa

Roman Ruins: The Leptis Magna theater, in Libya

High on the northwest shoulder of Africa sit the countries of Morocco, Algeria, Tunisia and Libya and the territory of Western Sahara. Since ancient times, conquerors—such as Vandals, Romans, Ottoman Turks and the French—have been drawn to the sparkling coast along the southern Mediterranean Sea. In modern times, the area retains Islamic and French influences.

The geography of Northwestern Africa is varied and dramatic. Along the fertile coast, crops of wheat, olives, figs and citrus fruits are grown, and the palm-fringed beaches of Morocco and Tunisia attract many tourists. Just south is a ribbon of mountains, called the Atlas, that stretches 1,200 mi (1,931 km) from Morocco across Algeria to Tunisia. And below this ridge is the great desert of the Sahara.

Tunisia, the small finger of land between Algeria and Libya, freed itself from French rule in 1956. Ruins of two great civilizations, the Phoenician and the Roman, can be viewed in Carthage, on the Tunisian coast. Other popular destinations for visitors to this region are the pink-walled city of Marrakech, in Morocco, and the Leptis Magna, in Libya, the site of impressive Roman ruins. The territory of Western Sahara, once held by Spain but now overseen by Morocco, has been the object of many conflicts.

Data Bank

ALGERIA
AREA: 919,586 sq mi (2,381,740 sq km)
POPULATION: 33,357,089
CAPITAL: Algiers
LANGUAGES: Arabic (official), French, Berber dialects

LIBYA
AREA: 679,358 sq mi (1,759,540 sq km)
POPULATION: 5,631,585
CAPITAL: Tripoli
LANGUAGES: Arabic, Italian, English

MOROCCO
AREA: 172,413 sq mi (446,550 sq km)
POPULATION: 32,209,101
CAPITAL: Rabat
LANGUAGES: Arabic (official), Berber dialects, French

TUNISIA
AREA: 63,170 sq mi (163,610 sq km)
POPULATION: 10,032,050
CAPITAL: Tunis
LANGUAGES: Arabic (official), French

Madeira Is. (Portugal)

ATLANTIC OCEAN

Canary Is. (Spain)
Santa Cruz de Tenerif
Tarf

el Aaiun

Sma

WESTERN SAHARA (occupied by Morocco)

Dakhla

Nouakchott

MAURITA

Senegal R.

Moroccan Market: Vendors display their wares in Marrakech.

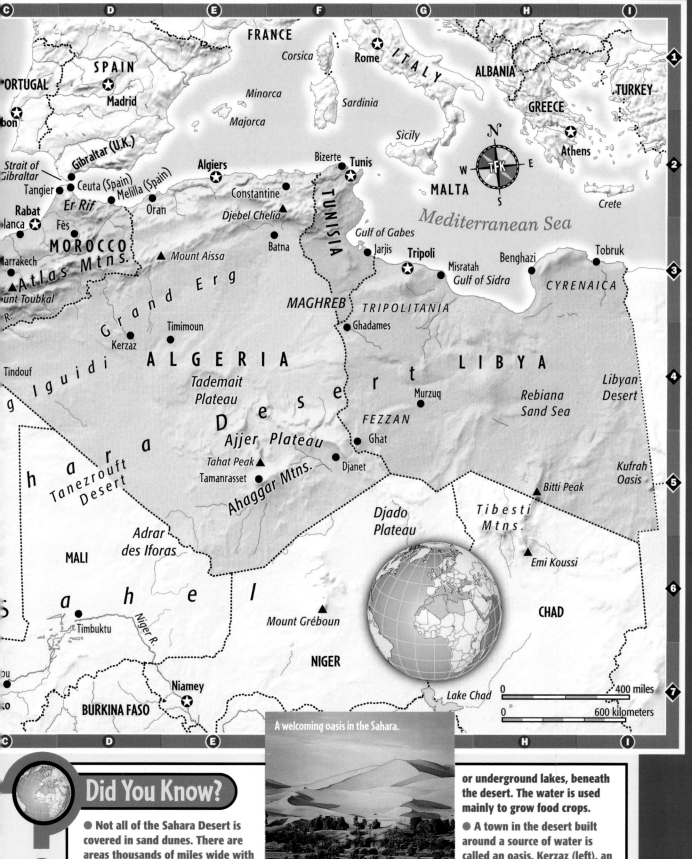

A welcoming oasis in the Sahara.

Did You Know?

● Not all of the Sahara Desert is covered in sand dunes. There are areas thousands of miles wide with nothing but rocks and pebbles.

● The deserts of Algeria and Libya sprout oil rigs and natural-gas pipelines that enrich their economies. With the Great Man-Made River project, begun in 1984, Libya tapped into aquifers, or underground lakes, beneath the desert. The water is used mainly to grow food crops.

● A town in the desert built around a source of water is called an oasis. Kerzaz (left), an oasis in the Algerian Sahara, has outdoor walkways with roofs for shade. It is surrounded by sand dunes up to 160 ft (50 m) high.

● A hot, dusty, unpleasant wind that blows from the Libyan desert toward Italy is called a sirocco.

Western Africa

Bustling Bridge: Commuters and traders in Lagos, Nigeria

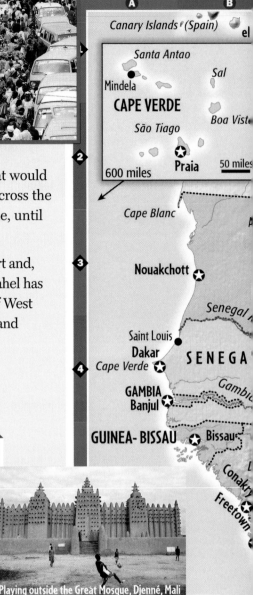

The western edge of Africa looks like a puzzle piece that would fit snugly against the eastern side of South America, across the Atlantic. And in fact, the two continents used to be one, until they broke up and drifted apart about 200 million years ago.

West Africa includes the southern stretch of the Sahara Desert and, just south of it, a vast swath of grasslands called the Sahel. The Sahel has been overfarmed and plagued by drought. The coastal regions of West Africa—from Senegal to the Niger River delta—have rain forests and crops of coffee, cotton, rubber and cacao.

Canary Islands (Spain)

Santa Antao

CAPE VERDE

Mindela

Sal

Boa Vist

São Tiago

Praia

600 miles   50 miles

Cape Blanc

Nouakchott

Senegal

Saint Louis

Dakar

SENEGA

Cape Verde

GAMBIA
Banjul

Gambi

GUINEA-BISSAU   Bissau

Conakr

Freetow

Data Bank

BENIN
AREA: 43,483 sq mi (112,620 sq km)
POPULATION: 7,250,033
CAPITAL: Porto-Novo
LANGUAGES: French (official), African languages

BURKINA FASO
AREA: 105,870 sq mi (274,200 sq km)
POPULATION: 13,574,820
CAPITAL: Ouagadougou
LANGUAGES: French (official), African languages

CAPE VERDE
AREA: 1,557 sq mi (4,033 sq km)
POPULATION: 415,294
CAPITAL: Praia
LANGUAGES: Portuguese, Crioulo

CÔTE D'IVOIRE
AREA: 124,502 sq mi (322,460 sq km)
POPULATION: 17,327,724
CAPITAL: Yamoussoukro
LANGUAGES: French (official), African languages

GAMBIA
AREA: 4,363 sq mi (11,300 sq km)
POPULATION: 1,546,848
CAPITAL: Banjul
LANGUAGES: English (official), native languages

GHANA
AREA: 92,456 sq mi (239,460 sq km)
POPULATION: 20,757,032
CAPITAL: Accra
LANGUAGES: English (official), African languages

GUINEA
AREA: 94,925 sq mi (245,857 sq km)
POPULATION: 9,246,462
CAPITAL: Conakry
LANGUAGES: French (official), native languages

GUINEA-BISSAU
AREA: 13,946 sq mi (36,120 sq km)
POPULATION: 1,388,363
CAPITAL: Bissau
LANGUAGES: Portuguese (official), Crioulo, African languages

LIBERIA
AREA: 43,000 sq mi (111,370 sq km)
POPULATION: 3,390,635
CAPITAL: Monrovia
LANGUAGES: English (official,) tribal dialects

MALI
AREA: 478,764 sq mi (1,240,000 sq km)
POPULATION: 11,956,788
CAPITAL: Bamako
LANGUAGES: French (official), Bambara

MAURITANIA
AREA: 397,953 sq mi (1,030,700 sq km)
POPULATION: 2,998,563
CAPITAL: Nouakchott
LANGUAGES: Hassaniya Arabic, Wolof (both official), Pulaar, Soninke, French

NIGER
AREA: 489,189 sq mi (1,267,000 sq km)
POPULATION: 11,360,538
CAPITAL: Niamey
LANGUAGES: French (official), Hausa, Djerma

Playing outside the Great Mosque, Djenné, Mali

NIGERIA
AREA: 356,700 sq mi (923,770 sq km)
POPULATION: 137,253,133
CAPITAL: Abuja
LANGUAGES: English (official), Hausa, Yoruba, Igbo, others

SENEGAL
AREA: 75,749 sq mi (196,190 sq km)
POPULATION: 10,852,147
CAPITAL: Dakar
LANGUAGES: French (official), Wolof, Pulaar

SIERRA LEONE
AREA: 27,699 sq mi (71,740 sq km)
POPULATION: 5,883,889
CAPITAL: Freetown
LANGUAGES: English (official), Mende, Temne, Krio

TOGO
AREA: 21,925 sq mi (56,785 sq km)
POPULATION: 5,556,812
CAPITAL: Lomé
LANGUAGES: French (official), Éwé, Mina, Kabyé, Dagomba

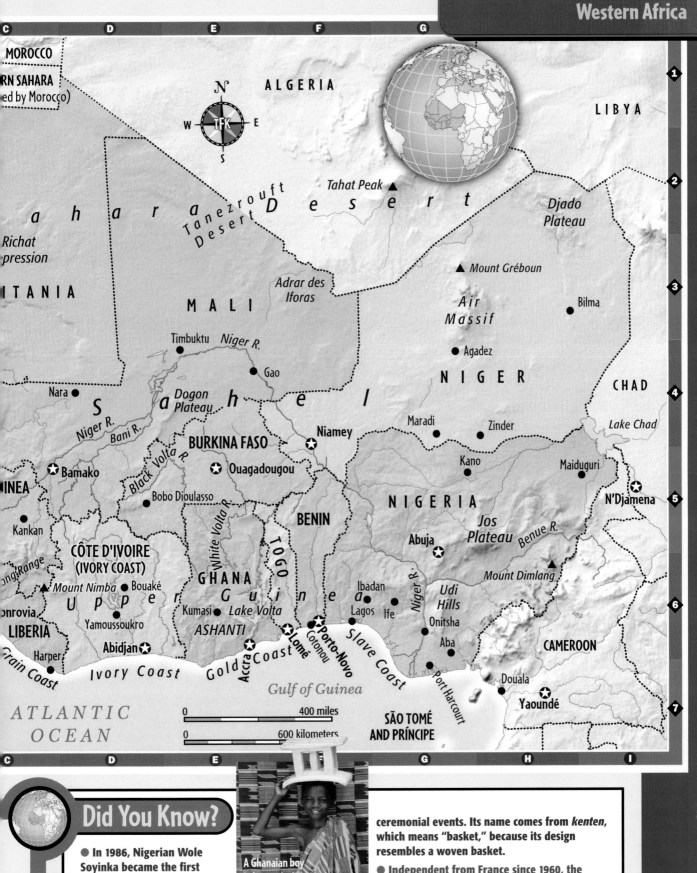

MOROCCO

RN SAHARA
ed by Morocco)

ALGERIA

LIBYA

Tanezrouft
Desert

Tahat Peak ▲

Djado
Plateau

a h a r a

Richat
pression

▲ Mount Gréboun

Air
Massif

Bilma

ITANIA

MALI

Adrar des
Iforas

Timbuktu   Niger R.

Gao

Dogon
Plateau

S   a   h   e   l

NIGER

CHAD

Nara ●

Niger R.

Agadez

Bani R.

BURKINA FASO

Niamey ⊛

Maradi ●

Zinder ●

Lake Chad

INEA

Bamako ⊛

Ouagadougou ⊛

Kano ●

Maiduguri ●

Kankan ●

Bobo Dioulasso ●

Black Volta R.

NIGERIA

N'Djamena ⊛

BENIN

Jos
Plateau

CÔTE D'IVOIRE
(IVORY COAST)

White Volta R.

GHANA

Abuja ⊛

Benue R.

Mount Dimlang ▲

▲ Mount Nimba   Bouaké ●

ongi Range

U p p e r

G u i n e a

Ibadan ●

Udi
Hills

Niger R.

onrovia

Kumasi ●   Lake Volta

Lagos ● Ife ●

Onitsha ●

LIBERIA

Yamoussoukro ●

ASHANTI

Lomé ⊛

Aba ●

CAMEROON

Harper ●

Abidjan ⊛

Accra ⊛

Porto-Novo ⊛
Cotonou

Slave Coast

Douala ●

Grain Coast

Ivory Coast

Gold Coast

Port Harcourt

Yaoundé ⊛

ATLANTIC
OCEAN

Gulf of Guinea

SÃO TOMÉ
AND PRÍNCIPE

0   400 miles

0   600 kilometers

TOGO

TFK

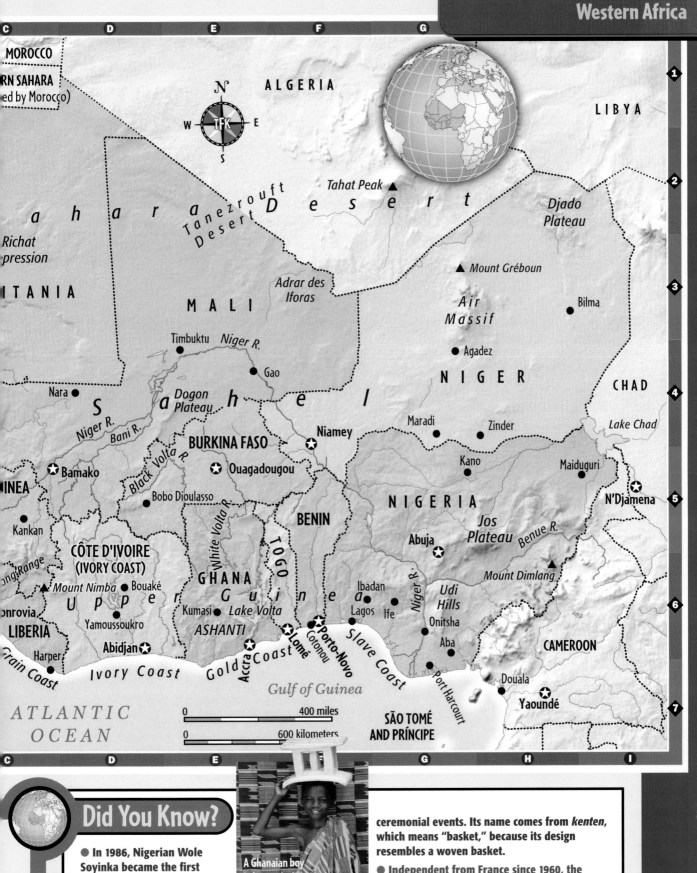
A Ghanaian boy
in kente cloth

Did You Know?

● In 1986, Nigerian Wole Soyinka became the first African to win the Nobel Prize for Literature.

● The Niger River flows east from Guinea through Mali and Niger and south to Nigeria. At 2,600 mi (4,181 km) long, it is West Africa's most vital river.

● Ghana is famous for its kente cloth. It was first woven in 12th-century Ghana, and clothing made from it was worn by African royalty during ceremonial events. Its name comes from *kenten*, which means "basket," because its design resembles a woven basket.

● Independent from France since 1960, the Côte d'Ivoire has a 500-year history of trading in elephant tusks, which were used to make ivory jewelry and piano keys. Today, elephants are protected, and the ivory trade is illegal.

● In 1987, freed slaves from the United States returned to Africa. They set up the first republic on the continent, which they named Liberia from the Latin word for "free."

Central Africa

The Kisangani: A tributary of the Congo River

River towns bustling with markets, untouched wilderness areas where lowland gorillas and forest elephants roam, barren deserts and dry grassland are all found in Central Africa. The Congo River and its tributaries form a lifeline for the people of Congo and the Democratic Republic of the Congo. Riverboats navigate the waters bringing people, food and trade.

Much of northern Chad is desert land. In recent years, long periods of drought have taken a heavy toll on the country and its people. The Sahara Desert is growing and moving southward. The Sahel, a semiarid grassland that stretches across south-central Chad, is expanding into neighboring savannas. To the south of Chad lies the Central African Republic, which forms a transitional area between the sub-Saharan zone in Chad and the equatorial zone to the south.

Dense forests cover large parts of Central African Republic, Congo, Democratic Republic of the Congo, Equatorial Guinea and Gabon. These countries lie near the equator, and their climate is hot and humid. Monkeys, baboons, gorillas, lions, leopards and a vast array of birds make their home in the jungle. Although natural resources are abundant in some of these lands, poverty, disease, government corruption and warfare are a sad fact of daily life for the people.

Women in Cameroon crush millet.

Data Bank

CAMEROON
AREA: 183,567 sq mi (475,440 sq km)
POPULATION: 16,063,678
CAPITAL: Yaoundé
LANGUAGES: African languages; English, French (both official)

CENTRAL AFRICAN REPUBLIC
AREA: 240,534 sq mi (622,984 sq km)
POPULATION: 3,742,482
CAPITAL: Bangui
LANGUAGES: French (official), Sangho, tribal languages

CHAD
AREA: 495,752 sq mi (1,284,000 sq km)
POPULATION: 9,538,544
CAPITAL: N'Djamena
LANGUAGES: French, Arabic (both official), Sara, African languages

CONGO (REPUBLIC OF THE)
AREA: 132,046, sq mi (342,000 sq km)
POPULATION: 2,998,040
CAPITAL: Brazzaville
LANGUAGES: French (official), Lingala, Monokutuba, other African languages

CONGO (DEMOCRATIC REPUBLIC OF THE)
AREA: 905,562 sq mi (2,345,410 sq km)
POPULATION: 58,317,930
CAPITAL: Kinshasa
LANGUAGES: French, Lingala, Kingwana, Kikongo, other African languages

EQUATORIAL GUINEA
AREA: 10,830 sq mi (28,051 sq km)
POPULATION: 523,051
CAPITAL: Malabo
LANGUAGES: Spanish, French (both official), pidgin English, Fang

GABON
AREA: 103,347 sq mi (267,667 sq km)
POPULATION: 1,355,246
CAPITAL: Libreville
LANGUAGES: French (official), Fang, Myene, Nzebi, Bapounou/Eschira, Bandjabi

SÃO TOMÉ AND PRÍNCIPE
AREA: 386 sq mi (1,001 sq km)
POPULATION: 181,565
CAPITAL: São Tomé
LANGUAGES: Portuguese

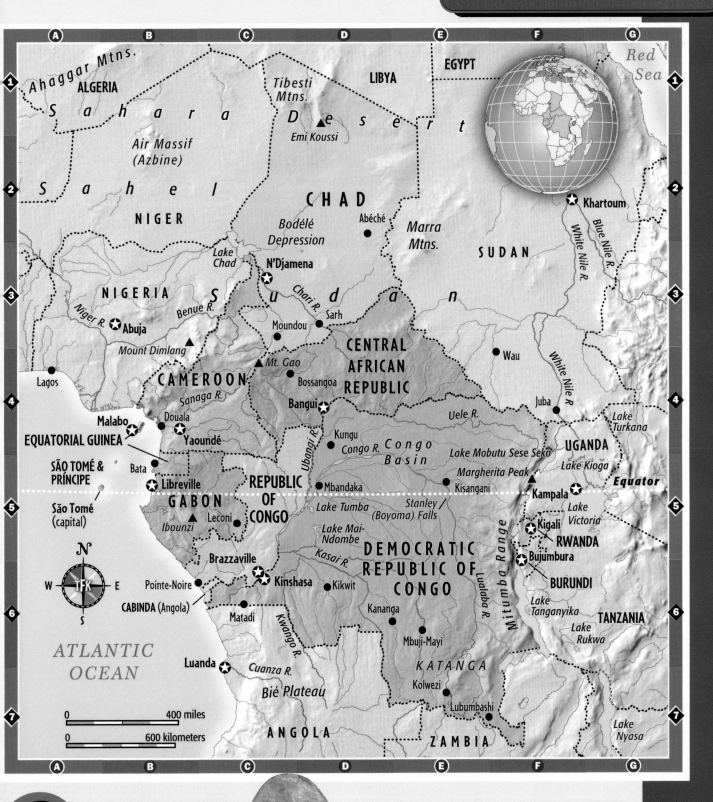

Red Sea

A B C D E F G

1 Ahaggar Mtns. ALGERIA
Tibesti Mtns.
LIBYA
EGYPT

S a h a r a   D e s e r t
Emi Koussi ▲

2 Sahel
Air Massif (Azbine)

NIGER
CHAD
Bodélé Depression
Abéché
Marra Mtns.

SUDAN
Khartoum ✪

White Nile R.
Blue Nile R.

3 NIGERIA
Lake Chad
N'Djamena ✪
S u d a n
Chari R.
Sarh

Niger R.
Benue R.
Moundou
Abuja ✪
Mount Dimlang ▲

Mt. Gao ▲
Bossangoa

CENTRAL AFRICAN REPUBLIC
Wau
White Nile R.

4 Lagos
CAMEROON
Sanaga R.
Douala
Bangui ✪
Kungu
Congo R.
Uele R.
Juba

Malabo ✪
Yaoundé
EQUATORIAL GUINEA
Bata
C o n g o   B a s i n
Lake Mobutu Sese Seko
Margherita Peak ▲
UGANDA
Lake Kioga
Lake Turkana

SÃO TOMÉ & PRÍNCIPE
Libreville ✪
REPUBLIC OF CONGO
Mbandaka
Kisangani
Kampala ✪
Equator

5 São Tomé (capital)
GABON
Leconi
Ibounzi ▲
Lake Tumba
Lake Mai-Ndombe
Stanley / (Boyoma) Falls
Kigali ✪
RWANDA
Lake Victoria

Brazzaville ✪
Kasai R.
DEMOCRATIC REPUBLIC OF CONGO
Bujumbura ✪
BURUNDI
Mitumba Range

6 Pointe-Noire
Kinshasa ✪
Kikwit
Kananga
Lualaba R.
Lake Tanganyika
Lake Rukwa
TANZANIA

CABINDA (Angola)
Matadi
Kwango R.
Mbuji-Mayi

7 ATLANTIC OCEAN
Luanda ✪
Cuanza R.
Bié Plateau
K A T A N G A
Kolwezi
Lubumbashi
Lake Nyasa

ANGOLA
ZAMBIA

N W E S (compass)

0   400 miles
0   600 kilometers

Did You Know?

● The Kota people of the Central African Republic believe that their ancestors help them communicate with God. Figures such as the one shown are used to protect the possessions of the dead.

● Pygmies, a group of people found through Central Africa, are an average height of 4 ft (120 cm).

● Name game: Equatorial Guinea was formerly known as Spanish Guinea. The Democratic Republic of the Congo was once known as the Belgian Congo. It was called Zaïre from 1971 to 1997. The country is often referred to as Congo (Kinshasa), while the other Congo is called Congo (Brazzaville).

East Central Africa

A Masai warrior

Spectacular highlands, rolling plains dotted with acacia trees, lush grasslands teeming with wildlife, and sparkling fresh- and saltwater lakes are the prominent features of this part of Africa. Clustered around Lake Victoria, which is the continent's largest lake, are Uganda, Kenya and Tanzania. Africa's deepest lake, Lake Tanganyika, lies at the western edge of Tanzania and Burundi. The small, landlocked country of Rwanda shares borders with Burundi, Tanzania and Uganda.

East Central Africa has many lakes, but water is still considered a precious gift. Kenyans often greet one another by asking "Does it rain where you live?" For many of the region's people, years of drought, grinding poverty, government corruption, ethnic rivalries and an AIDS epidemic have combined to make everyday life difficult.

In 1964, Tanganyika joined with the island of Zanzibar to form the country of Tanzania. South of Zanzibar, in the Indian Ocean, are the small island nations of Comoros and Seychelles. Still further south is Madagascar, the fourth-largest island in the world.

Heads Up: Serengeti National Park, in Tanzania, is home to this giraffe.

Data Bank

BURUNDI
AREA: 10,745 sq mi (27,830 sq km)
POPULATION: 6,231,221
CAPITAL: Bujumbura
LANGUAGES: Kirundi, French (both official), Swahili

COMOROS
AREA: 838 sq mi (2,170 sq km)
POPULATION: 651,901
CAPITAL: Moroni
LANGUAGES: Arabic, French (both official), Shikomoro

KENYA
AREA: 224,960 sq mi (582,650 sq km)
POPULATION: 32,021,856
CAPITAL: Nairobi
LANGUAGES: English, Kiswahili (both official), native languages

MADAGASCAR
AREA: 226,660 sq mi (587,040 sq km)
POPULATION: 17,501,871
CAPITAL: Antananarivo
LANGUAGES: Malagasy, French (both official)

MALAWI
AREA: 45,745 sq mi (118,480 sq km)
POPULATION: 11,906,855
CAPITAL: Lilongwe
LANGUAGES: English, Chichewa (both official)

MAURITIUS
AREA: 788 sq mi (2,040 sq km)
POPULATION: 1,220,481
CAPITAL: Port Louis
LANGUAGES: English, French (both official), Creole, Hindi, Urdu

MOZAMBIQUE
AREA: 309,494 sq mi (801,590 sq km)
POPULATION: 18,811,731
CAPITAL: Maputo
LANGUAGES: Portuguese (official), Bantu languages

RWANDA
AREA: 10,169 sq mi (26,338 sq km)
POPULATION: 7,954,013
CAPITAL: Kigali
LANGUAGES: Kinyarwanda, French, English (all official), Bantu, Kiswahili

SEYCHELLES
AREA: 176 sq mi (455 sq km)
POPULATION: 80,832
CAPITAL: Victoria
LANGUAGES: English, French (both official), Creole

TANZANIA
AREA: 364,898 sq mi (945,087 sq km)
POPULATION: 36,588,225
CAPITAL: Dar es Salaam
LANGUAGES: Kiswahili, English (both official), Arabic

UGANDA
AREA: 91,135 sq mi (236,040 sq km)
POPULATION: 26,404,543
CAPITAL: Kampala
LANGUAGES: English (official), Ganda, other native languages

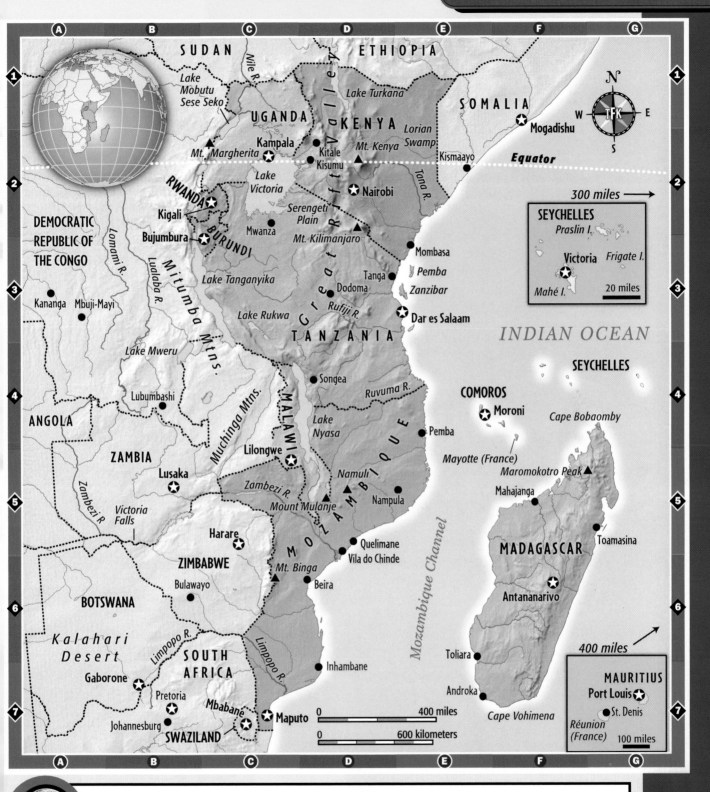

Map: East Central Africa

- SUDAN
- ETHIOPIA
- Nile R.
- Lake Mobutu Sese Seko
- Lake Turkana
- SOMALIA
- Mogadishu
- UGANDA
- KENYA
- Lorian Swamp
- Mt. Margherita ▲
- Kampala ★
- Kitale
- Mt. Kenya ▲
- Kisumu
- Kismaayo
- Equator
- 300 miles →
- RWANDA
- Lake Victoria
- Nairobi ★
- Tana R.
- Kigali ★
- Serengeti Plain
- DEMOCRATIC REPUBLIC OF THE CONGO
- Lomami R.
- BURUNDI
- Bujumbura ★
- Mwanza
- Mt. Kilimanjaro ▲
- Mombasa
- SEYCHELLES
- Praslin I.
- Victoria ★ Frigate I.
- Mahé I.
- 20 miles
- Kananga
- Mbuji-Mayi
- Lualaba R.
- Lake Tanganyika
- Dodoma
- Tanga
- Pemba
- Zanzibar
- Rufiji R.
- Lake Rukwa
- TANZANIA
- Dar es Salaam ★
- Mitumba Mtns.
- Great Rift Valley
- INDIAN OCEAN
- Lake Mweru
- Songea
- Ruvuma R.
- SEYCHELLES
- COMOROS
- Moroni ★
- Cape Bobaomby
- ANGOLA
- Lubumbashi
- Muchinga Mtns.
- MALAWI
- Lake Nyasa
- Pemba
- Mayotte (France)
- Maromokotro Peak ▲
- ZAMBIA
- Lilongwe ★
- MOZAMBIQUE
- Namuli ▲
- Mahajanga
- Lusaka ★
- Zambezi R.
- Nampula
- Zambezi R.
- Victoria Falls
- Mount Mulanje ▲
- MADAGASCAR
- Toamasina
- Harare ★
- Quelimane
- Vila do Chinde
- Mozambique Channel
- ZIMBABWE
- Mt. Binga ▲
- Beira
- Antananarivo ★
- Bulawayo
- BOTSWANA
- 400 miles
- Kalahari Desert
- Limpopo R.
- SOUTH AFRICA
- Inhambane
- Toliara
- MAURITIUS
- Port Louis ★
- Gaborone ★
- St. Denis
- Pretoria ★
- Mbabane ★
- Androka
- Cape Vohimena
- Réunion (France)
- 100 miles
- Johannesburg
- Maputo ★
- SWAZILAND
- 0 — 400 miles
- 0 — 600 kilometers

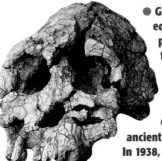

Did You Know?

- Scientists believe that our earliest human ancestors lived in Kenya. The skull shown at right is thought to be 3.5 million years old.

- Madagascar is a haven for chameleons. Half the world's chameleons are found on the island.

- Gorillas, which live in the rain forests of equatorial Africa, are the world's largest primates. A male gorilla can weigh up to 441 lbs (200 kg).

- A giraffe can run as fast as 32 mph (56 kph), and a stampeding elephant can cover 12 mi (19 km) in 30 minutes.

- The coelacanth (see-la-canth), an ancient type of fish, was believed to be extinct. In 1938, one was found swimming in the Indian Ocean, near Comoros.

137

Kenya

Jambo!

I'm Caroline, and I'm 12 years old. I live with my mom, brother and two sisters in Nairobi. I love Kenyan food, especially chai, which is tea with lots of milk, and somosas, which are fried triangular pastries with meat. I speak three languages: Kikuyu, my family's language; Swahili, which everyone in Kenya learns; and English. Enjoy my country!

The Kenyan Flag

Kenya adopted its flag shortly after gaining independence from Britain in 1963. The flag symbolizes the pride and traditions of its people.

Black represents the people of Kenya.

Red is for the blood shed in the struggle for independence.

Green stands for Kenya's fertile land.

White symbolizes peace.

The **warrior's shield** covering crossed spears represents Kenya's proud tribal heritage.

Dividing the Land

Many of Kenya's people are nomads. They travel from pasture to pasture to feed their cattle. Look at the chart to see how much of the land is used by nomadic people.

Forests and woodlands **30%**

Permanent pastures **37%**

Other, including cities **25%**

Permanent crops **1%**

Land that can be used for farming **7%**

The Economy

AGRICULTURE: Coffee, tea, corn, wheat, sugarcane, fruits, vegetables, dairy products

MANUFACTURING: Small consumer goods (batteries, furniture, plastics, soap, textiles)

MAJOR INDUSTRIES: Oil refining, cement, tourism

MAJOR EXPORTS: Tea, coffee, fruits, vegetables, flowers, petroleum and cement

MAJOR IMPORTS: Industrial machinery, iron and steel, petroleum products, cars and trucks

TRADING PARTNERS: United Arab Emirates, Britain, South Africa, Saudi Arabia, Uganda

Workers pick tea leaves.

Top 5 Tea-Producing Countries

Tea is one of Kenya's major exports. The country is the world's fourth-largest tea producer.

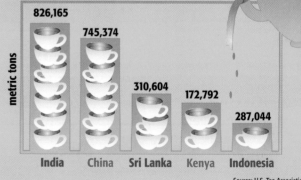

metric tons

India	China	Sri Lanka	Kenya	Indonesia
826,165	745,374	310,604	172,792	287,044

Source: U.S. Tea Association

Major Events in Kenya's History

6 million B.C. Early man appears in East Africa. (Fossils of human ancestors dating from this period have been found in the Rift Valley.)

500 B.C.–700 A.D. Bantu-speaking people settle in Kenya. (Their descendants make up 75% of modern Kenya's population.) In about 700, Arabs settle in coastal Kenya.

1498 Portuguese explorer Vasco da Gama reaches Kenya. Portuguese settlers later establish control of the coastal region.

1895 Britain takes over Kenya which is then known as British East Africa.

KENYA

Every year, tourists visit **Kenya's** 59 national parks and reserves. The parks are home to 844 types of birds and 359 mammal species.

SUDAN

UGANDA

ETHIOPIA

SOMALIA

TANZANIA

Lake Turkana

Rift Valley

Lake Victoria

Mount Kenya

Nairobi ★

Tsavo West National Park

Tsavo East National Park

Mount Kilimanjaro

Mombasa ●

INDIAN OCEAN

Marsabit National Reserve

Marsabit National Park

Marsabit National Park and Reserve was once home to an elephant with such long tusks that Kenya's president assigned guards to protect it.

Lake Nakuru National Park surrounds beautiful Lake Nakuru, where more than 1 million flamingos live.

Amboseli National Park lies at the foot of Africa's highest peak, Mount Kilimanjaro, which rises in neighboring Tanzania.

Tsavo East and West National Parks cover more than 8,000 sq mi (20,720 sq km). The crystal-clear water of Mzima Springs, in Tsavo West, provides a cool home for hippos and crocodiles.

Masai Mara National Reserve is the most popular game park in Kenya. During the dry, cold season, hundreds of thousands of wildebeest and zebras migrate from the plains of the Serengeti, in Tanzania, to the grasslands of the Masai Mara.

AFRICA
KENYA
ATLANTIC OCEAN
INDIAN OCEAN

Miles
0   50   100

Kilometers
0   100   200

Say It in Swahili

If you've seen *The Lion King*, then you've already learned a few words of Swahili! *Simba* means "lion"; *rafiki* is "friend." Swahili (or Kiswahili) is spoken throughout eastern Africa. Try saying the words at right. *Hakuna matata* (It's no trouble)!

Hello	→ Jambo
How are you?	→ Habari?
I'm fine.	→ Nzuri.
Thank you	→ Asante
Father	→ Baba
Mother	→ Mama
Sleep	→ Lala
Journey	→ Safari

KENYA Is Famous for ...

Nyama choma Kenya's national dish can be any type of barbecued meat, but it is usually goat. It is often served with ugali, a thick porridge.

Chai Kenyans drink a lot of tea. Chai is made by boiling together water, tea leaves, sugar and milk.

Safaris Kenyans and tourists enjoy the thrill of seeing wild animals in their habitats.

Running Kenya's long- and middle-distance runners are among the fastest in the world.

Soccer Kids across the country dream of being chosen for the national team, the Harambee Stars.

1940s Kenyan Africans form groups to fight for independence from British rule. A secret society called the Mau Mau favors violence.

1952-1956 Mau Mau rebellion. More than 13,000 people are killed .

1963 Kenya wins independence from Britain. Popular leader Jomo Kenyatta becomes president.

1978 Kenyatta dies. Vice President Daniel arap Moi begins a long reign as president.

For more about Kenya and its history, visit *timeforkids.com/gpkenya*.

Southern Africa

A rainbow over Victoria Falls, in Zimbabwe

Spotted cheetahs, lumbering elephants, magnificent lions and hundreds of bird species—these are the hallmarks of southern Africa. The region's vast savannas, mountains and plateaus host an astonishing array of plant and animal life. Tourists come from around the world to take safaris, adventures whose name means "journey" in Swahili. The southern part of Africa is also rich in natural resources, such as diamonds, gold and copper, and physical beauty. At Zimbabwe's spectacular Victoria Falls, the Zambezi River plunges nearly 355 ft (108 m) into a rain-forested gorge. Thundering over the rocks is some 33,000 cubic ft (935 cubic m) of water per second!

The richest, most modern country on the continent is South Africa. Comprising more than 30 ethnic groups, the country has undergone many political and social changes. For hundreds of years, a small white minority ruled a mostly black population. Following the country's first free election in 1994, South Africa entered a new era of equality and cooperation.

Johannesburg, South Africa

Data Bank

ANGOLA
AREA: 481,350 sq mi (1,246,700 sq km)
POPULATION: 10,978,552
CAPITAL: Luanda
LANGUAGES: Portuguese (official), Bantu, other African languages

BOTSWANA
AREA: 231,800 sq mi (600,370 sq km)
POPULATION: 1,561,973
CAPITAL: Gaborone
LANGUAGES: English (official), Setswana

LESOTHO
AREA: 11,720 sq mi (30,355 sq km)
POPULATION: 1,865,040
CAPITAL: Maseru
LANGUAGES: Sesotho (southern Sotho), English (official), Zulu, Xhosa

NAMIBIA
AREA: 318,694 sq mi (825,418 sq km)
POPULATION: 1,954,033
CAPITAL: Windhoek
LANGUAGES: English (official), Afrikaans, native languages

SOUTH AFRICA
AREA: 471,008 sq mi (1,219,912 sq km)
POPULATION: 42,718,530
CAPITAL: Pretoria
LANGUAGES: Afrikaans, English, Ndebele, Pedi, Sotho, Swazi, Tsonga, Tswana, Venda, Xhosa, Zulu (all official)

SWAZILAND
AREA: 6,704 sq mi (17,363 sq km)
POPULATION: 1,169,241
CAPITAL: Mbabane
LANGUAGES: siSwati, English (both official)

ZAMBIA
AREA: 290,583 sq mi (752,614 sq km)
POPULATION: 10,462,436
CAPITAL: Lusaka
LANGUAGES: English (official), Bemba, Kaonda, Lozi, Lunda, other native languages

ZIMBABWE
AREA: 150,802 sq mi (390,580 sq km)
POPULATION: 12,671,860
CAPITAL: Harare
LANGUAGES: English (official), Shona, Sindebele, native languages

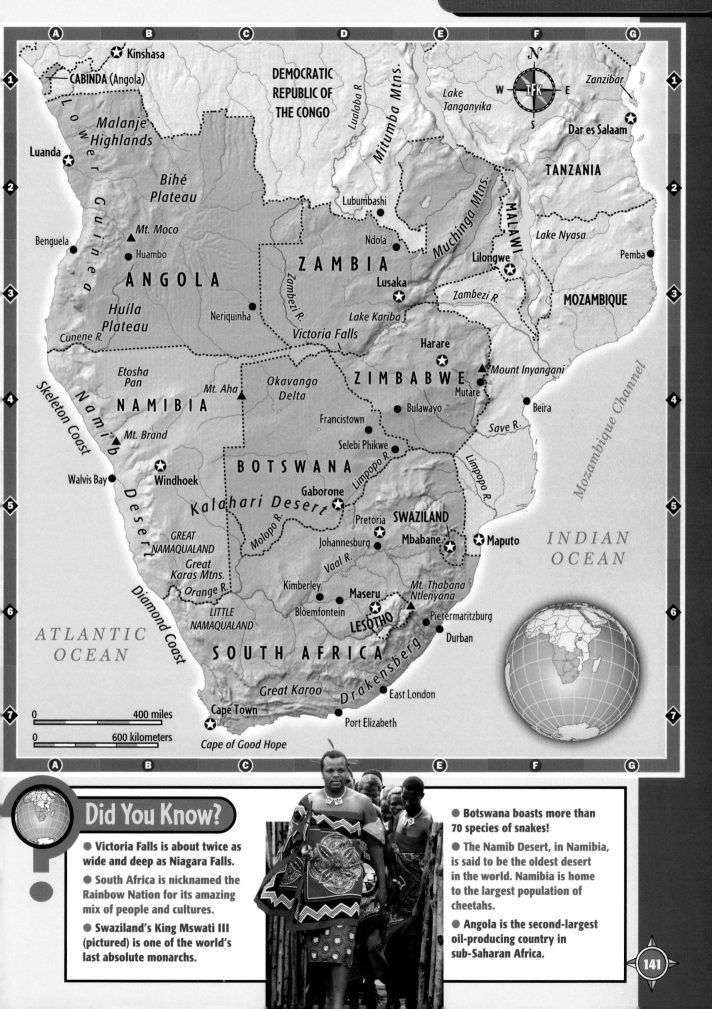

DEMOCRATIC REPUBLIC OF THE CONGO

Kinshasa

CABINDA (Angola)

Lower Guinea

Malanje Highlands

Luanda

Bihé Plateau

Benguela

Mt. Moco

Huambo

ANGOLA

Huíla Plateau

Cunene R.

Neriquinha

Zambezi R.

Lualaba R.

Mitumba Mtns.

Lake Tanganyika

Zanzibar

Dar es Salaam

TANZANIA

Lubumbashi

Ndola

ZAMBIA

Lusaka

Muchinga Mtns.

Lilongwe

MALAWI

Lake Nyasa

Pemba

MOZAMBIQUE

Zambezi R.

Lake Kariba

Victoria Falls

Harare

ZIMBABWE

Mount Inyangani

Mutare

Bulawayo

Beira

Save R.

Etosha Pan

Mt. Aha

Okavango Delta

Francistown

NAMIBIA

Mt. Brand

Skeleton Coast

Namib Desert

Windhoek

Walvis Bay

BOTSWANA

Selebi Phikwe

Limpopo R.

Kalahari Desert

Gaborone

Mozambique Channel

Molopo R.

Pretoria

SWAZILAND

Mbabane

Maputo

INDIAN OCEAN

GREAT NAMAQUALAND

Great Karas Mtns.

Orange R.

Johannesburg

Vaal R.

Diamond Coast

LITTLE NAMAQUALAND

Kimberley

Maseru

Mt. Thabana Ntlenyana

Bloemfontein

LESOTHO

Pietermaritzburg

Durban

ATLANTIC OCEAN

SOUTH AFRICA

Drakensberg

Great Karoo

East London

Cape Town

Port Elizabeth

Cape of Good Hope

0 400 miles

0 600 kilometers

A B C D E F G

1 2 3 4 5 6 7

N W E S

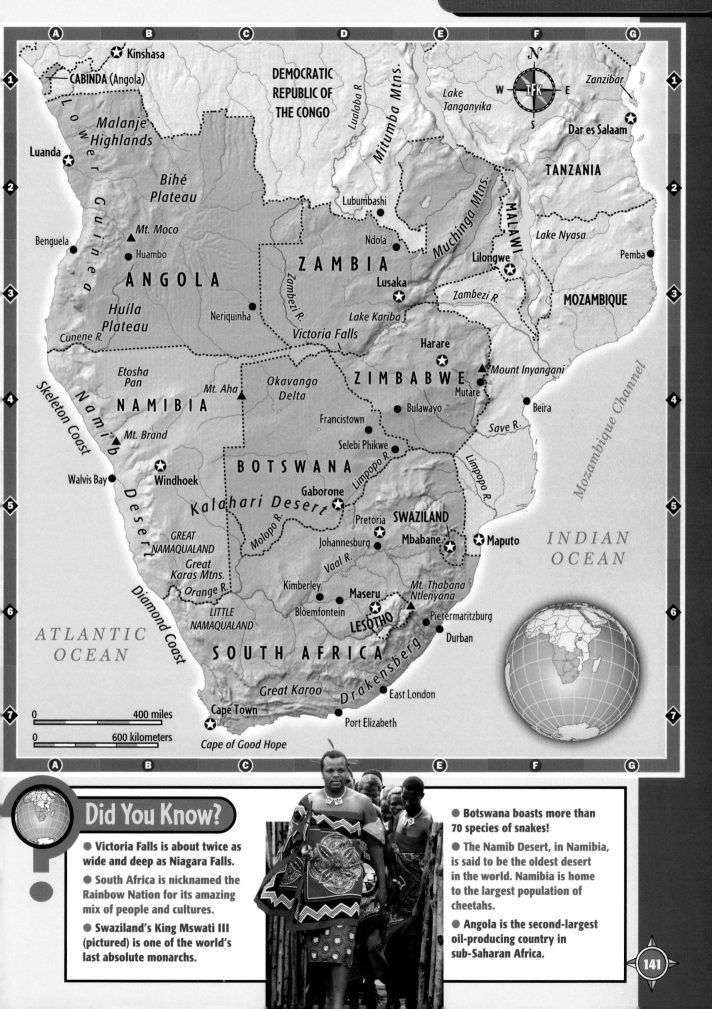

Did You Know?

● Victoria Falls is about twice as wide and deep as Niagara Falls.

● South Africa is nicknamed the Rainbow Nation for its amazing mix of people and cultures.

● Swaziland's King Mswati III (pictured) is one of the world's last absolute monarchs.

● Botswana boasts more than 70 species of snakes!

● The Namib Desert, in Namibia, is said to be the oldest desert in the world. Namibia is home to the largest population of cheetahs.

● Angola is the second-largest oil-producing country in sub-Saharan Africa.

South Africa

Sawubona!

My name is Tsholofelo (too-*loo*-fel-oh). My friends call me Tooloo. I am 10 years old. I live with my parents and two sisters in Soweto, near Johannesburg. My favorite meal is called samp and tripe—that's corn mush and cow stomach! Let me show you more about my country.
Sala kahle!

The South African Flag

This became the national flag after the country's first free elections in 1994. Before that, blacks used the flag as a symbol of freedom.

The **red, blue** and **black** colors represent the country's various ethnic and racial groups.

The **green V** turns into a single line. This shows how a once-divided land faces the future with its people united.

South Africa's Religions

Many South Africans follow tribal religions. But the influence of European settlers is represented by the large numbers of Christians in the country today.

Christian 68%

Tribal Religions 28.5%

Hindu 1.5%

Muslim 2%

The Economy

MINING: Gold, platinum metals, diamonds, coal

MANUFACTURING: Food products, iron, steel, boats

MAJOR INDUSTRIES: Tourism, energy, mining

MAJOR EXPORTS: Diamonds, pearls, semiprecious stones, chemicals, iron, steel

MAJOR IMPORTS: Machinery, appliances, chemical products

TRADING PARTNERS: Britain, Germany, U.S., Japan, France

Top 5 Gold-Producing Countries

More than one-fifth of the world's gold comes from South Africa.

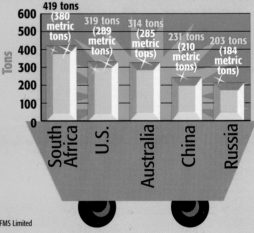

Country	Tons
South Africa	419 tons (380 metric tons)
U.S.	319 tons (289 metric tons)
Australia	314 tons (285 metric tons)
China	231 tons (210 metric tons)
Russia	203 tons (184 metric tons)

Source: GFMS Limited

Major Events in South Africa's History

1400s Zulu and Xhosa people establish large kingdoms.

1652 The Dutch establish the port of Cape Town. They are the first Europeans to settle in South Africa.

1852 The British take control of Cape Town. At the end of the Boer War, in 1902, Britain gains control of all South Africa.

1910 South Africa becomes an independent nation.

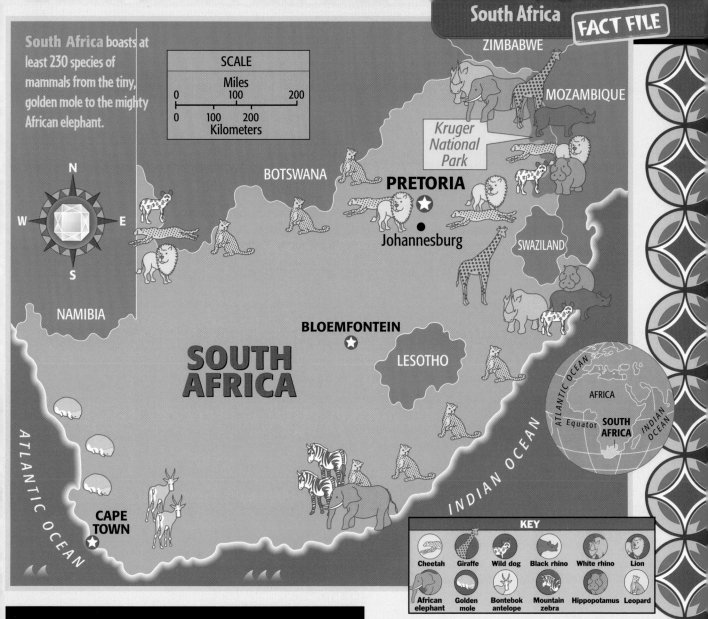

South Africa boasts at least 230 species of mammals from the tiny, golden mole to the mighty African elephant.

SCALE

Miles
0   100   200

0   100   200
Kilometers

ZIMBABWE

MOZAMBIQUE

Kruger National Park

BOTSWANA

PRETORIA ☆

● Johannesburg

SWAZILAND

NAMIBIA

BLOEMFONTEIN ☆

SOUTH AFRICA

LESOTHO

N
W   E
S

ATLANTIC OCEAN

INDIAN OCEAN

ATLANTIC OCEAN

AFRICA

SOUTH AFRICA

Equator

INDIAN OCEAN

CAPE TOWN ☆

KEY

| Cheetah | Giraffe | Wild dog | Black rhino | White rhino | Lion |
| African elephant | Golden mole | Bontebok antelope | Mountain zebra | Hippopotamus | Leopard |

SOUTH AFRICA Is Famous for ...

Soccer The country's most popular sport is played in dusty streets and professional clubs.

Kwaito This is a type of dance music. Popular with kids, it uses traditional African beats to create a sound similar to hip-hop.

Pap and vleis A hearty meal of porridge and meat is eaten almost every day in most middle-class South Africans' homes.

Brais A barbecue is one of the most popular ways to spend a weekend afternoon.

Sangomas Many people consult sangomas, or traditional tribal healers, when they are sick or have problems.

Ostriches South Africa has many ostrich farms.

Say It in Zulu

Zulu, also called isiZulu, is the most widely spoken language in South Africa. Zulu uses many tones and clicking sounds, made by pressing the tongue against different parts of the mouth.

Hello ⟶ Sawubona (sa-woo-*boh*-na)

Goodbye ⟶ Sala kahle (sah-la *kah*-leh)

Friend ⟶ Umngane (oom-*gan*-eh)

Thank you ⟶ Ngiyabonga (ngee-ya-*bon*-ga)

Excuse me ⟶ Uxulo (ooh-*khoo*-lo)

My name is ⟶ Igama lami ngu . . . (ee-gah-ma *lah*-me ngoo...)

1948 Apartheid (a-*par*-tate) is introduced. Laws physically separate different racial groups.

1952 The African National Congress begins a protest against apartheid. Nelson Mandela is one of its leaders.

1976 President F.W. DeKlerk announces the end of apartheid. Mandela is released from prison after serving 27 years.

1994 South Africa holds its first elections in which all races can vote. Nelson Mandela becomes president.

 Learn more about South Africa at *timeforkids.com/gpsouthafrica*.

Australia and the Pacific Islands

The Great Barrier Reef includes nearly 3,000 reefs.

Australia is the smallest, flattest and—with the exception of Antarctica—the driest continent. It is also a region with many different landscapes: parched deserts, vast grasslands, tropical rain forests and plains dotted with mammoth rocks.

Located between the Indian and Pacific Oceans, Australia is relatively isolated from other continents. It is home to unusual plant and animal life, including the only egg-laying mammals on earth, the platypus and the echidna. Off Australia's northeast coast, the Great Barrier Reef contains an unparalleled treasure of brilliant corals and marine life.

To the east of Australia lie the Pacific Islands, a collection of more than 10,000 islands, atolls and islets. The largest of this group are New Zealand and New Guinea. New Guinea is the world's second-largest island, after Greenland. Half the island forms part of Indonesia; the other half is the independent country Papua New Guinea. The Pacific Islands are known for their natural beauty. In New Zealand alone, the terrain ranges from snowy glaciers and sparkling fjords to active volcanoes, temperate rainforests and sandy beaches.

Regional Facts

AREA, AUSTRALIA:
2,967,893 sq mi (7,686,850 sq km)

LAND AREA, PACIFIC ISLANDS:
317,700 sq mi (822,800 sq km)

NUMBER OF COUNTRIES: 13 countries—
Fiji, Kiribati, Marshall Islands, Micronesia,
Nauru, New Zealand, Palau, Papua New
Guinea, Somoa, Solomon Islands, Tonga,
Tuvalu and Vanuatu.

HIGHEST POINT: Mount Wilhelm, Papua
New Guinea, 14,793 ft (4,509 m)

LOWEST POINT: Lake Eyre, Australia,
49 ft (15 m) below sea level

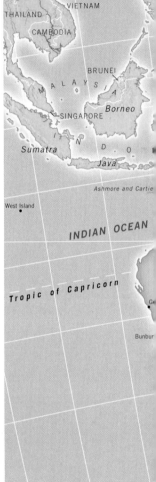

Uluru (Ayers Rock) is the world's largest monolith.

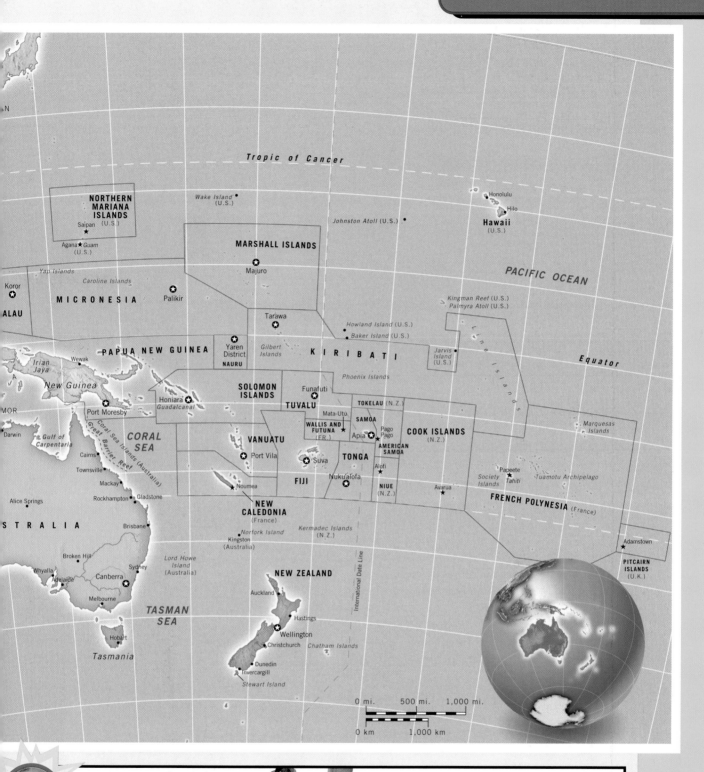

Tropic of Cancer

NORTHERN MARIANA ISLANDS
Saipan ★ (U.S.)
Agana ★ Guam (U.S.)

Wake Island • (U.S.)

Johnston Atoll (U.S.) •

Honolulu •
Hilo •
Hawaii (U.S.)

PACIFIC OCEAN

Yap Islands
Caroline Islands
Koror •
ALAU •
MICRONESIA
Palikir ✪

MARSHALL ISLANDS
Majuro ✪

Tarawa ✪

Kingman Reef (U.S.) •
Palmyra Atoll (U.S.) •

Howland Island (U.S.) •
Baker Island (U.S.) •

Yaren District
NAURU ✪

Gilbert Islands

K I R I B A T I

Jarvis Island (U.S.)

Equator

MOR
New Guinea
Irian Jaya
Wewak •
PAPUA NEW GUINEA
Port Moresby •

Phoenix Islands

SOLOMON ISLANDS
Honiara ✪ Guadalcanal

Funafuti ✪
TUVALU

TOKELAU (N.Z.)
Mata-Utu •
WALLIS AND FUTUNA (FR.)

SAMOA ✪
Apia •

Pago Pago •
AMERICAN SAMOA

COOK ISLANDS (N.Z.)

Marquesas Islands

Darwin •
Gulf of Carpentaria

CORAL SEA
Coral Sea Islands (Australia)

Cairns •
Townsville •
Mackay •

Great Barrier Reef

VANUATU
Port Vila ✪

Suva ✪
FIJI

TONGA
Nuku'alofa ✪
Alofi •

NIUE (N.Z.)

Avarua •

Papeete ★
Society Islands Tahiti
Tuamotu Archipelago

FRENCH POLYNESIA (France)

Alice Springs •
Rockhampton • Gladstone •

Nouméa ★
NEW CALEDONIA (France)

Kermadec Islands (N.Z.)

A U S T R A L I A
Broken Hill •
Brisbane •

Norfolk Island
Kingston (Australia)

Adamstown ★
PITCAIRN ISLANDS (U.K.)

Whyalla •
Adelaide •
Canberra ★
Sydney •
Melbourne •

Lord Howe Island (Australia)

NEW ZEALAND
Auckland •
Hastings •
Wellington ✪
Christchurch •
Chatham Islands

TASMAN SEA

International Date Line

Hobart •
Tasmania

Dunedin •
Invercargill •
Stewart Island

0 mi.   500 mi.   1,000 mi.

0 km   1,000 km

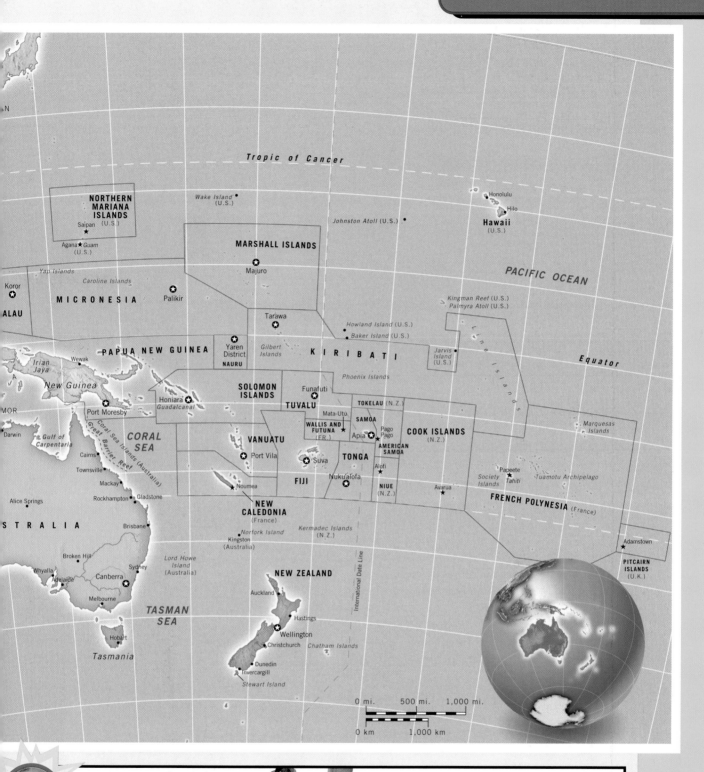

Wow Zone!

- The only land mammals native to New Zealand are bats.

- Australia is the only continent to contain just one country.

- There are no active volcanoes in Australia.

- Koalas are not bears. They are marsupials. They carry their young in a pouch.

- Fiji contains more than 800 islands and islets spread across 1,000,000 sq mi (3,000,000 sq km). Only 100 of Fiji's islands are inhabited.

- In 1789, sailors on the British ship *Bounty* took over the vessel and set their captain, William Bligh, adrift in a small boat. The incident was made famous in the novel—and subsequent movies—*Mutiny on the Bounty*. Bligh and 18 shipmates survived and traveled more than 3,600 mi (5,800 km) before arriving at the island of Java.

Australia and Papua New Guinea

Australia is a hot, dry country of stunning sunsets and vast plains. Known for its unusual animals and colorful birds, the land Down Under is home to kangaroos and koalas and lorrikeets and rosellas. Australia stretches across almost 3 million sq mi

Sydney Harbor: The majestic peaked roofs belong to the Sydney Opera House.

(8 million sq km), making it the world's sixth-largest country. It is almost as big as the United States, but its population is less than one-tenth the size of the United States' population. Most of Australia's interior, which is called the Outback, has so little water that hardly anyone can live there. Most Australians—some 70% of the population—live in the country's large coastal cities. Sydney has 4 million residents and is Australia's largest urban center. The island of Tasmania is located off Australia's southern coast. It is the only place on earth where you will find the fierce, little mammal aptly named the Tasmanian devil.

Off the northern coast of Australia lies Papua New Guinea. This rugged country occupies the eastern half of the island of New Guinea (the other half of the island belongs to Indonesia). Papua New Guinea was an Australian territory until it gained independence in 1975.

A Tasmanian devil lets out a screech.

Horseback riders enjoy the view from a Tasmanian beach.

Data Bank

AUSTRALIA
AREA: 2,967,893 sq mi (7,686,850 sq km)
POPULATION: 19,913,144
CAPITAL: Canberra
LANGUAGES: English, native languages

PAPUA NEW GUINEA
AREA: 178,703 sq mi (462,840 sq km)
POPULATION: 5,420,280
CAPITAL: Port Moresby
LANGUAGES: Motu, other native languages, English

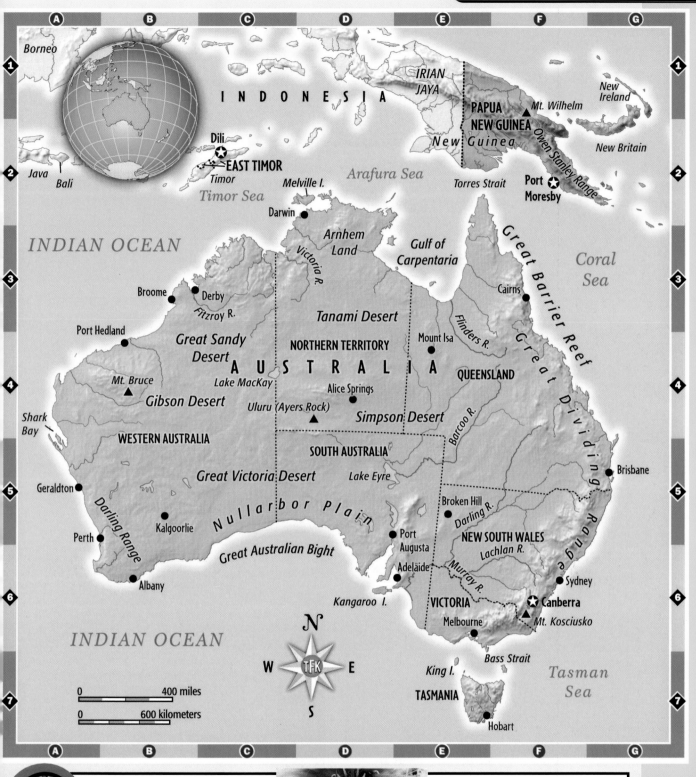

Map labels:

INDONESIA

IRIAN JAYA

PAPUA NEW GUINEA — Mt. Wilhelm

New Guinea — Owen Stanley Range — New Ireland — New Britain

Port Moresby — Torres Strait — Coral Sea

Dili ✈ EAST TIMOR — Timor

Java — Bali — Timor Sea — Melville I. — Arafura Sea

INDIAN OCEAN

Darwin — Arnhem Land — Victoria R. — Gulf of Carpentaria

Borneo

Broome — Derby — Fitzroy R. — Cairns — Great Barrier Reef

Port Hedland — Great Sandy Desert — Tanami Desert — NORTHERN TERRITORY — Mount Isa — Flinders R.

Mt. Bruce ▲ — Gibson Desert — Lake MacKay — A U S T R A L I A — QUEENSLAND — Great Dividing Range

Shark Bay — Uluru (Ayers Rock) ▲ — Alice Springs — Simpson Desert — Barcoo R.

WESTERN AUSTRALIA — SOUTH AUSTRALIA

Geraldton — Great Victoria Desert — Lake Eyre — Brisbane

Perth — Darling Range — Kalgoorlie — Nullarbor Plain — Broken Hill — Darling R.

Albany — Great Australian Bight — Port Augusta — NEW SOUTH WALES — Lachlan R.

Adelaide — Murray R. — Sydney

INDIAN OCEAN — Kangaroo I. — VICTORIA — Canberra ▲ Mt. Kosciusko

Melbourne — Bass Strait — Tasman Sea

N W E S — King I. — TASMANIA

400 miles
600 kilometers

Hobart

Australia

G'Day!

I'm Paul, and I'm 12 years old. I live in a suburb of Sydney with my parents, younger brother, Jake and my pet guinea pig. I like rugby or forcingsback, a kicking game with a rugby ball. But I also like cricket and soccer. Once a week, I take lessons for the E-flat horn and piano. Enjoy the Land Down Under!

The Australian Flag

The symbols on Australia's flag honor its history and geography.

Union Jack, from Britain's flag, represents Australia's ties to Britain.

Southern Cross Stars represent the country's position in the Southern Hemisphere.

Commonwealth Star includes seven points: six stand for the six states, the seventh for the country's two territories.

How the Land Is Used

Much of Australia's land is used for grazing sheep and cattle. Most people live along the coast where the cities are located.

Forests 19%
Permanent pastures 54%
Deserts 18%
6%
3%
Land that can be used for farming
Urban and other

The Economy

AGRICULTURE: Livestock, cotton, grapes, sugarcane, canola

MANUFACTURING: Food products, transportation equipment

MAJOR INDUSTRIES: Agriculture, wool production, food and wine, tourism, quarrying

MAJOR EXPORTS: Textile yarn and fabrics, iron ore and bauxite, food and livestock

MAJOR IMPORTS: Automobiles, office and telecommunications equipment, paper and paperboard products

TRADING PARTNERS: U.S., Japan, China, South Korea, Singapore

Australian sheep produce one-third of the world's wool.

Top 5 Largest Deserts

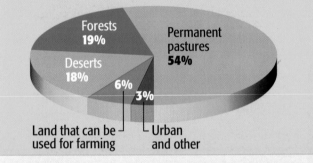

In Australia, the mountains of the Great Dividing Range block rainfall from the Pacific from reaching the country's interior. That's why there is so much desert!

1 **Sahara (Northern Africa):** 3,500,000 sq mi (5,632,700 sq km)

2 **Australian*:** 1,300,000 (2,092,150)

3 **Arabian Peninsula (Southwest Asia):** 1,000,000 (1,609,344)

4 **Turkestan (Central Asia):** 750,000 (1,207,000)

5 **Gobi (Central Asia); and North American:** 500,000 (804,672)

*Includes Gibson, Great Sandy, Great Victoria and Simpson

Major Events in Australia's History

60,000 B.C.-40,000 B.C. People from Southeast Asia travel and settle in Australia. Their descendants are the Aboriginal people.

8,000 B.C. Aborigines invent the boomerang. This wooden weapon, which is used for hunting, returns to its thrower.

1770 A.D. Britain claims Australia. It settles the first of six colonies in 1788.

1901 The six colonies join to form the Commonwealth of Australia. It has a democratic government. Britain's royalty has only a ceremonial role.

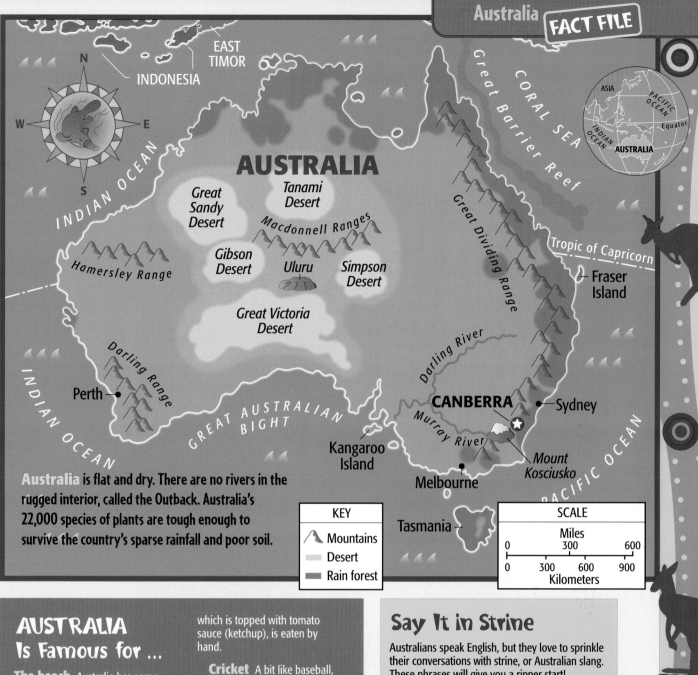

AUSTRALIA

INDONESIA

EAST TIMOR

N
W · E
S

INDIAN OCEAN

Great Sandy Desert

Tanami Desert

Macdonnell Ranges

Gibson Desert

Uluru

Simpson Desert

Great Victoria Desert

Hamersley Range

Darling Range

Perth

GREAT AUSTRALIAN BIGHT

INDIAN OCEAN

Kangaroo Island

CORAL SEA

Great Barrier Reef

Great Dividing Range

Tropic of Capricorn

Fraser Island

Darling River

CANBERRA · Sydney

Murray River

Mount Kosciusko

Melbourne

PACIFIC OCEAN

Tasmania

ASIA
PACIFIC OCEAN
INDIAN OCEAN
Equator
AUSTRALIA

Australia is flat and dry. There are no rivers in the rugged interior, called the Outback. Australia's 22,000 species of plants are tough enough to survive the country's sparse rainfall and poor soil.

KEY

⋀ Mountains
▢ Desert
▢ Rain forest

SCALE

Miles
0 — 300 — 600

0 — 300 — 600 — 900
Kilometers

AUSTRALIA Is Famous for ...

The beach Australia has some of the most beautiful beaches in the world! Australians flock to them in the hot summer months, from December to January.

Vegemite This salty dark-brown paste is made from yeast and is spread on toast and sandwiches. (Healthy, but not to everyone's taste!)

Meat pie This popular snack,

which is topped with tomato sauce (ketchup), is eaten by hand.

Cricket A bit like baseball, some visitors find it boring. A match can last for days with no result.

Australian-rules football This rough, free-flowing game is extremely popular in parts of the country.

Koalas and kangaroos These marsupials carry their young in their pouches.

Say It in Strine

Australians speak English, but they love to sprinkle their conversations with strine, or Australian slang. These phrases will give you a ripper start!

'Sarvo ⟶ This afternoon

Rippe ⟶ Terrific

G'day ⟶ Hello

Good on ya ⟶ Well done

Mackas ⟶ McDonald's

Dunny ⟶ Toilet

To spit the dummy ⟶ To really lose your temper

go Learn more strine and see the sights at *timeforkids.com/gpaustralia*.

1927 Canberra replaces Melbourne as the nation's capital city.

1962 Australia's native people are given the right to vote. Five years later, they're recognized as citizens.

1976 The Aboriginal Land Rights Act is passed. It is a legal turning point for the Aborigines, giving them the right to make claims on their traditional land in the Northern Territory.

2000 Sydney hosts the Summer Olympics.

New Zealand and the Pacific Islands

Pacific Paradise: A village in Fiji

More than 10,000 coral and volcanic islands dot the vast central Pacific Ocean. Within the Pacific Islands, also known as Oceania, are three groups: Melanesia, Polynesia, and Micronesia. Oceania—with its coral reefs, blue lagoons, soaring volcanic mountains and warm weather—is one of the most beautiful places in the world.

Most Pacific Island nations include many small islands—Micronesia has more than 600 islands and islets, Fiji has more than 800—and all share a similar mild climate. The people of Oceania speak dozens of different languages.

New Guinea and the islands of New Zealand make up 90% of the Pacific Islands' land area.

The kiwi is native to New Zealand.

Data Bank

FIJI
AREA: 7,054 sq mi (18,270 sq km)
POPULATION: 880,874
CAPITAL: Suva
LANGUAGES: English (official), Fijian, Hindustani

KIRIBATI
AREA: 313 sq mi (811 sq km)
POPULATION: 100,798
CAPITAL: Tarawa
LANGUAGES: English (official), I-Kiribati

MARSHALL ISLANDS
AREA: 70 sq mi (181 sq km)
POPULATION: 57,738
CAPITAL: Majuro
LANGUAGES: Marshallese, English (both official), Japanese

MICRONESIA
AREA: 271 sq mi (702 sq km)
POPULATION: 108,155
CAPITAL: Palikir
LANGUAGES: English (official), Trukese, Pohnpeian, Yapese, other native languages

NEW ZEALAND
AREA: 103,737 sq mi (268,680 sq km)
POPULATION: 3,993,817
CAPITAL: Wellington
LANGUAGES: English, Maori (both official)

SOLOMON ISLANDS
AREA: 10,985 sq mi (28,450 sq km)
POPULATION: 523,617
CAPITAL: Honiara
LANGUAGES: English, Solomon Pidgin, Melanesian languages

VANUATU
AREA: 4,719 sq mi (12,200 sq km)
POPULATION: 202,609
CAPITAL: Port-Vila
LANGUAGES: English, French, Bislama (all official), others

NAURU
AREA: 8 sq mi (21 sq km)
POPULATION: 12,909
CAPITAL: Yaren District
LANGUAGES: Nauruan, English

PALAU
AREA: 177 sq mi (458 sq km)
POPULATION: 20,016
CAPITAL: Koror
LANGUAGES: English, Palauan, Sonsoralese, Tobi, others

SAMOA
AREA: 1,136 sq mi (2,944 sq km)
POPULATION: 177,714
CAPITAL: Apia
LANGUAGES: Samoan (Polynesian), English

TONGA
AREA: 289 sq mi (748 sq km)
POPULATION: 110,237
CAPITAL: Nuku'alofa
LANGUAGES: Tongan, English

TUVALU
AREA: 10 sq mi (26 sq km)
POPULATION: 11,468
CAPITAL: Funafuti
LANGUAGES: Tuvalulan, English, Somoan, Kiribati

CHINA
TAIWAN
PHILIPPINES
Iwo (Jap
Okinawa (Japan)
North Maria Islands (U.S
Guam (
Yap
PALAU
INDONESNIA
AUSTRALIA

C D E F G H I

MEXICO

1

*Midway Is.
(U.S.)*

*Wake I.
(U.S.)* P O L Y

Hawaii
(U.S.)

Bikini I. **MARSHALL
ISLANDS**

NORTH PACIFIC
OCEAN N E

2

M I C R O S

oline
nds

TED STATES
CRONESIA

*Gilbert
Islands*

Equator

3

NAURU

KIRIBATI I

A

**SOLOMON
ISLANDS** **TUVALU** N E S

Wallis & Futuna (France)

Tokelau (N.Z.)

N *American Samoa (U.S.)*

*French Polynesia
(France)*

4

VANUATU E S I A

FIJI **SAMOA**

Tahiti

Pitcairn Is . (U.K.)

New Caledonia (France) **TONGA** *Cook Is. (N.Z.)*

● Brisbane SOUTH PACIFIC OCEAN

NEW ZEALAND Auckland

5

North Island

NEW ZEALAND

*Norfolk I.
(Australia)*

berra *Lord Howe I.
(Australia)* *North
Island*

N

*Tasman
Sea* *Mount Ruapehu* ▲

dney

Wellington ✪ W TFK E

ania *South
Island* *Chatham Is. (N.Z.)* S Southern Alps ✪ **Wellington**

6

South Island ● Christchurch

Auckland I. (N.Z.) **NEW ZEALAND**

● *Bounty Is. (N.Z.)*

Mt. Cook ▲

PACIFIC
OCEAN

uarie I. (Australia) ● *Antipodes Is. (N.Z.)*

● Dunedin

● *Campbell I. (N.Z.)*

1000 miles

SOUTHERN

0   200 miles

7

1500 kilometers

OCEAN

Stewart I. 0   300 kilometers

C D E F G H I

Did You Know?

● There are several extinct volcanoes within the borders of Auckland, New Zealand.

These girls in New Zealand are dressed as traditional Maori dancers.

● New Zealand was the first country to give women the vote.

● Flightless kiwi birds live only in New Zealand. "Kiwi" has become a friendly nickname for a person from New Zealand.

● When British explorer Captain James Cook first discovered New Zealand, the native Maori men stuck out their tongues at him. He learned that this was intended to scare him off. Eventually, he and the Maori people became friendly.

● Copra (dried coconut meat) is a food product throughout Oceania.

● The people of Oceania are well known for their music, dance and art. Their masks, costumes and sculptures are in museums all around the world.

Antarctica

King penguins on parade

Antarctica is the highest, driest, coldest and windiest place on earth. It is also the location of the South Pole—the southernmost point on earth. Almost all of Antarctica is covered by an ice sheet. The rest of the continent is barren rock. During the winter months, from June until August, the night lasts for 24 hours, and huge blizzards and windstorms sweep across the frozen plains. Yet with its soaring ice cliffs and amazing views of the aurora australis, or southern lights, Antarctica is one of the most beautiful places in the world. It is also home to an incredible array of animals, including many kinds of whales, birds, fish, insects and mammals. Penguins are probably Antarctica's most famous residents.

About 500 million years ago, the frozen land of Antarctica was located near the equator. As recently as 65 million years ago—during the age of dinosaurs—it was warm enough in Antarctica for many life forms to thrive. Now scientists are discovering suprisingly well-preserved fossils of dinosaurs and other ancient life forms on the continent.

No human beings are native to Antarctica. Since the first explorers reached the South Pole in 1911, scientists and adventurers have ventured to the frozen land to learn more about it. Each year, as many as 4,000 people from 27 nations live, work and study at research centers. An additional 1,000 scientists travel to the Antarctic seas to study marine life and oceanography.

McMurdo Station is Antarctica's largest research center.

Continent Facts

AREA: 5,405,430 sq mi (14,000,000 sq km)

NUMBER OF COUNTRIES AND TERRITORIES: There are no national governments in Antarctica. Instead, Antarctica is governed by a treaty signed by 45 nations. The treaty states that Antarctica is a free and peaceful territory. The treaty also supports open scientific exchange and protects Antarctica's natural environment.

LONGEST RIVER: There are no true rivers in Antarctica. The Onyx River, a snowmelt area, is only about 18 mi (29 km) long.

LONGEST MOUNTAIN RANGE: The Transantarctic Mountains are 3,000 mi long (4,800 km)

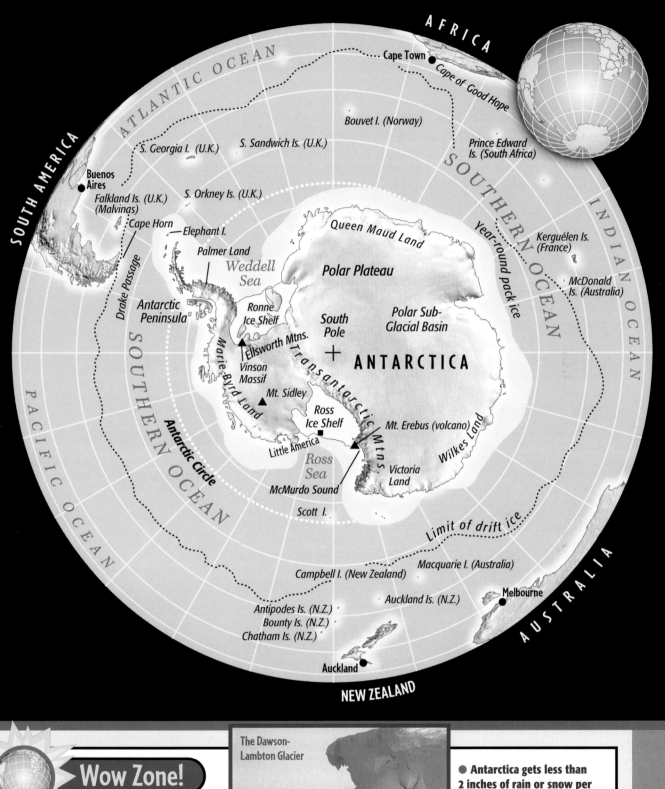

AFRICA

ATLANTIC OCEAN

Cape Town

Cape of Good Hope

Bouvet I. (Norway)

SOUTHERN OCEAN

S. Georgia I. (U.K.)

S. Sandwich Is. (U.K.)

Prince Edward
Is. (South Africa)

SOUTH AMERICA

Buenos
Aires

Falkland Is. (U.K.)
(Malvinas)

S. Orkney Is. (U.K.)

INDIAN OCEAN

Kerguélen Is.
(France)

Cape Horn

Elephant I.

Queen Maud Land

Year-round pack ice

McDonald
Is. (Australia)

Drake Passage

Palmer Land

Weddell
Sea

Polar Plateau

Antarctic
Peninsula

Ronne
Ice Shelf

South
Pole

Polar Sub-
Glacial Basin

Ellsworth Mtns.

+

ANTARCTICA

SOUTHERN OCEAN

Vinson
Massif

Mt. Sidley

Marie Byrd Land

Transantarctic Mtns.

Mt. Erebus (volcano)

Ross
Ice Shelf

PACIFIC OCEAN

Little America

Wilkes Land

Antarctic Circle

Ross
Sea

Victoria
Land

McMurdo Sound

Scott I.

Limit of drift ice

Macquarie I. (Australia)

Campbell I. (New Zealand)

Auckland Is. (N.Z.)

Melbourne

Antipodes Is. (N.Z.)
Bounty Is. (N.Z.)
Chatham Is. (N.Z.)

AUSTRALIA

Auckland

NEW ZEALAND

The Dawson-
Lambton Glacier

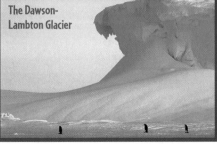

Wow Zone!

● On December 14, 1911,
Norwegian Roald Amundsen
became the first person to reach the
South Pole.

● Antarctica is 98% covered in ice and snow—that's
80% of the ice in the world! The remaining 2% of the
continent is rock.

● Antarctica gets less than
2 inches of rain or snow per
year. It is the world's
biggest desert.

● Scientists in Antarctica
recorded the coldest
temperature on earth:
−128.6°F (−88.0°C)!

● The biggest hole in Earth's ozone layer is located
over Antarctica.

World-at-a-Glance

AFGHANISTAN
AREA: 249,999 sq mi (647,500 sq km)
POPULATION: 29,547,078
CAPITAL: Kabul
LANGUAGES: Pashtu, Afghan Persian (Dari), other Turkic languages
GOVERNMENT: Transitional
RELIGIONS: Sunni Muslim, Shi'a Muslim
LITERACY RATE: 36%
CURRENCY: Afghani
MAIN EXPORTS: Fruits and nuts, carpets, wool, cotton, hides and pelts, precious and semiprecious gems

ALBANIA
AREA: 11,100 sq mi (28,748 sq km)
POPULATION: 3,544,808
CAPITAL: Tirana
LANGUAGES: Albanian (Tosk is the official dialect), Greek
GOVERNMENT: Emerging democracy
RELIGIONS: Muslim, Albanian Orthodox, Roman Catholic
LITERACY RATE: 87%
CURRENCY: Lek
MAIN EXPORTS: Textiles, footwear, asphalt, metals, crude oil, vegetables, fruits, tobacco

ALGERIA
AREA: 919,586 sq mi (2,381,740 sq km)
POPULATION: 33,357,089
CAPITAL: Algiers
LANGUAGES: Arabic (official), French, Berber dialects
GOVERNMENT: Republic
RELIGION: Sunni Muslim
LITERACY RATE: 70%
CURRENCY: Algerian dinar
MAIN EXPORTS: Petroleum, natural gas, petroleum products

ANDORRA
AREA: 181 sq mi (468 sq km)
POPULATION: 69,865
CAPITAL: Andorra la Vella
LANGUAGES: Catalan (official), French, Castilian, Portuguese
GOVERNMENT: Parliamentary democracy
RELIGION: Roman Catholic

LITERACY RATE: 100%
CURRENCY: Euro
MAIN EXPORTS: Tobacco products, furniture

ANGOLA
AREA: 481,350 sq mi (1,246,700 sq km)
POPULATION: 10,978,552
CAPITAL: Luanda
LANGUAGES: Portuguese (official), Bantu, other African languages
GOVERNMENT: Republic, nominally a multiparty democracy
RELIGIONS: Native beliefs, Roman Catholic, Protestant
LITERACY RATE: 42%
CURRENCY: Kwanza
MAIN EXPORTS: Crude oil, diamonds, refined petroleum products, gas, coffee, sisal, fish, timber, cotton

ANTIGUA AND BARBUDA
AREA: 171 sq mi (443 sq km)
POPULATION: 68,320
CAPITAL: Saint John's
LANGUAGES: English (official), local dialects
GOVERNMENT: Constitutional monarchy
RELIGIONS: Protestant, Roman Catholic
LITERACY RATE: 89%
CURRENCY: East Caribbean dollar
MAIN EXPORTS: Petroleum products, machinery and transport equipment, food, live animals

ARGENTINA
AREA: 1,068,296 sq mi (2,766,890 sq km)
POPULATION: 39,144,753
CAPITAL: Buenos Aires
LANGUAGES: Spanish (official), English, Italian, German
GOVERNMENT: Republic
RELIGIONS: Roman Catholic, Protestant, Jewish
LITERACY RATE: 97%
CURRENCY: Argentine peso
MAIN EXPORTS: Edible oils, fuels and energy, cereals, feed, motor vehicles

ARMENIA
AREA: 11,500 sq mi (29,800 sq km)
POPULATION: 3,325,307
CAPITAL: Yerevan

LANGUAGES: Armenian, Russian
GOVERNMENT: Republic
RELIGIONS: Armenian Apostolic, other Christian, Yezidi
LITERACY RATE: 99%
CURRENCY: Dram
MAIN EXPORTS: Diamonds, mineral products, foodstuffs, energy

AUSTRALIA
AREA: 2,967,893 sq mi (7,686,850 sq km)
POPULATION: 19,913,144
CAPITAL: Canberra
LANGUAGES: English, native languages
GOVERNMENT: Democracy
RELIGIONS: Protestant, Roman Catholic, other
LITERACY RATE: 100%
CURRENCY: Australian dollar
MAIN EXPORTS: Coal, gold, meat, wool, alumina, iron ore, wheat, machinery, transport equipment

AUSTRIA
AREA: 32,375 sq mi (83,858 sq km)
POPULATION: 8,174,762
CAPITAL: Vienna
LANGUAGE: German
GOVERNMENT: Republic
RELIGIONS: Roman Catholic, Protestant, Muslim
LITERACY RATE: 98%
CURRENCY: Euro
MAIN EXPORTS: Machinery, motor vehicles and parts, paper, metal goods, chemicals, iron, steel

AZERBAIJAN
AREA: 33,400 sq mi (86,000 sq km)
POPULATION: 7,868,385
CAPITAL: Baku
LANGUAGES: Azerbaijani (Azeri), Russian, Armenian
GOVERNMENT: Republic
RELIGIONS: Muslim, Russian Orthodox, Armenian Orthodox
LITERACY RATE: 97%
CURRENCY: Azerbaijani manat
MAIN EXPORTS: Oil and gas, machinery, cotton, foodstuffs

BAHAMAS
AREA: 5,380 sq mi
(13,940 sq km)
POPULATION:
299,697

CAPITAL: Nassau
LANGUAGE: English
GOVERNMENT: Parliamentary democracy
RELIGIONS: Protestant, Roman Catholic
LITERACY RATE: 96%
CURRENCY: Bahamian dollar
MAIN EXPORTS: Fish, rum, salt, chemicals, fruit and vegetables

BAHRAIN
AREA: 257 sq mi
(665 sq km)
POPULATION:
667,886

CAPITAL: Manama
LANGUAGES: Arabic, English, Farsi, Urdu
GOVERNMENT: Constitutional hereditary monarchy
RELIGIONS: Shi'a Muslim, Sunni Muslim
LITERACY RATE: 89%
CURRENCY: Bahraini dinar
MAIN EXPORTS: Petroleum and petroleum products, aluminum, textiles

BANGLADESH
AREA: 55,598 sq mi
(144,000 sq km)
POPULATION:
141,340,476

CAPITAL: Dhaka
LANGUAGES: Bangla (official), English
GOVERNMENT: Parliamentary democracy
RELIGIONS: Muslim, Hindu
LITERACY RATE: 43%
CURRENCY: Taka
MAIN EXPORTS: Clothing, jute, leather, frozen fish and seafood

BARBADOS
AREA: 166 sq mi
(431 sq km)
POPULATION:
278,289

CAPITAL: Bridgetown
LANGUAGE: English
GOVERNMENT: Parliamentary democracy
RELIGIONS: Protestant, Roman Catholic
LITERACY RATE: 97%
CURRENCY: Barbadian dollar
MAIN EXPORTS: Sugar and molasses, rum, foodstuffs, chemicals, electrical components

BELARUS
AREA: 80,154 sq mi
(207,600 sq km)
POPULATION:
10,310,520

CAPITAL: Minsk
LANGUAGES: Belarusian, Russian
GOVERNMENT: Republic

RELIGIONS: Eastern Orthodox, Roman Catholic, Protestant, Jewish, Muslim
LITERACY RATE: 100%
CURRENCY: Belarusian ruble
MAIN EXPORTS: Machinery and equipment, mineral products, chemicals, metals, textiles, foodstuffs

BELGIUM
AREA: 11,781 sq mi
(30,510 sq km)
POPULATION:
10,348,276

CAPITAL: Brussels
LANGUAGES: Dutch, French, German (all official)
GOVERNMENT: Federal parliamentary democracy under a constitutional monarch
RELIGIONS: Roman Catholic, Protestant
LITERACY RATE: 98%
CURRENCY: Euro
MAIN EXPORTS: Machinery and equipment, chemicals, diamonds, metals and metal products, foodstuffs

BELIZE
AREA: 8,865 sq mi
(22,966 sq km)
POPULATION:
272,945

CAPITAL: Belmopan
LANGUAGES: English (official), Spanish, Mayan, Garifuna (Carib)
GOVERNMENT: Parliamentary democracy
RELIGIONS: Roman Catholic, Protestant
LITERACY RATE: 94%
CURRENCY: Belizean dollar
MAIN EXPORTS: Sugar, bananas, citrus, clothing, fish products, molasses, wood

BENIN
AREA: 43,483 sq mi
(112,620 sq km)
POPULATION:
7,250,033

CAPITAL: Porto-Novo
LANGUAGES: French (official), African languages
GOVERNMENT: Republic under multiparty democratic rule
RELIGIONS: Native beliefs, Christian, Muslim
LITERACY RATE: 41%
CURRENCY: Communauté Financière Africaine franc
MAIN EXPORTS: Cotton, crude oil, palm products, cocoa

BHUTAN
AREA: 18,147 sq mi
(47,000 sq km)
POPULATION:
2,185,569

CAPITAL: Thimphu
LANGUAGES: Dzongkha (official)
GOVERNMENT: Monarchy
RELIGIONS: Buddhist, Hindu

LITERACY RATE: 42%
CURRENCIES: Ngultrum, Indian rupee
MAIN EXPORTS: Electricity, cardamom, gypsum, timber, handicrafts, cement, fruit, precious stones, spices

BOLIVIA
AREA: 424,162 sq mi
(1,098,580 sq km)
POPULATION:
8,724,156

CAPITAL: La Paz (seat of government); Sucre (legal capital)
LANGUAGES: Spanish, Quechua, Aymara (all official)
GOVERNMENT: Republic
RELIGIONS: Roman Catholic, Protestant
LITERACY RATE: 87%
CURRENCY: Boliviano
MAIN EXPORTS: Soybeans, natural gas, zinc, gold, wood

BOSNIA AND HERZEGOVINA
AREA: 19,741 sq mi
(51,129 sq km)
POPULATION:
4,007,608

CAPITAL: Sarajevo
LANGUAGES: Croatian, Serbian, Bosnian
GOVERNMENT: Emerging democracy
RELIGIONS: Muslim, Orthodox, Roman Catholic, Protestant
LITERACY RATE: NA
CURRENCY: Marka
MAIN EXPORTS: Metals, clothing, wood products

BOTSWANA
AREA: 231,800 sq mi
(600,370 sq km)
POPULATION:
1,561,973

CAPITAL: Gaborone
LANGUAGES: English (official), Setswana
GOVERNMENT: Parliamentary republic
RELIGIONS: Native beliefs, Christian
LITERACY RATE: 80%
CURRENCY: Pula
MAIN EXPORTS: Diamonds, copper, nickel, soda ash, meat, textiles

BRAZIL
AREA: 3,286,470 sq mi
(8,511,965 sq km)
POPULATION:
184,101,109

CAPITAL: Brasília
LANGUAGES: Portuguese (official), Spanish, English, French
GOVERNMENT: Federative republic
RELIGION: Roman Catholic
LITERACY RATE: 86%
CURRENCY: Real
MAIN EXPORTS: Transport equipment, iron ore, soybeans, footwear, coffee, motor vehicles

BRUNEI
AREA: 2,228 sq mi (5,770 sq km)
POPULATION: 365,251
CAPITAL: Bandar Seri Begawan
LANGUAGES: Malay (official), English, Chinese
GOVERNMENT: Constitutional sultanate
RELIGIONS: Muslim, Buddhist, Christian, other
LITERACY RATE: 92%
CURRENCY: Bruneian dollar
MAIN EXPORTS: Crude oil, natural gas, refined products

BULGARIA
AREA: 48,822 sq mi (110,910 sq km)
POPULATION: 7,517,973
CAPITAL: Sofia
LANGUAGE: Bulgarian
GOVERNMENT: Parliamentary democracy
RELIGIONS: Orthodox, Muslim, Roman Catholic, Protestant
LITERACY RATE: 99%
CURRENCY: Lev
MAIN EXPORTS: Clothing, footwear, iron and steel, machinery and equipment, fuels

BURKINA FASO
AREA: 105,870 sq mi (274,200 sq km)
POPULATION: 13,574,820
CAPITAL: Ouagadougou
LANGUAGES: French (official), African languages
GOVERNMENT: Parliamentary republic
RELIGIONS: Native beliefs, Muslim, Christian
LITERACY RATE: 27%
CURRENCY: Communauté Financière Africaine franc
MAIN EXPORTS: Cotton, livestock, gold

BURUNDI
AREA: 10,745 sq mi (27,830 sq km)
POPULATION: 6,231,221
CAPITAL: Bujumbura
LANGUAGES: Kirundi, French (both official), Swahili
GOVERNMENT: Republic
RELIGIONS: Roman Catholic, Protestant, native beliefs, Muslim
LITERACY RATE: 52%
CURRENCY: Burundi franc
MAIN EXPORTS: Coffee, tea, sugar, cotton

CAMBODIA
AREA: 69,900 sq mi (181,040 sq km)
POPULATION: 13,363,421
CAPITAL: Phnom Penh
LANGUAGES: Khmer (official), French, English
GOVERNMENT: Multiparty democracy under a constitutional monarchy
RELIGIONS: Buddhist, other
LITERACY RATE: 70%
CURRENCY: Riel
MAIN EXPORTS: Timber, garments, rubber, rice, fish

CAMEROON
AREA: 183,567 sq mi (475,440 sq km)
POPULATION: 16,063,678
CAPITAL: Yaoundé
LANGUAGES: African languages; English and French (both official),
GOVERNMENT: Unitary republic
RELIGIONS: Native beliefs, Christian, Muslim
LITERACY RATE: 79%
CURRENCY: Communauté Financière Africaine franc
MAIN EXPORTS: Crude oil and petroleum products, lumber, cocoa beans, aluminum

CANADA
AREA: 3,855,085 sq mi (9,984,670 sq km)
POPULATION: 32,507,874
CAPITAL: Ottawa
LANGUAGES: English and French (both official), other
GOVERNMENT: Confederation with parliamentary democracy
RELIGIONS: Roman Catholic, Protestant, others
LITERACY RATE: 97%
CURRENCY: Canadian dollar
MAIN EXPORTS: Motor vehicles, machinery, aircraft, chemicals, plastics, fertilizers, wood pulp, timber, crude petroleum

CAPE VERDE
AREA: 1,557 sq mi (4,033 sq km)
POPULATION: 415,294
CAPITAL: Praia
LANGUAGES: Portuguese, Crioulo
GOVERNMENT: Republic
RELIGIONS: Roman Catholic, Protestant
LITERACY RATE: 77%
CURRENCY: Cape Verdean escudo
MAIN EXPORTS: Fuel, shoes, garments, fish

CENTRAL AFRICAN REPUBLIC
AREA: 240,534 sq mi (622,984 sq km)
POPULATION: 3,742,482
CAPITAL: Bangui
LANGUAGES: French (official), Sangho, tribal languages
GOVERNMENT: Republic
RELIGIONS: Native beliefs, Protestant, Roman Catholic, Muslim
LITERACY RATE: 51%

CURRENCY: Communauté Financière Africaine franc
MAIN EXPORTS: Diamonds, timber, cotton, coffee, tobacco

CHAD
AREA: 495,752 sq mi (1,284,000 sq km)
POPULATION: 9,538,544
CAPITAL: N'Djamena
LANGUAGES: French and Arabic (both official), Sara, African languages
GOVERNMENT: Republic
RELIGIONS: Muslim, Chrisitian, animist, others
LITERACY RATE: 48%
CURRENCY: Communauté Financière Africaine franc
MAIN EXPORTS: Cotton, cattle, gum arabic

CHILE
AREA: 292,258 sq mi (756,950 sq km)
POPULATION: 15,827,180
CAPITAL: Santiago
LANGUAGE: Spanish
GOVERNMENT: Republic
RELIGIONS: Roman Catholic, Protestant, Jewish
LITERACY RATE: 96%
CURRENCY: Chilean peso
MAIN EXPORTS: Copper, fish, fruits, paper and pulp, chemicals

CHINA
AREA: 3,705,386 sq mi (9,596,960 sq km)
POPULATION: 1,294,629,555
CAPITAL: Beijing
LANGUAGES: Chinese (Mandarin), local dialects
GOVERNMENT: Communist state
RELIGIONS: Daoist (Taoist), Buddhist, Muslim, Christian
LITERACY RATE: 86%
CURRENCY: Yuan
MAIN EXPORTS: Machinery and equipment, textiles and clothing, footwear, toys, sporting goods, mineral fuels

COLOMBIA
AREA: 439,733 sq mi (1,138,910 sq km)
POPULATION: 42,310,775
CAPITAL: Bogotá
LANGUAGE: Spanish
GOVERNMENT: Republic
RELIGION: Roman Catholic
LITERACY RATE: 93%
CURRENCY: Colombian peso
MAIN EXPORTS: Petroleum, coffee, coal, clothing, bananas, flowers

COMOROS
AREA: 838 sq mi (2,170 sq km)
POPULATION: 651,901
CAPITAL: Moroni
LANGUAGES: Arabic, French (both official), Shikomoro
GOVERNMENT: Independent republic
RELIGIONS: Sunni Muslim, Roman Catholic
LITERACY RATE: 57%
CURRENCY: Comoran franc
MAIN EXPORTS: Vanilla, ylang-ylang, cloves, perfume oil, copra

CONGO, DEMOCRATIC REPUBLIC OF THE
AREA: 905,562 sq mi (2,345,410 sq km)
POPULATION: 58,317,930
CAPITAL: Kinshasa
LANGUAGES: French (official), Lingala, Kingwana, Kikongo, other African languages
GOVERNMENT: Dictatorship
RELIGIONS: Roman Catholic, Protestant, Kimbanguist, Muslim, native beliefs
LITERACY RATE: 66%
CURRENCY: Congolese franc
MAIN EXPORTS: Diamonds, copper, crude oil, coffee, cobalt

CONGO, REPUBLIC OF THE
AREA: 132,046 sq mi (342,000 sq km)
POPULATION: 2,998,040
CAPITAL: Brazzaville
LANGUAGES: French (official), Lingala, Monokutuba, other African languages
GOVERNMENT: Republic
RELIGIONS: Christian, animist, Muslim
LITERACY RATE: 84%
CURRENCY: Communauté Financière Africaine franc
MAIN EXPORTS: Petroleum, lumber, plywood, sugar, cocoa, coffee, diamonds

COSTA RICA
AREA: 19,730 sq mi (51,100 sq km)
POPULATION: 3,956,507
CAPITAL: San José
LANGUAGE: Spanish (official)
GOVERNMENT: Democratic republic
RELIGIONS: Roman Catholic, Protestant, other
LITERACY RATE: 96%
CURRENCY: Costa Rican colón
MAIN EXPORTS: Coffee, bananas, sugar, pineapples, textiles, electronic components, medical equipment

CÔTE D'IVOIRE
AREA: 124,502 sq mi (322,460 sq km)
POPULATION: 17,327,724
CAPITAL: Yamoussoukro
LANGUAGES: French (official), African languages
GOVERNMENT: Republic
RELIGIONS: Muslim, Christian
LITERACY RATE: 51%
CURRENCY: Communauté Financière Africaine franc
MAIN EXPORTS: Cocoa, coffee, timber, petroleum, cotton, bananas, pineapples

CROATIA
AREA: 21,829 sq mi (56,542 sq km)
POPULATION: 4,435,960
CAPITAL: Zagreb
LANGUAGE: Croatian
GOVERNMENT: Presidential/parliamentary democracy
RELIGIONS: Roman Catholic, Orthodox, Muslim
LITERACY RATE: 99%
CURRENCY: Kuna
MAIN EXPORTS: Transport equipment, textiles, chemicals, foodstuffs, fuels

CUBA
AREA: 42,803 sq mi (110,860 sq km)
POPULATION: 11,308,764
CAPITAL: Havana
LANGUAGE: Spanish
GOVERNMENT: Communist state
RELIGIONS: Roman Catholic, Protestant
LITERACY RATE: 97%
CURRENCY: Cuban peso
MAIN EXPORTS: Sugar, nickel, tobacco, fish, medical products, citrus, coffee

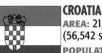

CYPRUS
AREA: 3,572 sq mi (9,250 sq km)
POPULATION: 775,927
CAPITAL: Nicosia
LANGUAGES: Greek, Turkish, English
GOVERNMENT: Republic
RELIGIONS: Greek Orthodox, Muslim, Maronite, Armenian Apostolic
LITERACY RATE: 98%
CURRENCIES: Cypriot pound, Turkish lira
MAIN EXPORTS: Citrus, potatoes, pharmaceuticals, cement, textiles

CZECH REPUBLIC
AREA: 30,450 sq mi (78,866 sq km)
POPULATION: 10,246,178
CAPITAL: Prague
LANGUAGE: Czech
GOVERNMENT: Parliamentary democracy
RELIGIONS: Roman Catholic, Protestant
LITERACY RATE: 100%
CURRENCY: Koruna
MAIN EXPORTS: Machinery and transport equipment, manufactured goods, chemicals

DENMARK
AREA: 16,639 sq mi (43,094 sq km)
POPULATION: 5,413,392
CAPITAL: Copenhagen
LANGUAGES: Danish, Faroese, Greenlandic, German
GOVERNMENT: Constitutional monarchy
RELIGIONS: Protestant, Roman Catholic, Muslim
LITERACY RATE: 100%
CURRENCY: Krone
MAIN EXPORTS: Machinery and instruments, meat, dairy products, fish, chemicals, furniture, ships, windmills

DJIBOUTI
AREA: 8,800 sq mi (23,000 sq km)
POPULATION: 466,900
CAPITAL: Djibouti
LANGUAGES: French, Arabic (both official), Somali, Afar
GOVERNMENT: Republic
RELIGIONS: Muslim, Christian
LITERACY RATE: 68%
CURRENCY: Djiboutian franc
MAIN EXPORTS: Re-exports, hides and skins, coffee

DOMINICA
AREA: 290 sq mi (754 sq km)
POPULATION: 69,278
CAPITAL: Roseau
LANGUAGES: English (official), French patois
GOVERNMENT: Parliamentary democracy
RELIGIONS: Roman Catholic, Protestant
LITERACY RATE: 94%
CURRENCY: East Caribbean dollar
MAIN EXPORTS: Bananas, soap, bay oil, vegetables, grapefruit, oranges

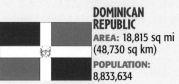

DOMINICAN REPUBLIC
AREA: 18,815 sq mi (48,730 sq km)
POPULATION: 8,833,634
CAPITAL: Santo Domingo
LANGUAGE: Spanish
GOVERNMENT: Representative democracy
RELIGION: Roman Catholic
LITERACY RATE: 85%
CURRENCY: Dominican peso
MAIN EXPORTS: Ferronickel, sugar, gold, silver, coffee, cocoa, tobacco, meats

EAST TIMOR
AREA: 5,814 sq mi
(15,007 sq km)
POPULATION:
1,019,252
CAPITAL: Dili
LANGUAGES: Tetum, Portuguese (both
official), Indonesian, English
GOVERNMENT: Republic
RELIGIONS: Roman Catholic, Muslim,
Protestant
LITERACY RATE: 48%
CURRENCY: U.S. dollar
MAIN EXPORTS: Coffee, sandalwood, marble

ECUADOR
AREA: 109,483 sq mi
(283,560 sq km)
POPULATION:
13,971,798
CAPITAL: Quito
LANGUAGES: Spanish (official),
Amerindian languages
GOVERNMENT: Republic
RELIGION: Roman Catholic
LITERACY RATE: 93%
CURRENCY: U.S. dollar
MAIN EXPORTS: Petroleum, bananas,
shrimp, coffee, cocoa, flowers, fish

EGYPT
AREA: 386,660 sq mi
(1,001,450 sq km)
POPULATION:
76,117,421
CAPITAL: Cairo
LANGUAGE: Arabic (official)
GOVERNMENT: Republic
RELIGIONS: Muslim (mostly Sunni), Coptic
Christian
LITERACY RATE: 58%
CURRENCY: Egyptian pound
MAIN EXPORTS: Crude oil and petroleum
products, cotton, textiles, metal products

EL SALVADOR
AREA: 8,124 sq mi
(21,040 sq km)
POPULATION:
6,587,541
CAPITAL: San Salvador
LANGUAGES: Spanish, Nahua
GOVERNMENT: Republic
RELIGION: Roman Catholic
LITERACY RATE: 80%
CURRENCY: U.S. dollar
MAIN EXPORTS: Offshore assembly
exports, coffee, sugar, shrimp, textiles,
chemicals, electricity

EQUATORIAL GUINEA
AREA: 10,830 sq mi
(28,051 sq km)
POPULATION: 523,051
CAPITAL: Malabo
LANGUAGES: Spanish, French (both
official), Pidgin English, Fang

GOVERNMENT: Republic
RELIGION: Christian
LITERACY RATE: 86%
CURRENCY: Communauté Financière
Africaine franc
MAIN EXPORTS: Petroleum, methanol,
timber, cocoa

ERITREA
AREA: 46,842 sq mi
(121,320 sq km)
POPULATION:
4,447,307
CAPITAL: Asmara
LANGUAGES: Afar, Arabic, Tigre, Kunama,
other languages
GOVERNMENT: Transitional
RELIGIONS: Muslim, Coptic Christian,
Roman Catholic, Protestant
LITERACY RATE: 59%
CURRENCY: Nakfa
MAIN EXPORTS: Livestock, sorghum,
textiles, food, small manufactured goods

ESTONIA
AREA: 17,462 sq mi
(45,226 sq km)
POPULATION:
1,401,945
CAPITAL: Tallinn
LANGUAGES: Estonian (official), Russian,
Ukrainian, Finnish
GOVERNMENT: Parliamentary republic
RELIGIONS: Protestant, Russian Orthodox,
Estonian Orthodox
LITERACY RATE: 100%
CURRENCY: Estonian kroon
MAIN EXPORTS: Machinery and
equipment, wood and paper, textiles, food
products, furniture, metals

ETHIOPIA
AREA: 485,184 sq mi
(1,256,634 sq km)
POPULATION:
67,851,281
CAPITAL: Addis Ababa
LANGUAGES: Amharic, Tigrinya, Oromigna,
other local languages
GOVERNMENT: Federal republic
RELIGIONS: Muslim, Ethiopian Orthodox,
animist
LITERACY RATE: 43%
CURRENCY: Birr
MAIN EXPORTS: Coffee, qat, gold, leather
products, live animals, oilseeds

FIJI
AREA: 7,054 sq mi
(18,270 sq km)
POPULATION:
880,874
CAPITAL: Suva
LANGUAGES: English (official), Fijian,
Hindustani
GOVERNMENT: Republic
RELIGIONS: Christian, Hindu, Muslim
LITERACY RATE: 94%

CURRENCY: Fijian dollar
MAIN EXPORTS: Sugar, garments, gold,
timber, fish, molasses, coconut oil

FINLAND
AREA: 130,127 sq mi
(337,030 sq km)
POPULATION:
5,214,512
CAPITAL: Helsinki
LANGUAGES: Finnish, Swedish
(both official)
GOVERNMENT: Republic
RELIGIONS: Evangelical Lutheran, Russian
Orthodox
LITERACY RATE: 100%
CURRENCY: Euro
MAIN EXPORTS: Machinery and
equipment, chemicals, metals, timber,
paper, pulp

FRANCE
AREA: 211,208 sq mi
(547,030 sq km)
POPULATION:
60,424,213
CAPITAL: Paris
LANGUAGE: French
GOVERNMENT: Republic
RELIGIONS: Roman Catholic, Protestant,
Jewish, Muslim
LITERACY RATE: 99%
CURRENCY: Euro
MAIN EXPORTS: Machinery and
transportation equipment, aircraft, plastics,
chemicals, pharmaceutical products, iron
and steel, beverages

GABON
AREA: 103,347 sq mi
(267,667 sq km)
POPULATION:
1,355,246
CAPITAL: Libreville
LANGUAGES: French (official), Fang,
Myene, Nzebi, Bapounou/Eschira, Bandjabi
GOVERNMENT: Republic
RELIGIONS: Christian, animist, Muslim
LITERACY RATE: 63%
CURRENCY: Communauté Financière
Africaine franc
MAIN EXPORTS: Crude oil, timber,
manganese, uranium

GAMBIA
AREA: 4,363 sq mi
(11,300 sq km)
POPULATION:
1,546,848
CAPITAL: Banjul
LANGUAGES: English (official), native
languages
GOVERNMENT: Republic
RELIGIONS: Muslim, Christian, other
LITERACY RATE: 40%
CURRENCY: Dalasi
MAIN EXPORTS: Peanut products, fish,
cotton lint, palm kernels, re-exports

GEORGIA
AREA: 26,911 sq mi (69,700 sq km)
POPULATION: 4,909,633
CAPITAL: Tbilisi
LANGUAGES: Georgian (official), Russian, Armenian, Azeri
GOVERNMENT: Republic
RELIGIONS: Georgian Orthodox, Muslim, Russian Orthodox, Armenian Apostolic
LITERACY RATE: 99%
CURRENCY: Lari
MAIN EXPORTS: Scrap metal, machinery, chemicals, fuel re-exports, citrus fruits, tea

GERMANY
AREA: 137,846 sq mi (357,021 sq km)
POPULATION: 82,424,609
CAPITAL: Berlin
LANGUAGE: German
GOVERNMENT: Federal republic
RELIGIONS: Protestant, Roman Catholic, Muslim
LITERACY RATE: 99%
CURRENCY: Euro
MAIN EXPORTS: Machinery, vehicles, chemicals, metals, manufactured goods, foodstuffs, textiles

GHANA
AREA: 92,456 sq mi (239,460 sq km)
POPULATION: 20,757,032
CAPITAL: Accra
LANGUAGES: English (official), African languages
GOVERNMENT: Constitutional democracy
RELIGIONS: Native beliefs, Muslim, Christian
LITERACY RATE: 75%
CURRENCY: Cedi
MAIN EXPORTS: Gold, cocoa, timber, tuna, bauxite, aluminum, diamonds

GREECE
AREA: 50,942 sq mi (131,940 sq km)
POPULATION: 10,647,529
CAPITAL: Athens
LANGUAGES: Greek (official), English, French
GOVERNMENT: Parliamentary republic
RELIGIONS: Greek Orthodox, Muslim
LITERACY RATE: 98%
CURRENCY: Euro
MAIN EXPORTS: Food and beverages, petroleum products, chemicals, textiles

GRENADA
AREA: 133 sq mi (344 sq km)
POPULATION: 89,357
CAPITAL: St. George's

LANGUAGES: English (official), French patois
GOVERNMENT: Constitutional monarchy
RELIGIONS: Roman Catholic, Protestant
LITERACY RATE: 98%
CURRENCY: East Caribbean dollar
MAIN EXPORTS: Bananas, cocoa, nutmeg, fruits and vegetables, clothing, mace

GUATEMALA
AREA: 42,042 sq mi (108,890 sq km)
POPULATION: 14,280,596
CAPITAL: Guatemala City
LANGUAGES: Spanish, Amerindian languages
GOVERNMENT: Constitutional democratic republic
RELIGIONS: Roman Catholic, Protestant, native Mayan beliefs
LITERACY RATE: 71%
CURRENCIES: Quetzal, U.S. dollar
MAIN EXPORTS: Coffee, sugar, bananas, fruits and vegetables, cardamom, meat, apparel, petroleum, electricity

GUINEA
AREA: 94,925 sq mi (245,857 sq km)
POPULATION: 9,246,462
CAPITAL: Conakry
LANGUAGES: French (official), native languages
GOVERNMENT: Republic
RELIGIONS: Muslim, Christian, native beliefs
LITERACY RATE: 36%
CURRENCY: Guinean franc
MAIN EXPORTS: Bauxite, alumina, gold, diamonds, coffee, fish

GUINEA-BISSAU
AREA: 13,946 sq mi (36,120 sq km)
POPULATION: 1,388,363
CAPITAL: Bissau
LANGUAGES: Portuguese (official), Crioulo, African languages
GOVERNMENT: Republic
RELIGIONS: Native beliefs, Muslim, Christian
LITERACY RATE: 42%
CURRENCY: Communauté Financière Africaine franc
MAIN EXPORTS: Cashew nuts, shrimp, peanuts, palm kernels, sawn lumber

GUYANA
AREA: 83,000 sq mi (214,970 sq km)
POPULATION: 705,803
CAPITAL: Georgetown
LANGUAGES: English, Amerindian dialects, Creole, Hindi, Urdu
GOVERNMENT: Republic

RELIGIONS: Christian, Hindu, Muslim, other
LITERACY RATE: 99%
CURRENCY: Guyanese dollar
MAIN EXPORTS: Sugar, gold, rice, shrimp, bauxite/alumina, molasses, rum, timber

HAITI
AREA: 10,714 sq mi (27,750 sq km)
POPULATION: 7,656,166
CAPITAL: Port-au-Prince
LANGUAGES: French, Creole (both official)
GOVERNMENT: Elected government
RELIGIONS: Roman Catholic, Protestant, others
LITERACY RATE: 53%
CURRENCY: Gourde
MAIN EXPORTS: Manufactured goods, coffee, oils, cocoa

HONDURAS
AREA: 43,278 sq mi (112,090 sq km)
POPULATION: 6,823,568
CAPITAL: Tegucigalpa
LANGUAGES: Spanish, Amerindian dialects
GOVERNMENT: Democratic constitutional republic
RELIGIONS: Roman Catholic, Protestant
LITERACY RATE: 76%
CURRENCY: Lempira
MAIN EXPORTS: Coffee, bananas, shrimp, lobster, meat, zinc, lumber

HUNGARY
AREA: 35,919 sq mi (93,030 sq km)
POPULATION: 10,032,375
CAPITAL: Budapest
LANGUAGE: Hungarian
GOVERNMENT: Parliamentary democracy
RELIGIONS: Roman Catholic, Calvinist, Lutheran
LITERACY RATE: 99%
CURRENCY: Forint
MAIN EXPORTS: Machinery and equipment, manufactured goods, food products, raw materials, fuels, electricity

ICELAND
AREA: 39,768 sq mi (103,000 sq km)
POPULATION: 282,151
CAPITAL: Reykjavik
LANGUAGES: Icelandic, English, Nordic languages, German
GOVERNMENT: Constitutional republic
RELIGION: Evangelical Lutheran
LITERACY RATE: 100%
CURRENCY: Icelandic krona
MAIN EXPORTS: Fish and fish products, animal products, aluminum, diatomite, ferrosilicon

INDIA
AREA: 1,269,338 sq mi (3,287,590 sq km)
POPULATION: 1,065,070,607
CAPITAL: New Delhi
LANGUAGES: Hindi (official), English, native languages
GOVERNMENT: Federal republic
RELIGIONS: Hindu, Muslim, Christian, Sikh
LITERACY RATE: 60%
CURRENCY: Indian rupee
MAIN EXPORTS: Textile goods, gems and jewelry, engineering goods, chemicals, leather manufactured goods

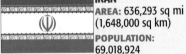

INDONESIA
AREA: 741,096 sq mi (1,919,440 sq km)
POPULATION: 238,452,952
CAPITAL: Jakarta
LANGUAGES: Bahasa Indonesian, English, Dutch, local dialects
GOVERNMENT: Republic
RELIGIONS: Muslim, Protestant, Roman Catholic, Hindu, Buddhist
LITERACY RATE: 89%
CURRENCY: Indonesian rupiah
MAIN EXPORTS: Oil and gas, electrical appliances, plywood, textiles, rubber

IRAN
AREA: 636,293 sq mi (1,648,000 sq km)
POPULATION: 69,018,924
CAPITAL: Tehran
LANGUAGES: Persian, Turkic, Kurdish
GOVERNMENT: Theocratic republic
RELIGIONS: Shi'a Muslim, Sunni Muslim, Zoroastrianism, Jewish, Christian
LITERACY RATE: 79%
CURRENCY: Iranian rial
MAIN EXPORTS: Petroleum, carpets, fruits and nuts, iron and steel, chemicals

IRAQ
AREA: 168,753 sq mi (437,072 sq km)
POPULATION: 25,374,691
CAPITAL: Baghdad
LANGUAGES: Arabic, Kurdish, Assyrian, Armenian
GOVERNMENT: Transitional
RELIGIONS: Muslim, Christian
LITERACY RATE: 40%
CURRENCY: Iraqi dinar
MAIN EXPORTS: Crude oil

IRELAND
AREA: 27,136 sq mi (70,280 sq km)
POPULATION: 3,969,558
CAPITAL: Dublin

LANGUAGES: English, Irish (Gaelic)
GOVERNMENT: Republic
RELIGIONS: Roman Catholic, Church of Ireland
LITERACY RATE: 98%
CURRENCY: Euro
MAIN EXPORTS: Machinery and equipment, computers, chemicals, pharmaceuticals, live animals

ISRAEL
AREA: 8,020 sq mi (20,770 sq km)
POPULATION: 6,199,008
CAPITAL: Jerusalem
LANGUAGES: Hebrew, Arabic (both official), English
GOVERNMENT: Parliamentary democracy
RELIGIONS: Jewish, Muslim, Christian
LITERACY RATE: 95%
CURRENCY: New Israeli shekel
MAIN EXPORTS: Machinery and equipment, software, cut diamonds, agricultural products, chemicals, textiles

ITALY
AREA: 116,305 sq mi (301,230 sq km)
POPULATION: 58,057,477
CAPITAL: Rome
LANGUAGES: Italian (official), German, French, Slovene
GOVERNMENT: Republic
RELIGIONS: Roman Catholic, Protestant, Jewish, Muslim
LITERACY RATE: 99%
CURRENCY: Euro
MAIN EXPORTS: Engineering products, textiles, production machinery, motor vehicles, transport equipment, chemicals, food, beverages, tobacco, minerals

JAMAICA
AREA: 4,244 sq mi (10,991 sq km)
POPULATION: 2,713,130
CAPITAL: Kingston
LANGUAGES: English, patois English
GOVERNMENT: Constitutional parliamentary democracy
RELIGIONS: Protestant, Roman Catholic
LITERACY RATE: 88%
CURRENCY: Jamaican dollar
MAIN EXPORTS: Alumina, bauxite, sugar, bananas, rum

JAPAN
AREA: 145,882 sq mi (377,835 sq km)
POPULATION: 127,333,002
CAPITAL: Tokyo
LANGUAGE: Japanese
GOVERNMENT: Constitutional monarchy with a parliamentary government

RELIGIONS: Shinto, Buddhist
LITERACY RATE: 99%
CURRENCY: Yen
MAIN EXPORTS: Motor vehicles, semiconductors, office machinery, chemicals

JORDAN
AREA: 35,637 sq mi (92,300 sq km)
POPULATION: 5,611,202
CAPITAL: Amman
LANGUAGES: Arabic (official), English
GOVERNMENT: Constitutional monarchy
RELIGIONS: Sunni Muslim, Christian
LITERACY RATE: 91%
CURRENCY: Jordanian dinar
MAIN EXPORTS: Phosphates, fertilizers, potash, agricultural products, manufactured goods, pharmaceuticals

KAZAKHSTAN
AREA: 1,049,150 sq mi (2,717,300 sq km)
POPULATION: 16,798,552
CAPITAL: Astana
LANGUAGES: Russian (official), Kazakh
GOVERNMENT: Republic
RELIGIONS: Muslim, Russian Orthodox, Protestant
LITERACY RATE: 98%
CURRENCY: Tenge
MAIN EXPORTS: Oil and oil products, ferrous metals, chemicals, machinery, grain, wool, meat, coal

KENYA
AREA: 224,960 sq mi (582,650 sq km)
POPULATION: 32,021,856
CAPITAL: Nairobi
LANGUAGES: English, Kiswahili (both official), native languages
GOVERNMENT: Republic
RELIGIONS: Protestant, Roman Catholic, native beliefs
LITERACY RATE: 85%
CURRENCY: Kenyan shilling
MAIN EXPORTS: Tea, horticultural products, coffee, petroleum products, fish

KIRIBATI
AREA: 313 sq mi (811 sq km)
POPULATION: 100,798
CAPITAL: Tarawa
LANGUAGES: English (official), I-Kiribati
GOVERNMENT: Republic
RELIGIONS: Roman Catholic, Protestant, Muslim, Baha'i
LITERACY RATE: NA
CURRENCY: Australian dollar
MAIN EXPORTS: Copra, coconuts, seaweed

KOREA, NORTH
AREA: 46,540 sq mi (120,540 sq km)
POPULATION: 22,697,553
CAPITAL: Pyongyang
LANGUAGE: Korean
GOVERNMENT: Authoritarian socialist
RELIGIONS: Buddhist, Confucianist, Christian, Chondogyo (Religion of the Heavenly Way)
LITERACY RATE: 99%
CURRENCY: North Korean won
MAIN EXPORTS: Minerals, fish products

KOREA, SOUTH
AREA: 38,023 sq mi (98,480 sq km)
POPULATION: 48,598,175
CAPITAL: Seoul
LANGUAGE: Korean
GOVERNMENT: Republic
RELIGIONS: Christian, Buddhist, Confucianist, Shamanist, Chondogyo
LITERACY RATE: 98%
CURRENCY: South Korean won
MAIN EXPORTS: Electronic products, machinery and equipment, cars, steel, ships, clothing, footwear, fish

KUWAIT
AREA: 6,880 sq mi (17,820 sq km)
POPULATION: 2,257,549
CAPITAL: Kuwait
LANGUAGES: Arabic (official), English
GOVERNMENT: Nominal constitutional monarchy
RELIGIONS: Muslim, Christian, Hindu, Parsi
LITERACY RATE: 84%
CURRENCY: Kuwaiti dinar
MAIN EXPORTS: Oil and refined products

KYRGYZSTAN
AREA: 76,641 sq mi (198,500 sq km)
POPULATION: 4,965,081
CAPITAL: Bishkek
LANGUAGES: Kyrgyz and Russian (both official)
GOVERNMENT: Republic
RELIGIONS: Muslim, Russian Orthodox
LITERACY RATE: 97%
CURRENCY: Kyrgyzstani som
MAIN EXPORTS: Cotton, wool, meat, tobacco, gold, mercury, uranium

LAOS
AREA: 91,429 sq mi (236,800 sq km)
POPULATION: 6,068,117
CAPITAL: Vientiane
LANGUAGES: Lao (official), French, English, ethnic languages
GOVERNMENT: Communist state
RELIGIONS: Buddhist, animist, Christian
LITERACY RATE: 53%
CURRENCY: Kip
MAIN EXPORTS: Wood products, clothes, electricity, coffee, tin

LATVIA
AREA: 24,938 sq mi (64,589 sq km)
POPULATION: 2,332,078
CAPITAL: Riga
LANGUAGES: Latvian (official), Lithuanian, Russian
GOVERNMENT: Parliamentary democracy
RELIGIONS: Lutheran, Roman Catholic, Russian Orthodox
LITERACY RATE: 100%
CURRENCY: Latvian lat
MAIN EXPORTS: Wood and wood products, machinery and equipment

LEBANON
AREA: 4,015 sq mi (10,400 sq km)
POPULATION: 3,777,218
CAPITAL: Beirut
LANGUAGES: Arabic (official), French, English, Armenian
GOVERNMENT: Republic
RELIGIONS: Muslim, Christian
LITERACY RATE: 87%
CURRENCY: Lebanese pound
MAIN EXPORTS: Foodstuffs, tobacco, textiles, chemicals, precious stones

LESOTHO
AREA: 11,720 sq mi (30,355 sq km)
POPULATION: 1,865,040
CAPITAL: Maseru
LANGUAGES: Sesotho (southern Sotho), English (official), Zulu, Xhosa
GOVERNMENT: Parliamentary constitutional monarchy
RELIGIONS: Christian, native beliefs
LITERACY RATE: 85%
CURRENCY: Loti; South African rand
MAIN EXPORTS: Manufactured clothing, road vehicles, footwear, wool and mohair

LIBERIA
AREA: 43,000 sq mi (111,370 sq km)
POPULATION: 3,390,635
CAPITAL: Monrovia
LANGUAGES: English (official), tribal dialects
GOVERNMENT: Republic
RELIGIONS: Native beliefs, Christian, Muslim
LITERACY RATE: 58%
CURRENCY: Liberian dollar
MAIN EXPORTS: Rubber, timber, iron, diamonds, cocoa, coffee

LIBYA
AREA: 679,358 sq mi (1,759,540 sq km)
POPULATION: 5,631,585
CAPITAL: Tripoli
LANGUAGES: Arabic, Italian, English
GOVERNMENT: Military dictatorship
RELIGION: Sunni Muslim
LITERACY RATE: 83%
CURRENCY: Libyan dinar
MAIN EXPORTS: Crude oil, refined petroleum products

LIECHTENSTEIN
AREA: 62 sq mi (160 sq km)
POPULATION: 33,436
CAPITAL: Vaduz
LANGUAGES: German (official), Alemannic dialect
GOVERNMENT: Hereditary constitutional monarchy
RELIGIONS: Roman Catholic, Protestant
LITERACY RATE: 100%
CURRENCY: Swiss franc
MAIN EXPORTS: Parts for motor vehicles, dental products, prepared foodstuffs

LITHUANIA
AREA: 25,174 sq mi (65,200 sq km)
POPULATION: 3,584,836
CAPITAL: Vilnius
LANGUAGES: Lithuanian (official), Polish, Russian
GOVERNMENT: Parliamentary democracy
RELIGIONS: Roman Catholic, Protestant, Russian Orthodox, Muslim, Jewish
LITERACY RATE: 100%
CURRENCY: Litas
MAIN EXPORTS: Mineral products, textiles, clothing, machinery and equipment

LUXEMBOURG
AREA: 998 sq mi (2,586 sq km)
POPULATION: 462,690
CAPITAL: Luxembourg
LANGUAGES: Luxembourgish, German, French
GOVERNMENT: Constitutional monarchy
RELIGIONS: Roman Catholic, Protestant, Jewish, Muslim
LITERACY RATE: 100%
CURRENCY: Euro
MAIN EXPORTS: Machinery and equipment, steel products, chemicals

MACEDONIA
AREA: 9,781 sq mi (25,333 sq km)
POPULATION: 2,071,210
CAPITAL: Skopje
LANGUAGES: Macedonian, Albanian, Turkish, Serbo-Croatian
GOVERNMENT: Parliamentary democracy
RELIGIONS: Macedonian Orthodox, Muslim
LITERACY RATE: NA
CURRENCY: Denar
MAIN EXPORTS: Food, beverages, tobacco, iron and steel

MADAGASCAR
AREA: 226,655 sq mi (587,040 sq km)
POPULATION: 17,501,871
CAPITAL: Antananarivo
LANGUAGES: Malagasy, French (both official)
GOVERNMENT: Republic
RELIGIONS: Native beliefs, Christian, Muslim
LITERACY RATE: 69%
CURRENCY: Malagasy franc
MAIN EXPORTS: Coffee, vanilla, shellfish, sugar, cotton, cloth, petroleum products

MALAWI
AREA: 45,745 sq mi (118,480 sq km)
POPULATION: 11,906,855
CAPITAL: Lilongwe
LANGUAGES: English, Chichewa (both official)
GOVERNMENT: Multiparty democracy
RELIGIONS: Protestant, Roman Catholic, Muslim, native beliefs
LITERACY RATE: 63%
CURRENCY: Malawian kwacha
MAIN EXPORTS: Tobacco, tea, sugar, cotton, coffee, peanuts, wood products, clothing

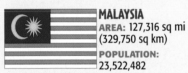

MALAYSIA
AREA: 127,316 sq mi (329,750 sq km)
POPULATION: 23,522,482
CAPITAL: Kuala Lumpur
LANGUAGES: Bahasa Melayu (official), English, Chinese, Tamil, Telugu, Malayalam
GOVERNMENT: Constitutional monarchy
RELIGIONS: Muslim, Buddhist, Daoist, Hindu, Christian
LITERACY RATE: 89%
CURRENCY: Ringgit
MAIN EXPORTS: Electronic equipment, petroleum and liquefied natural gas, wood and wood products, palm oil, rubber

MALDIVES
AREA: 116 sq mi (300 sq km)
POPULATION: 339,330
CAPITAL: Malé
LANGUAGES: Dhivehi, English
GOVERNMENT: Republic
RELIGION: Sunni Muslim
LITERACY RATE: 97%
CURRENCY: Maldivian rufiyaa
MAIN EXPORTS: Fish, clothing

MALI
AREA: 478,764 sq mi (1,240,000 sq km)
Population: 11,956,788
CAPITAL: Bamako
LANGUAGES: French (official), Bambara
GOVERNMENT: Republic
RELIGIONS: Muslim, native beliefs, Christian
LITERACY RATE: 46%
CURRENCY: Communauté Financière Africaine franc
MAIN EXPORTS: Cotton, gold, livestock

MALTA
AREA: 122 sq mi (316 sq km)
POPULATION: 403,342
CAPITAL: Valletta
LANGUAGES: Maltese, English (both official)
GOVERNMENT: Republic
RELIGION: Roman Catholic
LITERACY RATE: 93%
CURRENCY: Maltese lira
MAIN EXPORTS: Machinery, transportation equipment

MARSHALL ISLANDS
AREA: 70 sq mi (181 sq km)
POPULATION: 57,738
CAPITAL: Majuro
LANGUAGES: Marshallese, English (both official), Japanese
GOVERNMENT: Constitutional government
RELIGION: Christian
LITERACY RATE: 94%
CURRENCY: U.S. dollar
MAIN EXPORTS: Copra cake, coconut oil, handcrafts, fish

MAURITANIA
AREA: 397,953 sq mi (1,030,700 sq km)
POPULATION: 2,998,563
CAPITAL: Nouakchott
LANGUAGES: Hassaniya Arabic, Wolof (both official), Pulaar, Soninke, French
GOVERNMENT: Republic
RELIGION: Muslim
LITERACY RATE: 42%
CURRENCY: Ouguiya
MAIN EXPORTS: Iron ore, fish and fish products, gold

MAURITIUS
AREA: 788 sq mi (2,040 sq km)
POPULATION: 1,220,481
CAPITAL: Port Louis
LANGUAGES: English, French (both official), Creole, Hindi, Urdu
GOVERNMENT: Parliamentary democracy
RELIGIONS: Hindu, Roman Catholic, Protestant, Muslim
LITERACY RATE: 86%
CURRENCY: Mauritian rupee
MAIN EXPORTS: Clothing and textiles, sugar, cut flowers, molasses

MEXICO
AREA: 761,600 sq mi (1,972,550 sq km)
POPULATION: 104,959,594
CAPITAL: Mexico City
LANGUAGES: Spanish, Mayan, Nahuatl and other native languages
GOVERNMENT: Federal republic
RELIGIONS: Roman Catholic, Protestant
LITERACY RATE: 92%
CURRENCY: Mexican peso
MAIN EXPORTS: Manufactured goods, oil and oil products, silver, fruit, vegetables

MICRONESIA
AREA: 271 sq mi (702 sq km)
POPULATION: 108,155
CAPITAL: Palikir
LANGUAGES: English (official), Trukese, Pohnpeian, Yapese, other native languages
GOVERNMENT: Constitutional government
RELIGIONS: Roman Catholic, Protestant
LITERACY RATE: 89%
CURRENCY: U.S. dollar
MAIN EXPORTS: Fish, garments, bananas, black pepper

MOLDOVA
AREA: 13,067 sq mi (33,843 sq km)
POPULATION: 4,446,455
CAPITAL: Chisinau
LANGUAGES: Moldovan (official), Russian, Gagauz
GOVERNMENT: Republic
RELIGIONS: Eastern Orthodox, Jewish, Baptist
LITERACY RATE: 99%
CURRENCY: Moldovan leu
MAIN EXPORTS: Foodstuffs, textiles, machinery

MONACO
AREA: .75 sq mi (1.95 sq km)
POPULATION: 32,270
CAPITAL: Monaco
LANGUAGES: French (official), English, Italian, Monégasque
GOVERNMENT: Constitutional monarchy
RELIGION: Roman Catholic
LITERACY RATE: 99%
CURRENCY: Euro
MAIN EXPORTS: NA

MONGOLIA
AREA: 604,250 sq mi (1,565,000 sq km)
POPULATION: 2,751,314
CAPITAL: Ulaanbaatar
LANGUAGES: Khalkha Mongol, Turkic, Russian
GOVERNMENT: Parliamentary
RELIGIONS: Tibetan Buddhist, Lamaism, Muslim, Shamanism, Christian
LITERACY RATE: 99%
CURRENCY: Togrog/tugrik
MAIN EXPORTS: Copper, livestock, animal products, cashmere, wool, hides, fluorspar

MOROCCO
AREA: 172,413 sq mi (446,550 sq km)
POPULATION: 32,209,101
CAPITAL: Rabat
LANGUAGES: Arabic (official), Berber dialects, French
GOVERNMENT: Constitutional monarchy
RELIGIONS: Muslim, Christian, Jewish
LITERACY RATE: 52%
CURRENCY: Dirham
MAIN EXPORTS: Clothing, fish, inorganic chemicals, transistors, crude minerals, fertilizers, petroleum products, fruit

MOZAMBIQUE
AREA: 309,494 sq mi (801,590 sq km)
POPULATION: 18,811,731
CAPITAL: Maputo
LANGUAGES: Portuguese (official), Bantu languages
GOVERNMENT: Republic
RELIGIONS: Native beliefs, Christian, Muslim
LITERACY RATE: 48%
CURRENCY: Metical
MAIN EXPORTS: Aluminum, prawns, cashews, cotton, sugar, citrus, timber

MYANMAR (BURMA)
AREA: 261,969 sq mi (678,500 sq km)
POPULATION: 42,720,196
CAPITAL: Rangoon
LANGUAGES: Burmese, minority languages
GOVERNMENT: Military regime
RELIGIONS: Buddhist, Baptist, Roman Catholic, Muslim, animist
LITERACY RATE: 83%
CURRENCY: Kyat
MAIN EXPORTS: Gas, wood products, pulses, beans, fish, rice

NAMIBIA
AREA: 318,694 sq mi (825,418 sq km)
POPULATION: 1,954,033
CAPITAL: Windhoek
LANGUAGES: English (official), Afrikaans, German, native languages
GOVERNMENT: Republic
RELIGIONS: Christian, native beliefs
LITERACY RATE: 84%
CURRENCY: Namibian dollar, South African rand
MAIN EXPORTS: Diamonds, copper, gold, zinc, lead, uranium, cattle, processed fish

NAURU
AREA: 8 sq mi (21 sq km)
POPULATION: 12,909
CAPITAL: Yaren District
LANGUAGES: Nauruan, English
GOVERNMENT: Republic
RELIGIONS: Protestant, Roman Catholic
LITERACY RATE: NA
CURRENCY: Australian dollar
MAIN EXPORT: Phosphates

NEPAL
AREA: 54,363 sq mi (140,800 sq km)
POPULATION: 27,070,666
CAPITAL: Kathmandu
LANGUAGES: Nepali, English
GOVERNMENT: Parliamentary democracy, constitutional monarchy
RELIGIONS: Hinduism, Buddhism, Muslim
CURRENCY: Nepalese rupee
MAIN EXPORTS: Carpets, clothing, leather goods, jute goods, grain

NETHERLANDS
AREA: 16,033 sq mi (41,526 sq km)
POPULATION: 16,318,199
CAPITAL: Amsterdam
LANGUAGES: Dutch, Frisian (both official)
GOVERNMENT: Constitutional monarchy
RELIGIONS: Roman Catholic, Protestant, Muslim
LITERACY RATE: 99%
CURRENCY: Euro
MAIN EXPORTS: Machinery and equipment, chemicals, fuels, foodstuffs

NEW ZEALAND
AREA: 103,737 sq mi (268,680 sq km)
POPULATION: 3,993,817
CAPITAL: Wellington
LANGUAGES: English, Maori (both official)
GOVERNMENT: Parliamentary democracy
RELIGIONS: Protestant, Roman Catholic
LITERACY RATE: 99%
CURRENCY: New Zealand dollar

MAIN EXPORTS: Dairy products, meat, wood and wood products, fish, machinery

NICARAGUA
AREA: 49,998 sq mi (129,494 sq km)
POPULATION: 5,232,216
CAPITAL: Managua
LANGUAGE: Spanish (official)
GOVERNMENT: Republic
RELIGIONS: Roman Catholic, Protestant
LITERACY RATE: 68%
CURRENCY: Gold cordoba
MAIN EXPORTS: Coffee, shrimp and lobster, cotton, tobacco, bananas, beef

NIGER
AREA: 489,189 sq mi (1,267,000 sq km)
POPULATION: 11,360,538
CAPITAL: Niamey
LANGUAGES: French (official), Hausa, Djerma
GOVERNMENT: Republic
RELIGIONS: Muslim, native beliefs, Christian
LITERACY RATE: 18%
CURRENCY: Communauté Financière Africaine franc
MAIN EXPORTS: Uranium ore, livestock, cowpeas, onions

NIGERIA
AREA: 356,700 sq mi (923,770 sq km)
POPULATION: 137,253,133
CAPITAL: Abuja
LANGUAGES: English (official), Hausa, Yoruba, Igbo, others
GOVERNMENT: Republic transitioning from military to civilian rule
RELIGIONS: Muslim, Christian, native beliefs
LITERACY RATE: 68%
CURRENCY: Naira
MAIN EXPORTS: Petroleum and petroleum products, cocoa, rubber

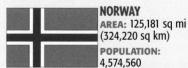

NORWAY
AREA: 125,181 sq mi (324,220 sq km)
POPULATION: 4,574,560
CAPITAL: Oslo
LANGUAGE: Norwegian (official)
GOVERNMENT: Constitutional monarchy
RELIGIONS: Protestant, Roman Catholic
LITERACY RATE: 100%
CURRENCY: Norwegian krone
MAIN EXPORTS: Petroleum and petroleum products, machinery and equipment, metals, chemicals, ships, fish

OMAN
AREA: 82,030 sq mi (212,460 sq km)
POPULATION: 2,903,165

CAPITAL: Muscat
LANGUAGES: Arabic (official), English, Indian languages
GOVERNMENT: Monarchy
RELIGIONS: Ibadhi Muslim, Sunni Muslim, Shi'a Muslim, Hindu
LITERACY RATE: 76%
CURRENCY: Omani rial
MAIN EXPORTS: Petroleum, fish, metals, textiles

PAKISTAN
AREA: 310,400 sq mi (803,940 sq km)
POPULATION: 153,705,278

CAPITAL: Islamabad
LANGUAGES: Urdu (official), Punjabi, Sindhi, Siraiki, Pashtu, others
GOVERNMENT: Federal republic
RELIGIONS: Muslim, Christian, Hindu
LITERACY RATE: 46%
CURRENCY: Pakistani rupee
MAIN EXPORTS: Textiles, rice, leather, sports goods, carpets

PALAU
AREA: 177 sq mi (458 sq km)
POPULATION: 20,016
CAPITAL: Koror

LANGUAGES: English, Palauan, Sonsoralese, Tobi, others
GOVERNMENT: Constitutional government
RELIGIONS: Roman Catholic, Protestant
LITERACY RATE: 92%
CURRENCY: U.S. dollar
MAIN EXPORTS: Shellfish, tuna, copra, garments

PANAMA
AREA: 30,193 sq mi (78,200 sq km)
POPULATION: 3,000,463

CAPITAL: Panama City
LANGUAGES: Spanish (official), English
GOVERNMENT: Constitutional democracy
RELIGIONS: Roman Catholic, Protestant
LITERACY RATE: 93%
CURRENCIES: Balboa, U.S. dollar
MAIN EXPORTS: Bananas, shrimp, sugar, coffee, clothing

PAPUA NEW GUINEA
AREA: 178,703 sq mi (462,840 sq km)
POPULATION: 5,420,280

CAPITAL: Port Moresby
LANGUAGES: Motu, other native languages, English

GOVERNMENT: Constitutional monarchy with parliamentary democracy
RELIGIONS: Roman Catholic, Protestant, native beliefs
LITERACY RATE: 66%
CURRENCY: Kina
MAIN EXPORTS: Oil, gold, copper ore, logs, palm oil, coffee, cocoa, crayfish, prawns

PARAGUAY
AREA: 157,046 sq mi (406,750 sq km)
POPULATION: 6,191,368

CAPITAL: Asunción
LANGUAGES: Spanish, Guarani (both official)
GOVERNMENT: Constitutional republic
RELIGIONS: Roman Catholic, Protestant
LITERACY RATE: 94%
CURRENCY: Guaraní
MAIN EXPORTS: Soybeans, feed, cotton, meat, edible oils, electricity

PERU
AREA: 496,223 sq mi (1,285,220 sq km)
POPULATION: 28,863,494

CAPITAL: Lima
LANGUAGES: Spanish, Quechua (both official), Aymara
GOVERNMENT: Constitutional republic
RELIGION: Roman Catholic
LITERACY RATE: 91%
CURRENCY: Nuevo sol
MAIN EXPORTS: Fish and fish products, gold, copper, zinc, crude petroleum, lead, coffee, sugar, cotton

PHILIPPINES
AREA: 115,830 sq mi (300,000 sq km)
POPULATION: 86,241,697

CAPITAL: Manila
LANGUAGES: Filipino, English (both official), Tagalog, other native languages
GOVERNMENT: Republic
RELIGIONS: Roman Catholic, Protestant, Muslim, Buddhist
LITERACY RATE: 96%
CURRENCY: Philippine peso
MAIN EXPORTS: Electronic equipment, machinery and transport equipment, garments, coconut products, chemicals

POLAND
AREA: 120,727 sq mi (312,685 sq km)
POPULATION: 38,626,349

CAPITAL: Warsaw
LANGUAGE: Polish
GOVERNMENT: Republic
RELIGIONS: Roman Catholic, Eastern Orthodox, Protestant

LITERACY RATE: 100%
CURRENCY: Zloty
MAIN EXPORTS: Machinery and transport equipment, manufactured goods, food

PORTUGAL
AREA: 35,672 sq mi (92,391 sq km)
POPULATION: 10,119,250

CAPITAL: Lisbon
LANGUAGE: Portuguese
GOVERNMENT: Parliamentary democracy
RELIGIONS: Roman Catholic, Protestant
LITERACY RATE: 93%
CURRENCY: Euro
MAIN EXPORTS: Clothing and footwear, machinery, chemicals, cork, paper products, hides

QATAR
AREA: 4,416 sq mi (11,437 sq km)
POPULATION: 840,290

CAPITAL: Doha
LANGUAGES: Arabic (official), English
GOVERNMENT: Monarchy
RELIGION: Muslim
LITERACY RATE: 83%
CURRENCY: Qatari rial
MAIN EXPORTS: Petroleum products, fertilizers, steel

ROMANIA
AREA: 91,700 sq mi (237,500 sq km)
POPULATION: 22,355,551

CAPITAL: Bucharest
LANGUAGES: Romanian (official), Hungarian, German
GOVERNMENT: Republic
RELIGIONS: Eastern Orthodox, Protestant, Catholic
LITERACY RATE: 98%
CURRENCY: Leu
MAIN EXPORTS: Textiles, footwear, metals and metal products, machinery and equipment, minerals, fuels

RUSSIA
AREA: 6,592,735 sq mi (17,075,200 sq km)
POPULATION: 144,112,353

CAPITAL: Moscow
LANGUAGES: Russian, others
GOVERNMENT: Federation
RELIGIONS: Russian Orthodox, Muslim
LITERACY RATE: 100%
CURRENCY: Russian ruble
MAIN EXPORTS: Petroleum and petroleum products, natural gas, wood and wood products, metals, chemicals

RWANDA

AREA: 10,169 sq mi (26,338 sq km)

POPULATION: 7,954,013

CAPITAL: Kigali

LANGUAGES: Kinyarwanda, French, English (all official), Bantu, Kiswahili

GOVERNMENT: Republic

RELIGIONS: Roman Catholic, Protestant, Muslim, native beliefs

LITERACY RATE: 70%

CURRENCY: Rwandan franc

MAIN EXPORTS: Coffee, tea, hides, tin ore

SAINT KITTS AND NEVIS

AREA: 101 sq mi (261 sq km)

POPULATION: 38,836

CAPITAL: Basseterre

LANGUAGE: English

GOVERNMENT: Constitutional monarchy

RELIGIONS: Protestant, Roman Catholic

LITERACY RATE: 97%

CURRENCY: East Caribbean dollar

MAIN EXPORTS: Machinery, food, electronics, beverages, tobacco

SAINT LUCIA

AREA: 238 sq mi (616 sq km)

POPULATION: 164,213

CAPITAL: Castries

LANGUAGES: English (official), French patois

GOVERNMENT: Parliamentary democracy

RELIGIONS: Roman Catholic, Protestant

LITERACY RATE: 67%

CURRENCY: East Caribbean dollar

MAIN EXPORTS: Bananas, clothing, cocoa, vegetables, fruits, coconut oil

SAINT VINCENT AND THE GRENADINES

AREA: 150 sq mi (389 sq km)

POPULATION: 117,193

CAPITAL: Kingstown

LANGUAGES: English, French patois

GOVERNMENT: Parliamentary democracy

RELIGIONS: Protestant, Roman Catholic, Hindu

LITERACY RATE: 96%

CURRENCY: East Caribbean dollar

MAIN EXPORTS: Bananas, eddoes and dasheen (taro), arrowroot starch, tennis racquets

SAMOA

AREA: 1,136 sq mi (2,944 sq km)

POPULATION: 177,714

CAPITAL: Apia

LANGUAGES: Samoan (Polynesian), English

GOVERNMENT: Constitutional monarchy under native chief

RELIGIONS: Protestant, Roman Catholic

LITERACY RATE: 100%

CURRENCY: Tala

MAIN EXPORTS: Fish, coconut oil and cream, copra, taro, garments, beer

SAN MARINO

AREA: 24 sq mi (61 sq km)

POPULATION: 28,503

CAPITAL: San Marino

LANGUAGE: Italian

GOVERNMENT: Independent republic

RELIGION: Roman Catholic

LITERACY RATE: 96%

CURRENCY: Euro

MAIN EXPORTS: Building stone, lime, wood, chestnuts, wheat, wine, hides

SÃO TOMÉ AND PRÍNCIPE

AREA: 386 sq mi (1,001 sq km)

POPULATION: 181,565

CAPITAL: São Tomé

LANGUAGE: Portuguese

GOVERNMENT: Republic

RELIGION: Christian

LITERACY RATE: 79%

MAIN EXPORTS: Cocoa, copra, coffee, palm oil

SAUDI ARABIA

AREA: 756,981 sq mi (1,960,582 sq km)

POPULATION: 25,100,425

CAPITAL: Riyadh

LANGUAGE: Arabic

GOVERNMENT: Monarchy

RELIGION: Muslim

LITERACY RATE: 79%

CURRENCY: Saudi riyal

MAIN EXPORTS: Petroleum and petroleum products

SENEGAL

AREA: 75,749 sq mi (196,190 sq km)

POPULATION: 10,852,147

CAPITAL: Dakar

LANGUAGES: French (official), Wolof, Pulaar

GOVERNMENT: Republic under multiparty democratic rule

RELIGIONS: Muslim, indigenous beliefs, Christian

LITERACY RATE: 40%

CURRENCY: Communauté Financière Africaine franc

MAIN EXPORTS: Fish, groundnuts (peanuts), petroleum products, phosphates, cotton

SERBIA AND MONTENEGRO

AREA: 39,517 sq mi (102,350 sq km)

POPULATION: 10,663,022

CAPITAL: Belgrade

LANGUAGES: Serbian, Albanian

GOVERNMENT: Republic

RELIGIONS: Orthodox, Muslim, Roman Catholic, Protestant

LITERACY RATE: 93%

CURRENCY: New Yugoslav dinar

MAIN EXPORTS: Manufactured goods, food, live animals, raw materials

SEYCHELLES

AREA: 176 sq mi (455 sq km)

POPULATION: 80,832

CAPITAL: Victoria

LANGUAGES: English, French (both official), Creole

GOVERNMENT: Republic

RELIGIONS: Roman Catholic, Anglican, other Christian

LITERACY RATE: 58%

CURRENCY: Seychelles rupee

MAIN EXPORTS: Canned tuna, frozen fish, cinnamon bark, copra, petroleum products

SIERRA LEONE

AREA: 27,699 sq mi (71,740 sq km)

POPULATION: 5,883,889

CAPITAL: Freetown

LANGUAGES: English (official), Mende, Temne, Krio

GOVERNMENT: Constitutional democracy

RELIGIONS: Muslim, native beliefs, Christian

LITERACY RATE: 31%

CURRENCY: Leone

MAIN EXPORTS: Diamonds, rutile, cocoa, coffee, fish

SINGAPORE

AREA: 267 sq mi (692 sq km)

POPULATION: 4,767,974

CAPITAL: Singapore

LANGUAGES: Malay, Chinese, Tamil, English (all official)

GOVERNMENT: Parliamentary republic

RELIGIONS: Buddhist, Muslim, Christian, Hindu, Sikh, Taoist, Confucianist

LITERACY RATE: 93%

CURRENCY: Singapore dollar

MAIN EXPORTS: Machinery and equipment (including electronics), consumer goods, chemicals, mineral fuels

SLOVAKIA
AREA: 18,859 sq mi (48,845 sq km)
POPULATION: 5,423,567
CAPITAL: Bratislava
LANGUAGES: Slovak (official), Hungarian
GOVERNMENT: Parliamentary republic
RELIGIONS: Roman Catholic, Protestant, Orthodox
LITERACY RATE: NA
CURRENCY: Slovak koruna
MAIN EXPORTS: Machinery and transport equipment, chemicals

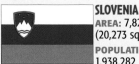

SLOVENIA
AREA: 7,827 sq mi (20,273 sq km)
POPULATION: 1,938,282
CAPITAL: Ljubljana
LANGUAGES: Slovenian, Serbo-Croatian
GOVERNMENT: Parliamentary democratic republic
RELIGIONS: Roman Catholic, Lutheran, Muslim
LITERACY RATE: 100%
CURRENCY: Tolar
MAIN EXPORTS: Manufactured goods, machinery and transport equipment

SOLOMON ISLANDS
AREA: 10,985 sq mi (28,450 sq km)
POPULATION: 523,617
CAPITAL: Honiara
LANGUAGES: English, Solomon Pidgin, Melanesian languages
GOVERNMENT: Parliamentary republic tending toward anarchy
RELIGIONS: Anglican, Roman Catholic, Protestant, native beliefs
LITERACY RATE: NA
CURRENCY: Solomon Islands dollar
MAIN EXPORTS: Timber, fish, copra, palm oil, cocoa

SOMALIA
AREA: 246,199 sq mi (637,657 sq km)
POPULATION: 8,304,601
CAPITAL: Mogadishu
LANGUAGES: Somali (official), Arabic, English, Italian
GOVERNMENT: Transitional parliamentary
RELIGION: Sunni Muslim
LITERACY RATE: 38%
CURRENCY: Somali shilling
MAIN EXPORTS: Livestock, bananas, hides, fish, charcoal, scrap metal

SOUTH AFRICA
AREA: 471,008 sq mi (1,219,912 sq km)
POPULATION: 42,718,530
CAPITAL: Pretoria
LANGUAGES: Afrikaans, English, Ndebele, Pedi, Sotho, Swazi, Tsonga, Tswana, Venda, Xhosa, Zulu (all official)
GOVERNMENT: Republic
RELIGIONS: Christian, Muslim, Hindu, native beliefs, animist
LITERACY RATE: 86%
CURRENCY: Rand
MAIN EXPORTS: Gold, diamonds, platinum, machinery and equipment

SPAIN
AREA: 194,896 sq mi (504,782 sq km)
POPULATION: 40,280,780
CAPITAL: Madrid
LANGUAGES: Castilian Spanish, Catalan, Galician, Basque
GOVERNMENT: Parliamentary monarchy
RELIGION: Roman Catholic
LITERACY RATE: 98%
CURRENCY: Euro
MAIN EXPORTS: Machinery, motor vehicles, foodstuffs, other consumer goods

SRI LANKA
AREA: 23,332 sq mi (65,610 sq km)
POPULATION: 19,905,165
CAPITAL: Colombo
LANGUAGES: Sinhala (official), Tamil, English
GOVERNMENT: Republic
RELIGIONS: Buddhist, Hindu, Christian, Muslim
LITERACY RATE: 92%
CURRENCY: Sri Lankan rupee
MAIN EXPORTS: Textiles, apparel, tea, diamonds, coconut products

SUDAN
AREA: 967,493 sq mi (2,505,810 sq km)
POPULATION: 39,148,162
CAPITAL: Khartoum
LANGUAGES: Arabic, Nubian, dialects of Nilotic, Nilo-Hamitic, Sudanic languages, English
GOVERNMENT: Authoritarian regime
RELIGIONS: Sunni Muslim, native beliefs, Christian
LITERACY RATE: 61%
CURRENCY: Sudanese dinar
MAIN EXPORTS: Oil and petroleum products, cotton, sesame, livestock

SURINAME
AREA: 63,039 sq mi (163,270 sq km)
POPULATION: 436,935
CAPITAL: Paramaribo
LANGUAGES: Dutch (official), Surinamese, English
GOVERNMENT: Constitutional democracy
RELIGIONS: Hindu, Muslim, Roman Catholic, Protestant, native beliefs
LITERACY RATE: 93%
CURRENCY: Surinamese guilder
MAIN EXPORTS: Alumina, crude oil, lumber, shrimp and fish, rice, bananas

SWAZILAND
AREA: 6,704 sq mi (17,363 sq km)
POPULATION: 1,169,241
CAPITAL: Mbabane
LANGUAGES: siSwati, English (both official)
GOVERNMENT: Monarchy
RELIGIONS: Zionist, Roman Catholic, Muslim, Anglican, Bahai, Methodist
LITERACY RATE: 82%
CURRENCY: Lilangeni
MAIN EXPORTS: Soft-drink concentrates, sugar, wood pulp, cotton yarn

SWEDEN
AREA: 173,731 sq mi (449,964 sq km)
POPULATION: 8,986,400
CAPITAL: Stockholm
LANGUAGE: Swedish
GOVERNMENT: Constitutional monarchy
RELIGIONS: Lutheran, Roman Catholic, Orthodox, Baptist, Muslim, Jewish
LITERACY RATE: 99%
CURRENCY: Swedish krona
MAIN EXPORTS: Machinery, motor vehicles, paper products, pulp, wood

SWITZERLAND
AREA: 15,942 sq mi (41,290 sq km)
POPULATION: 7,450,867
CAPITAL: Bern
LANGUAGES: German, French, Italian, Romansch (all official)
GOVERNMENT: Federal republic
RELIGIONS: Roman Catholic, Protestant
LITERACY RATE: 99%
CURRENCY: Swiss franc
MAIN EXPORTS: Machinery, chemicals, metals, watches, agricultural products

SYRIA
AREA: 71,498 sq mi (185,180 sq km)
POPULATION: 18,016,874
CAPITAL: Damascus
LANGUAGES: Arabic (official), French, English
GOVERNMENT: Republic under military regime
RELIGIONS: Sunni Muslim, Alawite, Druze, and other Muslim sects, Christian, Jewish
LITERACY RATE: 77%
CURRENCY: Syrian pound
MAIN EXPORTS: Crude oil, petroleum products, fruits and vegetables, cotton fiber, clothing, meat and live animals

TAIWAN
AREA: 13,892 sq mi (35,980 sq km)
POPULATION: 22,749,838
CAPITAL: Taipei
LANGUAGES: Chinese (Mandarin), Taiwanese, Hakka dialects
GOVERNMENT: Multiparty democratic regime
RELIGIONS: Buddhist, Confucian, Taoist, Christian
LITERACY RATE: 86%
CURRENCY: New Taiwan dollar
MAIN EXPORTS: Machinery and electrical equipment, metals, textiles, plastics

TAJIKISTAN
AREA: 55,251 sq mi (143,100 sq km)
POPULATION: 7,011,556
CAPITAL: Dushanbe
LANGUAGES: Tajik (official), Russian
GOVERNMENT: Republic
RELIGIONS: Sunni Muslim, Shi'a Muslim
LITERACY RATE: 99%
CURRENCY: Somoni
MAIN EXPORTS: Aluminum, electricity, cotton, fruits, vegetable oil, textiles

TANZANIA
AREA: 364,898 sq mi (945,087 sq km)
POPULATION: 36,588,225
CAPITAL: Dar es Salaam
LANGUAGES: Kiswahili, English (both official), Arabic
GOVERNMENT: Republic
RELIGIONS: Christian, Muslim, native beliefs
LITERACY RATE: 78%
CURRENCY: Tanzanian shilling
MAIN EXPORTS: Gold, coffee, cashew nuts, manufactured goods, cotton

THAILAND
AREA: 198,455 sq mi (514,000 sq km)
POPULATION: 64,865,523
CAPITAL: Bangkok
LANGUAGES: Thai, English
GOVERNMENT: Constitutional democracy
RELIGIONS: Buddhism, Muslim, Christianity, Hinduism
LITERACY RATE: 96%
CURRENCY: Baht
MAIN EXPORTS: Computers, transistors, seafood, clothing, rice

TOGO
AREA: 21,925 sq mi (56,785 sq km)
POPULATION: 5,556,812
CAPITAL: Lomé

LANGUAGES: French (official), Éwé, Mina, Kabyé, Dagomba
GOVERNMENT: Republic under transition to democratic rule
RELIGIONS: Native beliefs, Christian, Muslim
LITERACY RATE: 61%
CURRENCY: Communauté Financière Africaine franc
MAIN EXPORTS: Cotton, phosphates, coffee, cocoa

TONGA
AREA: 289 sq mi (748 sq km)
POPULATION: 110,237
CAPITAL: Nuku'alofa
LANGUAGES: Tongan, English
GOVERNMENT: Constitutional monarchy
RELIGION: Christian
LITERACY RATE: 99%
CURRENCY: Pa'anga
MAIN EXPORTS: Squash, fish, vanilla beans, root crops

TRINIDAD AND TOBAGO
AREA: 1,980 sq mi (5,128 sq km)
POPULATION: 1,096,585
CAPITAL: Port-of-Spain
LANGUAGES: English (official), Hindi, French, Spanish, Chinese
GOVERNMENT: Parliamentary democracy
RELIGIONS: Roman Catholic, Hindu, Protestant, Muslim, other
LITERACY RATE: 99%
CURRENCY: Trinidad and Tobago dollar
MAIN EXPORTS: Petroleum and petroleum products, chemicals, steel products

TUNISIA
AREA: 63,170 sq mi (163,610 sq km)
POPULATION: 10,032,050
CAPITAL: Tunis
LANGUAGES: Arabic (official), French
GOVERNMENT: Republic
RELIGION: Muslim
LITERACY RATE: 74%
CURRENCY: Tunisian dinar
MAIN EXPORTS: Textiles, mechanical goods, phosphates and chemicals, agricultural products, hydrocarbons

TURKEY
AREA: 301,381 sq mi (780,580 sq km)
POPULATION: 68,893,918
CAPITAL: Ankara
LANGUAGES: Turkish (official), Kurdish, Arabic, Armenian, Greek
GOVERNMENT: Republican parliamentary democracy

RELIGION: Muslim
LITERACY RATE: 87%
CURRENCY: Turkish lira
MAIN EXPORTS: Clothing, foodstuffs, textiles, metal manufactured goods

TURKMENISTAN
AREA: 188,455 sq mi (488,100 sq km)
POPULATION: 4,863,169
CAPITAL: Ashgabat
LANGUAGES: Turkmen, Russian, Uzbek, other
GOVERNMENT: Republic
RELIGIONS: Muslim, Eastern Orthodox
LITERACY RATE: 98%
CURRENCY: Turkmen manat
MAIN EXPORTS: Gas, oil, cotton, textiles

TUVALU
AREA: 10 sq mi (26 sq km)
POPULATION: 11,468
CAPITAL: Funafuti
LANGUAGES: Tuvaluan, English, Samoan, Kiribati
GOVERNMENT: Constitutional monarchy with a parliamentary democracy
RELIGION: Protestant
LITERACY RATE: NA
CURRENCIES: Australian dollar, Tuvaluan dollar
MAIN EXPORTS: Copra, fish

UGANDA
AREA: 91,135 sq mi (236,040 sq km)
POPULATION: 26,404,543
CAPITAL: Kampala
LANGUAGES: English (official), Ganda, other native languages
GOVERNMENT: Republic
RELIGIONS: Roman Catholic, Protestant, Muslim, native beliefs
LITERACY RATE: 70%
CURRENCY: Ugandan shilling
MAIN EXPORTS: Coffee, fish and fish products, tea, gold, cotton, flowers

UKRAINE
AREA: 233,088 sq mi (603,700 sq km)
POPULATION: 47,732,079
CAPITAL: Kiev
LANGUAGES: Ukrainian, Russian, Romanian, Polish, Hungarian
GOVERNMENT: Republic
RELIGIONS: Ukrainian Orthodox, Ukrainian Catholic, Protestant, Jewish
LITERACY RATE: 100%
CURRENCY: Hryvnia
MAIN EXPORTS: Ferrous and nonferrous metals, fuel and petroleum products, chemicals, machinery, transport equipment

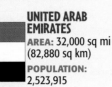

UNITED ARAB EMIRATES
AREA: 32,000 sq mi (82,880 sq km)

POPULATION: 2,523,915

CAPITAL: Abu Dhabi

LANGUAGES: Arabic (official), Persian, English, Hindi, Urdu

GOVERNMENT: Federation

RELIGIONS: Muslim, Christian, Hindu, others

LITERACY RATE: 78%

CURRENCY: Emirati dirham

MAIN EXPORTS: Crude oil, natural gas, re-exports, dried fish, dates

UNITED KINGDOM
AREA: 94,525 sq mi (244,820 sq km)

POPULATION: 60,270,708

CAPITAL: London

LANGUAGES: English, Welsh, Gaelic

GOVERNMENT: Constitutional monarchy

RELIGIONS: Anglican, Roman Catholic, Protestant, Muslim, Sikh, Hindu, Jewish

LITERACY RATE: 99%

CURRENCY: British pound

MAIN EXPORTS: Manufactured goods, fuels, chemicals, food, beverages, tobacco

UNITED STATES
AREA: 3,717,776 sq mi (9,629,091 sq km)

POPULATION: 293,027,571

CAPITAL: Washington, D.C.

LANGUAGES: English, Spanish

GOVERNMENT: Federal republic

RELIGIONS: Protestant, Roman Catholic, Jewish, others

LITERACY RATE: 97%

CURRENCY: U.S. dollar

MAIN EXPORTS: Capital goods, automobiles, industrial supplies, raw materials, consumer goods

URUGUAY
AREA: 68,038 sq mi (176,220 sq km)

POPULATION: 3,440,205

CAPITAL: Montevideo

LANGUAGES: Spanish, Portunol

GOVERNMENT: Republic

RELIGIONS: Roman Catholic, Protestant, Jewish, others

LITERACY RATE: 98%

CURRENCY: Uruguayan peso

MAIN EXPORTS: Meat, rice, leather products, wool, vehicles, dairy products

UZBEKISTAN
AREA: 172,740 sq mi (447,400 sq km)

POPULATION: 26,410,416

CAPITAL: Tashkent

LANGUAGES: Uzbek, Russian, Tajik, others

GOVERNMENT: Republic

RELIGIONS: Muslim, Eastern Orthodox, others

LITERACY RATE: 99%

CURRENCY: Uzbekistani sum

MAIN EXPORTS: Cotton, gold, energy products, mineral fertilizers, ferrous metals, textiles, food products, automobiles

VANUATU
AREA: 4,719 sq mi (12,200 sq km)

POPULATION: 202,609

CAPITAL: Port-Vila

LANGUAGES: English, French, Bislama (all official), others

GOVERNMENT: Parliamentary repubulic

RELIGIONS: Protestant, Roman Catholic, native beliefs

LITERACY RATE: 53%

CURRENCY: Vatu

MAIN EXPORTS: Copra, beef, cocoa, timber, kava, coffee

VATICAN CITY (HOLY SEE)
AREA: .17 sq mi (.44 sq km)

POPULATION: 890

CAPITAL: None

LANGUAGES: Latin, Italian, others

GOVERNMENT: Ecclesiastical

RELIGION: Roman Catholic

LITERACY RATE: 100%

CURRENCY: Euro

MAIN EXPORTS: NA

VENEZUELA
AREA: 352,141 sq mi (912,050 sq km)

POPULATION: 25,017,387

CAPITAL: Caracas

LANGUAGES: Spanish (official), native dialects

GOVERNMENT: Federal republic

RELIGIONS: Roman Catholic, Protestant, others

LITERACY RATE: 93%

CURRENCY: Bolivar

MAIN EXPORTS: Petroleum, bauxite and aluminum, steel, chemicals, agricultural products

VIETNAM
AREA: 127,243 sq mi (329,560 sq km)

POPULATION: 82,689,518

CAPITAL: Hanoi

LANGUAGES: Vietnamese (official), English, French, Chinese, Khmer, others

GOVERNMENT: Communist state

RELIGIONS: Buddhist, Hoa Hao, Cao Dai, Roman Catholic, Protestant, others

LITERACY RATE: 94%

CURRENCY: Dong

MAIN EXPORTS: Crude oil, marine products, rice, coffee, rubber, tea, garments, shoes

YEMEN
AREA: 203,848 sq mi (527,970 sq km)

POPULATION: 20,024,867

CAPITAL: Sanaa

LANGUAGE: Arabic

GOVERNMENT: Republic

RELIGION: Muslim

LITERACY RATE: 50%

CURRENCY: Yemeni rial

MAIN EXPORTS: Crude oil, coffee, dried and salted fish

ZAMBIA
AREA: 290,583 sq mi (752,614 sq km)

POPULATION: 10,462,436

CAPITAL: Lusaka

LANGUAGES: English (official), Bemba, Kaonda, Lozi, Lunda, other native languages

GOVERNMENT: Republic

RELIGIONS: Christian, Muslim, Hindu, native beliefs

LITERACY RATE: 81%

CURRENCY: Zambian kwacha

MAIN EXPORTS: Copper, cobalt, electricity, tobacco, flowers, cotton

ZIMBABWE
AREA: 150,802 sq mi (390,580 sq km)

POPULATION: 12,671,860

CAPITAL: Harare

LANGUAGES: English (official), Shona, Sindebele, native languages

GOVERNMENT: Parliamentary democracy

RELIGIONS: Syncretic, Christian, Muslim, others

LITERACY RATE: 91%

CURRENCY: Zimbabwean dollar

MAIN EXPORTS: Tobacco, gold, ferroalloys, textiles, clothing

Index

Credits

KEY:
LPI: Lonely Planet Images
AP/WW: Associated Press/Wide World Pictures
TIW: The Image Works
RF: Royalty Free

All photos and illustrations clockwise from top left:

Front Cover: Atlas logo–Pascal Menanad for TIME For Kids (left), Tara Murphy for TIME For Kids (center), Bob Daemmrich–TIW, NASA (earth), Julian Abram Wainwright–EPA/AP/WW (girl in green dress)
Back Cover: Atlas logo–see front cover; Mark Leong for TIME For Kids (boy in snapshot)
Title Page: Atlas logo–Pascal Menanad for TIME For Kids (left), Tara Murphy for TIME For Kids (center), Bob Daemmrich–TIW, NASA (earth)
2-3: (in contents-page order) NASA; Imelda Medina–EPA/AP/WW; Norbert Rosing–UNEP/TIW;Nicholas Reuss–LPI (bear); Getty Photodisc; Kevin Schafer–Corbis; Getty Brand X; Punchstock (toucan); Corbis (RF); Shaun Best–Reuters (skier); Richard I'Anson–LPI; Gregory Adams–LPI; Jose Fuste Raga–Corbis; Charles Lenars–Corbis (sculpture); Corbis (RF); David Tipling–LPI; Jonathan Chester–LPI (penguins)
6: Atlas logo–see Title Page; Continent spread–see pages 58-59
8-9: NASA (earth); Getty Photodisc; Phil Coale–AP/WW; Corbis (RF); Getty Photodisc (lithosphere); Yukichika Murayama–AP/WW (dinosaur); Illustration by Brad Hamman
10-11: Ed Wray–AP/WW (lava); Joe Lertola for TIME For Kids (volcano and earthquake graphics); Imelda Medina–EPA/EFE/AP/WW; Douglas C. Pizac–AP/WW; Wang Yuan-Mao–AP/WW (earthquake)
12-13: Brent Winebrenner–LPI (rain forest); Joe Zeff for TIME For Kids (hurricane graphic); John Borthwick–LPI; Anthony Ham–LPI; Chart by Brad Hamman
14-15: Joe Lertola for TIME For Kids (universe graphic); NASA (2)
16-17: Norbert Rosing–UNEP/TIW; Martel–ICONE/TIW; Nicholas Reuss–LPI
18-19: Getty Photodisc; J. Pat Carter–AP/WW
20-21: Eoin Clarke–LPI; Cheryl Conlon–LPI; Eastcott-Momatiuk/TIW
22-23: Getty Photodisc; Alison Wright–TIW; Kevin Frayer–AP/WW
24-25: Brooke McDonald for TIME For Kids; Lee Foster–LPI; Rick Rudnicki–LPI
26-27: Khue Bui–AP/WW; Dan Reiland–Eau Claire Leader-Telegram/AP/WW; Getty Photodisc
28-29: Jon Davison–LPI (lighthouse); Kim Grant–LPI; Toby Talbot–AP/WW; Jamie Harron–Papilio/Corbis
30-31: Kent Meireis–TIW (New York City); Joseph Sohm–TIW; Townsend P. Dickinson–TIW; Getty Photodisc
32-33: Rick Gerharter–LPI; Wausau Daily Herald/AP/WW; Ryan Soderlin–The Salina Journal/AP/WW
34-35: Clinton Lewis–Bowling Green Daily News/AP/WW; Neil Brake–AP/WW; John Elk III–LPI
36-37: John Hay–LPI; John Elk III–LPI; NASA

38-39: Getty Photodisc; Hideo Haga–HAGA/TIW; Ann Cecil–LPI
40-41: Charlotte Hindle–LPI (Mexico City); Michael & Patricia Fogden–Corbis (bird); Kevin Schafer–Corbis; Getty Brand X;
42-43: Bob Daemmrich–TIW; Werner Bertsch–Bruce Coleman; Sergio Dorantes–Corbis
44-45: Alfredo Maiquez–LPI (Richard I'Anson–LPI; Kevin Schafer–Corbis;
46-47: Punchstock (toucan); Tony Savino–TIW; Pablo Corral Vega–Corbis
48-49: Getty Brand X (2); Ann Johansson–Corbis (emeralds); Jeff Greenberg–LPI (tortoise)
50-51: Sengo Perez for TIME For Kids; Jackson Vereen–Foodpix; Frans Lanting–Minden Pictures; Courtesy International Potato Center.
52-53: Antonio Lacerda–EPA/EFE/AP/WW; John Hay–LPI; Reuters
54-55: John Maier Jr. for TIME For Kids; John Maier Jr.–TIW; Getty Photodisc
56-57: Oliver Strewe–LPI; Getty Photodisc; Wes Walker–LPI (glacier)
58-59: Craig Pershouse–LPI; Richard Nebesky–LPI; Diana Mayfield–LPI
60-61: Lee Snider–TIW (2); Getty Photodisc (bridge)
62-63: Ned Friary–LPI (midnight sun); Sonda Dawes–TIW; Topham Picturepoint–TIW (Lapps)
64-65: Rob Crandall–TIW; Jose Manuel Ribeiro–Reuters; Hideo Haga–HAGA/TIW; Marcelo Del Pozo–Reuters (flamenco)
66-67: Corbis (RF); Marcel & Eva Malherbe–TIW; Corbis (RF)
68-69: Pascal Menand for TIME For Kids; Getty Photodisc; Punchstock
70-71: Paul Beinssen–LPI; Thierry Roge–Reuters; Rick Gerharter–LPI; Jeremy Gray–LPI
72-73: Corbis (RF); Stephan Jansen–EPA/DPA/AP/WW; Wolfgang Kumm–EPA/DPA/AP/WW (wall); Hermann Dornhege–Plus 49/TIW
74-75: Shaun Best–Reuters (skier); Olivier Rogery–ROQUES/Corbis; Clem Lindenmayer–LPI; Klaus Titzer–Reuters;
76-77: Christopher Wood–LPI; Hideo Haga–HAGA/TIW; Jonathan Smith–LPI
78-79: Uppa–Topham/TIW; Russell Mountford–LPI; Jon Davison–LPI
80-81: Adam Tanner–TIW; Paul David Hellander–LPI; Lee Foster–LPI; Sasa Maricic–EPA/AP/WW (salt)
82-83: Corbis (RF); Rhonda Gutenberg–LPI; Hideo Haga–HAGA/Corbis
84-85: Argyropoulous–SIPA for TIME For Kids; Gjon Mili–TIME Picture Collection; Punchstock
86-87: Ludovic Maisant–Corbis; Jonathan Smith–LPI; Vasily Fedosenko–Reuters; Jonathan Smith–LPI (girls)
88-89: Bruce Edwards–The Flint Journal/AP/WW; Christina Dameyer–LPI (musician and Kiev)
90-91: Henry Groskinsky–Time-Life Pictures/Getty Images (egg); Alain Tomasini–LPI; Martin Moos–LPI
92-93: Jeremy Nicholl–Polaris for TIME For Kids (2); Bogden Cristel–Reuters; Philippe Wojazer–Reuters
94-95: Jeff Cantarutti–LPI; Felicity Volk–LPI; Michael J. Doolittle–TIW
96-97: Wolfgang Kaehler–Corbis; Gideon Mendel–Corbis; Jim Brandenberg–Minden Pictures (tiger); Reuters
98-99: Greg Elms–LPI; John Biemer–AP/WW; Getty Photodisc

100-101: Russell Mountford–LPI (Jerusalem and Syria); Laura Sivell–Corbis; Clint Lucas–LPI (Petra)
102-103: Bazuki Muhammad–Reuters; Gustavo Ferrari–AP/WW; Ludovic Maisant–Corbis
104-105: Shamil Zhumatov–Reuters; Yuri Kocketkov–EPA/AP/WW (rocket); Ludovic Maisant–Corbis (2)
106-107: Vahid Salemi–AP/WW; Ilyas Dean–Dean Pictures/TIW; Alexander Zemlianichenko–AP/WW
108-109: Corbis (RF); Thomas Easley–AP/WW; Elizabeth Dalziel–AP/WW
110-111: Angelique LeDoux for TIME For Kids; Jayanta Shaw–Reuters; Greg Elms–LPI
112-113: Corbis (RF); Paul Hilton–EPA/AP/WW; Corbis (RF)
114-115: Mark Leong for TIME For Kids; Reuters; Michael S. Yamashita–Corbis
116-117: Fujifotos–TIW; Dallas & John Heaton–Corbis; Andy Rain–EPA/AP/WW (cell phone); Ahn Young-Joon–AP/WW
118-119: Chris Mellor–LPI (floating market); Getty Photodisc; Richard I'Anson–LPI
120-121: Peter Charlesworth–Asiaworks for TIME For Kids (2); Julian Abram Wainwright–EPA/AP/WW; Juliet Coombe–LPI
122-123: Manfred Gottschalk–LPI; Richard I'Anson–LPI; Gregory Adams–LPI
124-125: Doug McKinlay–LPI (gorillas); David Else–LPI; Dushan Cooray–LPI
126-127: Eric L. Wheater–LPI; Corbis (RF); Frances Linzee Gordon–LPI
128-129: Thomas Hartwell–Polaris for TIME For Kids; Mohamed El-Dakhakhny–AP/WW; Norbert Schiller–AP/WW
130-131: Doug McKinlay–LPI; Hinata Haga–HAGA/TIW; Jose Fuste Raga–Corbis
132-133: George Esiri–Reuters; Margaret Courtney-Clarke–Corbis; Yves Herman–Reuters
134-135: Jock Fistick–TIW; Charles Lenars–Corbis; Ascani–ICONE/TIW
136-137: Mitch Reardon–LPI; Fred Spoor–National Museums of Kenya; Ariadne Van Zandbergen–LPI
138-139: Tara Murphy for TIME For Kids; Getty Photodisc; Illustration by Jane Sanders; George Mulala–Reuters
140-141: Richard I'Anson–LPI; Themba Hadebe–AP/WW; Getty Photodisc
142-143: Per-Anders Pettersson for TIME For Kids; Martin Thomas–Reuters; Louise Gubb–TIW
144-145: Great Barrier Reef National Park Authority/Reuters; Daniel Birks–LPI; Corbis (RF)
146-147: Getty Photodisc; Mary L. Peachin–LPI; Getty Photodisc; Grant Dixon–LPI (beach)
148-149: Michael Amendolia for TIME For Kids; John Banagan–LPI (kangaroo); Paul A. Souders–Corbis (desert); Mark Newman–LPI
150-151: Philip Game–LPI; Herbert Knosowski–AP/WW; Rob Griffith–AP/WW; Tui De Roi–Minden Pictures (kiwi)
152-153: Jonathan Chester–LPI; David Tipling–LPI; Tom Szlukovenyi–Reuters

Maps: Joe LeMonnier for TIME For Kids Atlas
Continent maps (except Antarctica): Joe Lertola for TIME For Kids
Fact File maps: Jean Weisenbaugh for TIME For Kids
Time-line illustrations: Rita Lascaro for TIME For Kids